Ted HISCOCK

BRINDLEY OUT TELFORD HOME

Volume 2:   MADE IN SMETHWICK NEAR BIRMINGHAM

Birmingham Canal with Boulton & Watt's 18th century Soho Foundry in background

Ted HISCOCK

DEDICATION

As with Volume 1 of **"Brindley Out Telford Home – A Journey along the Birmingham Canal"**, Volume 2, **Brindley Out Telford Home – Made In Smethwick Near Birmingham"** is also dedicated to the thousands of anonymous and forgotten toilers as well as those titans whose names changed the way of the industrial world. Also, those men, women and children and their ponies, who worked the traffic, steered the boats and lived their simple but hard lives travelling the murky waters of our canal system of Britain. Once more, I thank Kate, my lovely wife for permitting me the time for such indulgence to research and write this second volume.

Ted Hiscock; 2020

Photographs and material used in the preparation of this book have been obtained from a variety of sources. Those obtained directly from an original source or library have been duly acknowledged, but some may have been obtained on the open market and despite attempts at tracing their origins, many remain anonymous, to my knowledge. If, through no fault of mine, photographs, images and material have been used without due credit or acknowledgement, I humbly apologise. If anyone believes that due acknowledgement or permission has not been accredited or sought, please do inform me as soon as possible.

Copyright: Ted Hiscock

Edwardhiscock6@gmail.com www.tedhiscock.com

23/11/2020

ISBN 978-1-78996-249-9

Copyright strictly the property of the author

The Author

Ted HISCOCK was born in 1946 at Wellington, Somerset, a small town in the South-West of England. His father, a country banker and amateur painter and his mother's cousin Tony Griffin, a professional painter, were a constant source of inspiration in Ted's artistic development.

After having gone to Birmingham in 1966 to attend the Medical School, Ted was privileged to have a career for 40 years in general medical practice in that great city before retiring to the city centre, where he lived with his wife Kate for 20 years. During the last quarter of a century, he has developed his passions as a painter and writer, frequently finding inspiration from the canal network of the West Midlands. He learned a great deal of his artistic techniques with the late sorely missed, David Mynett, firstly in Majorca (2002) and Venice (2011) and has held several sole exhibitor exhibitions in central Birmingham and the south of France.

Currently, his creative attention has become more focussed on sculpting and historical writing. When the canal side Flapper pub first became threatened with demolition and development, he commenced researching the history of the Birmingham Canal and realised the potential plight that faced these important 'un-conserved' waterways in these days of avaricious redevelopment. (This is in no way a reflection on the superb maintenance by the Canal and River Trust, whose dedication to the waterways is second to none). One thing led to another and after the success of Volume 1, which consisted of a virtual journey from the city centre to the Winson Green Stop and back into Birmingham, Volume 2 explores the continuation of the Birmingham Canals beyond Winson Green as the two limbs pass through Smethwick and West Bromwich and then the journey returns to Winson Green. The canals are the catalyst in this journey which permits a route of exploration of the industries that sprung up, brought greatness, some disappearing without trace and others absorbed into the grasp of competitors whilst others that simply moved on.

PERSONAL PREFACE

When "Brindley Out Telford Home – A Journey along the Birmingham Canal" was published in 2019 I was always aware that the story did not conveniently end at the Winson Green stop and this feature was an arbitrary turning point as well as being the boundary for Birmingham in a north-westerly direction. Encouraged by the popular success of this first canal travelogue combined with the Covid19 first lockdown, when we were permitted one trip dedicated to exercise, our route for daily canine ramble took us beyond this point and the importance of the Smethwick canal banks became very apparent.

Smethwick, like so many industrial towns that mushroomed at the end of the 18th century and throughout the 19th Century continued to grow like some rapidly spreading malignancy and became a workshop to Britain and the Empire. Factories of every conceivable size and function sprang up all over the town but particularly concentrated along the two parallel canals built by the two titans, James Brindley and Thomas Telford. Many of them had spilled over from adjacent Birmingham as expansion had created an urgent need for more space for bigger and better. The facility of the canal routes for quick in and out transportation was essential so it was inevitable these shores became so contaminated with the noise, filth and grime of rapid manufacturing.

A third canal engineer, John Smeaton, came into the forefront of contextual importance within a few years of James Brindley building the first route. John Smeaton had invented the chemical reaction of cement which enabled engineering feats, previously thought to be impossible, to happen. Brindley's embarrassment had been the lack of water as the canal passed over the Smethwick Summit, where six locks could not adequately be supplied from the trickle that was the Hockley Brook. Smeaton confronted the problem, reduced Brindley's original canal height, removed three locks and pushed the canal through his newly formed Summit cutting.

There were numerous companies that sprung up along these two canals, that changed the world. GKN, Soho Foundry, W & T Avery, Cornwall Works, Surrey Works, Chance Brothers, Muntz's Metals to name but a few. Associated with these vast sites were the names of Guest, Keen, Nettlefold, Chamberlain, Boulton, Watt, Murdoch, Keir, Avery Brothers, Tangye Brothers. To whet the thirst of the work force, Mitchells & Butler saw a rapid expansion of their brewery at Cape Hill and their distinctive pubs spread throughout the West Midlands. Many of these entrepreneurs were non-conformist in their beliefs and according to Sir Richard Tangye, often shunned by the mainstream protestant pillars of society, which was a double-edged sword of as this elite group were able to progress their research without putting their heads above the parapet of expected convention until success had been achieved.

It used to be said that Birmingham was 'the home of a thousand trades': Smethwick has always been in the shadow of that global reputation but many 'Made in Birmingham' items originated in this town at the elbow of its glorious neighbour. Many of the owners of these great industries lived in Birmingham, with mansions scattered throughout the city; leafy Edgbaston being extremely popular and a few of these great houses still stand.

What is fascinating about these 'cheek by jowl' industries along the murky waters through Smethwick, is the inter-dependence that existed between them. If a manufacturer needed a special design and did not possess the skill to produce the product, it was a fair chance that one of the neighbours would oblige. An example of this was the combined effort between Muntz and Chance Brothers in the design of glass houses, e.g. The Crystal Palace. Another frequent aspect was the gobbling up by one of the other. One extraordinary and exemplary creation of these pioneers of the late 18th and early 19th centuries was the Birmingham Lunar Society, of which many were members.

They met regularly, reflecting, discussing and exploring inspired new ideas over dinners, bolstering their mutual courage for progress.

A striking characteristic of the wealthier among them was their altruistic re-injection of massive funds back into the communities that kept their factories going. The Tangye Brothers gave Birmingham its School of Art and Art Gallery after Sir Richard had returned form an Australian trip, where he marvelled at the innovative manner that the wealthy of Melbourne supported the community with setting up arts' centres. One of Matthew Boulton's altruistic contribution was to sponsor the building of the Birmingham General Hospital by starting a series of Triennial fund-raising concerts that ultimately achieved their goal. Arthur Keen was a major benefactor of Smethwick, assisting with the provision of a municipal gas works, construction of public baths, free libraries and parks and was also a generous supporter and Life Governor of Birmingham University. Many of these driven men went into local and national politics: William Avery became Mayor of Birmingham a couple of times, the Chamberlain fame needs no extra mention, Henry Wiggin became an MP.

The intention of this book is to continue the journey of Volume 1 by exploring the realms of Smethwick and West Bromwich that many will have forgotten or like me, have never known. The town of Smethwick and its canal banks will never be the same as new generations of industries come and go on the sites previously occupied by the pioneers. It is important to record the facts into a compilation of chapters that recognises this part of British Heritage. Most of the contained material is gleaned from the same sources as the first book; Richard Dean's "Maps of Birmingham Canals 1989" [REF: 119], Grace's Guide, [REF: 2] Wikipedia, Ordnance Survey Maps, Historic England's excellent portfolio of historic Britain From Above of aerial photographs, Google Earth, Birmingham and other Black Country Museums and Libraries and archives, Historic England's fine list of Graded properties, anecdotal conversations with local characters who remember 'the days when ….' After 54 years of living in Birmingham, I have now moved away to the South-West of England to leafier realms and the coincidence of being locked down by Covid19 threats has enabled progress on this compilation. In my time working in Birmingham, I have watched a half century of changes occurring throughout the conurbation, (much of it not particularly savoury) and mourn the loss of modern society's lack of interest in the history that made the region and the Empire so great. I came to Birmingham as a student and stayed for the duration growing to love the people and heritage but now, it has become time for new pastures in the more rural setting of Dorset.

I wish to record my sincere thanks to two good friends who were persuaded to perform the tedious task of proof-reading the manuscript. Their input was invaluable – thank you both Mike Williams and Graham Wigley. Also, Ray Shill, (a name well-known in the BCN), has been invaluable providing information and researching some aspects of the route, in particular, that pertaining to the widening of Spon Lane Bridge (p. 119).

The title of **"Brindley Out Telford Home – Made in Smethwick, near Birmingham"** seemed to me to be so appropriate.

Ted Hiscock January 2021

CONTENTS

PERSONAL PREFACE	**4**
PART 1 – WINSON GREEN TO THE JUNCTION	**10**
1.1 Winson Green Stop – Gauging Station & Toll House	11
A. Canal Feeder Conduit	12
1.2 Cape Hill Brewery – Mitchells & Butlers Ltd	14
1.3 Guest, Keen & Nettlefolds	17
A. Guest & Co	18
B. Nettlefolds	20
C. Patent Iron & Brass Tube Co	22
D. Arthur Keen	23
E. Modern Times	26
1.4 Thomas Adkins, Soap Works Junction, Henry Wiggin & Ludwig Mond	29
1.5 Soho Foundry	32
A. Soho Foundry: An 'At Risk' Scheduled Monument	33
B. Boulton & The Soho Manufactory	36
C. The Unique History of Heritage : Boulton & Watt	37
D. W & T Avery	43
E. Into the 20th Century	45
F. Corollary	49
1.6 Smethwick Gas Works at Rabone Lane	50
1.7 Cornwall Works – Tangye Brothers	53
1.8 British Tube Mills	68
A. British Tube Works	68
B. Incandescent Heat Company Works	70
PART 2 – SMETHWICK TO STEWART AQUEDUCT	**72**
2.1 Surrey Works – Richard Evered & Co Ltd	74
2.2 Birmingham Carriage & Wagon Co – British Railway Carriage & Wagon Co.	78
2.3 Sandwell Iron & Axle Works	81
2.4 District Iron Works - J. Brockhouse & Co (West Bromwich)	82
2.5 Smethwick Pumping Station No. 3	84
2.6 John Smeaton & Summit Bridge (1788/9)	87
2.7 Sandwell Park Colliery Co.	90
A. Sandwell Hall & the Earls of Dartmouth	90
B. Sandwell Park Colliery Co	91
2.8 Archibald Kenrick Works	93
2.9 Spon Lane Foundry & Horseley Iron Works	96
A. Horseley Iron Works	96
B. Spon Lane Foundry	99
2.10 Blakeley Hall, Bromford & Spon Lane Collieries, Jensen Motor Ltd	102
A. Blakeley Hall, Bromford & Spon Lane Collieries	102
B. Jensen Brothers & Jensen Motors Ltd	103
2.11 Oldbury Railway Carriage & Wagon Works	105
2.12 Stewart Aqueduct – Grade 2 Listed Historic Aqueduct	107
PART 3 – STEWART AQUEDUCT BACK TO THE GREEN	**109**
3.1 Chance Brothers	110

A. Blakeley Hall	110
B. British Crown Glass Co	110
C. Chance Brothers	111
3.2 Ruskin Pottery	117
Spon Lan Bridge	119
3.3 Galton Bridge & the Galton Family	120
3.4 Engine Arm & Aqueduct	123
3.5 Iron Works of Smethwick	127
Anchor Iron, Eagle Iron, Etna Iron, Sandwell Iron & Axle, Smethwick Iron Foundry	127
3.6 Credenda Works	128
3.7 Kingston Metal Works – Allen Everitt & Sons	133
3.8 French Walls – George Muntz, Muntz's Metals, George Burn Ltd	135
A. French Walls, George Muntz & Muntz's Metal	135
B. George Burn Ltd	138
3.9 London Works	139
A. Smethwick Grove, Jean Moilliet & James Keir	139
B. Fox Henderson & Co	141
C. Thomas Astbury & Son; Patent Nut & Bolt Co, Watkins & Keen	143

4. THREE TITANIC CANAL ENGINEERS – BRINDLEY, SMEATON & TELFORD   **145**
    A. James Brindley   145
    B. John Smeaton   148
    C. Thomas Telford   150

5. OTHER MEN OF THE BIRMINGHAM LUNAR SOCIETY   **152**
    A. Lunar Society of Birmingham   152
    B. Members of the Lunar Society   154
        a. Erasmus Darwin   154
        b. Matthew Boulton   155
        c. James Watt   158
        d. William Murdoch   160
        e. William Small   162
        f. James Keir   163

6. APPENDIX   **165**

PART A	a. The Statutory Legislation for declaring a scheduled Monument	166
	b. Resumé of legislative criteria for scheduled monument : Soho Foundry	169
PART B	Historic England Listed Properties along the Birmingham Canal	171
PART C	1888 Surveyed Ordnance Survey 6" : Mile Maps (annotated)	173
PART D	Paintings & Sketches by the author www.tedhiscock.com	180
PART E	Timeline	181
	A W & T Avery bill	187
PART F.	References	188

INDEX   **192**

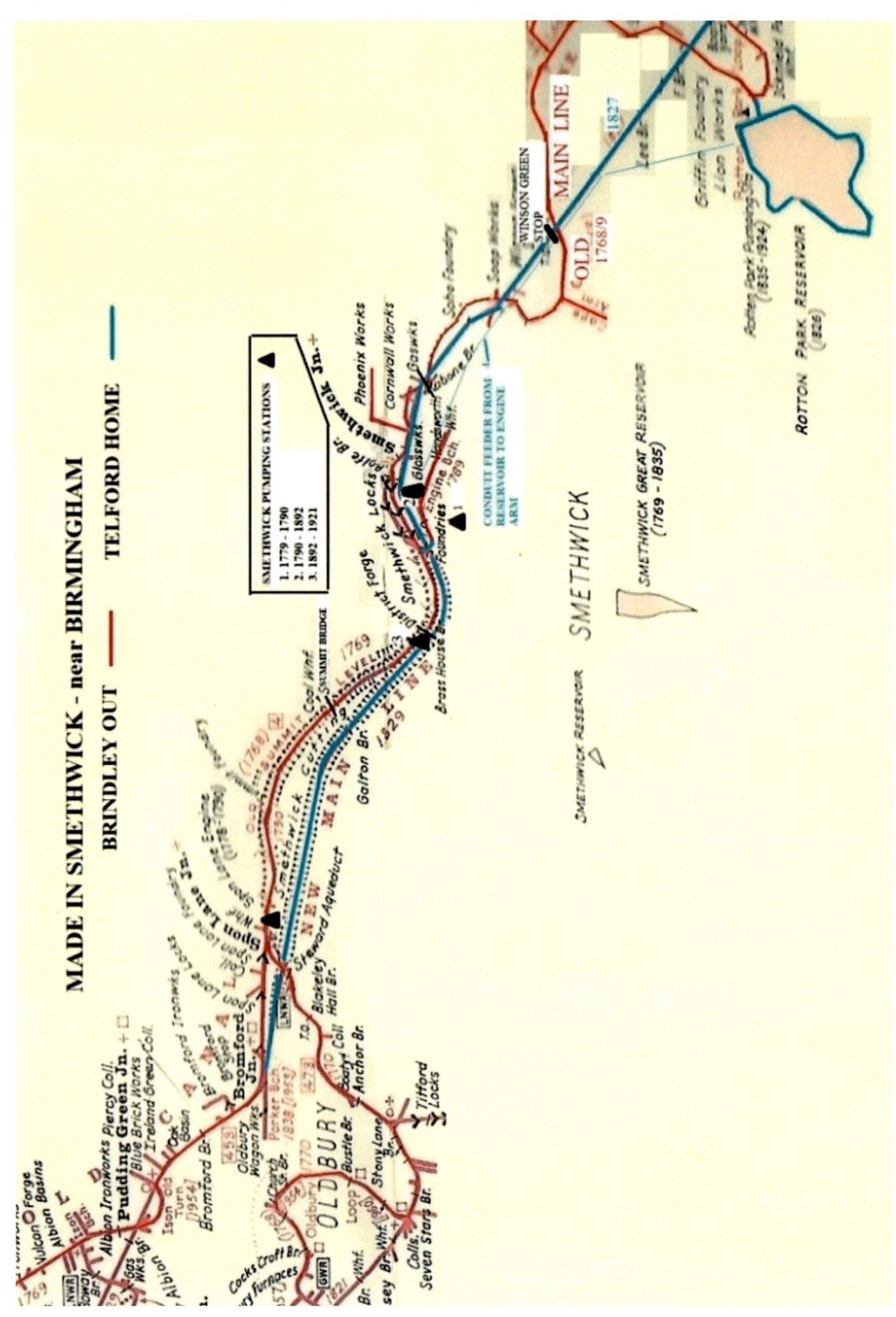

It was the cutting of the Birmingham Canal in 1768-9 that eventually brought manufacturing industry to Smethwick; the firms which from the late 18th century set up works along its banks were concerned mainly with metalworking, which has ever since played a predominant role in the town's economy. The primary production of metals from ores has never been of any significance, but many forms of engineering have flourished. In the early 1870s Smethwick and Dudley Port, 'with a thousand swarming hives of metallurgical industries . . . too numerous to mention', were contrasted with other Black Country towns which specialized in one or two specific types of metalware.

British History of Smethwick

PART 1
WINSON GREEN TO THE JUNCTION

249. Soho Foundry from the towpath, Birmingham Canal (2006) Oil on canvas

The traveller needs to reach the northern canal junction of the **Soho Loop** emerging to Telford's straight Main Line Canal. From a modern-day perspective, the starting point of this virtual journey is not a particularly easy place to reach but it is strategically important for the canals in historical and economic terms. It was here that not only the Birmingham Smethwick border commenced but where cargoes were forced to pay their dues. Originally Brindley's winding route on an east – west axis was unimpeded but subsequent changes led to the closure of the Cape Arm Loop, that would have passed to the right margin of this painting below.

--X--

1.1 WINSON GREEN STOP – GAUGING STATION & TOLL HOUSE

"243. Only a mile to go to Birmingham" (2006) Oil on Canvas   www.tedhiscock.com

The first roving bridge is a Grade 2 Listed item, (as its partner to the left of the painting where Brindley's original canal passes beneath as it emerges on to the Telford Main Line).

HISTORIC ENGLAND LISTING
ROVING BRIDGE* OVER BIRMINGHAM/WOLVERHAMPTON CANAL JUST WEST OF WEST SOHO LOOP ENTRANCE
Grade 2
LIST ENTRY 1289686
5104 SP 08 NW 6/7
HEATH STREET
Winson Green B18
Roving Bridge* over Birmingham/Wolverhampton Canal just west of west Soho Loop entrance.
 "Cast iron roving bridge serving double tow path of Telford's New Line. Single shallow segmental arch. Parapets pierced in saltire cross pattern and each formed from three castings. Stone dressed brick abutments. Inscribed: "THE HORSELEY COMPANY TIPTON 1848".
roving bridge is one where the ponies pulling boats could change canal towpaths without being disconnected

There are several striking features immediately from the site of the Stop: the straightness of Telford's route, the extremely high banks and bridges, the considerable width of the canal and today, the rural reclamation by nature herself, helped by deliberate planting in the 1980s. It is an amazing contemplation that heavy industry used to pump foulness into the water and the whole area echoed with deafening noise, noxious fumes pervaded the air, smoke and filth from machines adjacent to these waters generated a very unhealthy environment. Now, it is the domain of birds, butterflies and wildflowers, with walkers, cyclists, runners and holiday boats generating the bulk of traffic. The brick base of this toll house still remains, although in a sorry state, it is gradually returning to nature and occupied by bullrushes, water plants, geese, ducks and herons.

For a more comprehensive information concerning this site; read Ray Shill's: 'Birmingham's Canals' [2001] ISBN 0-7509-2077-7 Sutton Publishing Ltd [REF: 12 p.27]

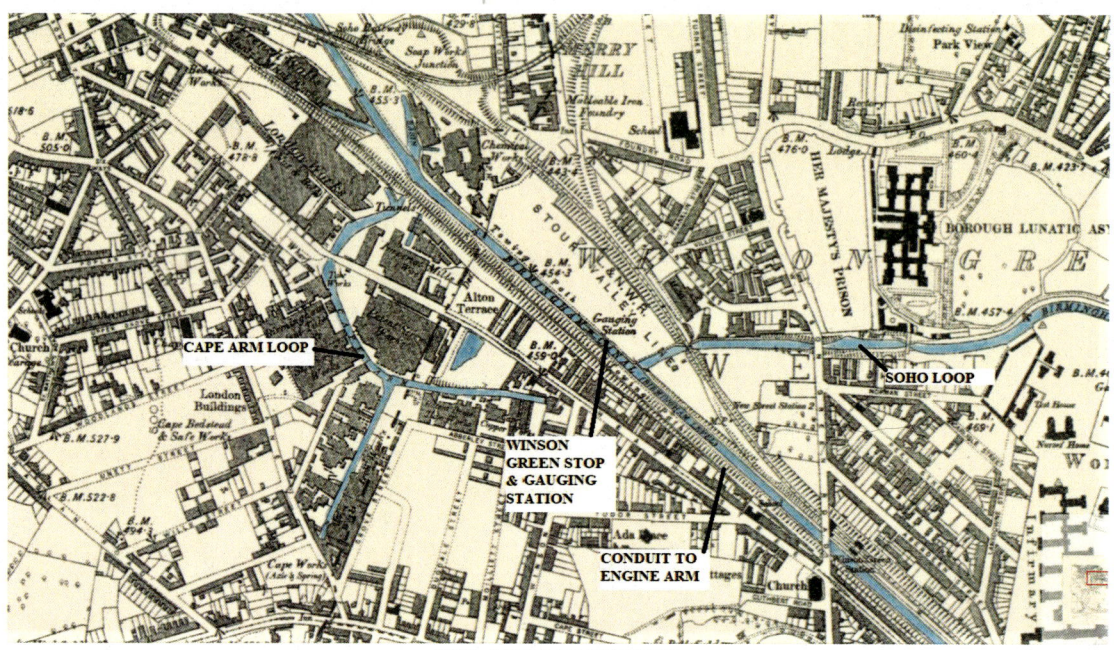

1888 O/S MAP SURVEY

CANAL FEEDER CONDUIT The ingenious interdependence of two parallel canals to the North of this point, collectively built by Brindley and Telford permitted many products of the industrial revolution to reach the outside world. Boulton and Watt's Soho Foundry was one that relied on the Brindley route of export. It was no accident that the same firm of Boulton & Watt who built two steam engines in 1779 – (one remains today in Birmingham's **Thinktank Museum** and is the world's oldest working engine) should have secured the task of providing the power of shifting water uphill! This couple of steam engines could pump water from both directions to maintain water levels at the highest point where water feed was poor; one was close to Spon Locks and the other was fed by this **conduit feeder** from Rotton Park Reservoir to Telford's **Engine Arm** and adjacent Aqueduct, dating from 1825 close to **Smethwick Locks.** *[REF: 78]*

LEFT; The Toll house and gauging station as it used to be when in use with Winson Green Prison in distance on the left. Note the stopping boards on the bank to the left, which were used (& still can be) to stop the water, allowing maintenance to the bed of the canal. [Birmingham Library].
RIGHT: "268.1 Soho Loop Junction" (Immediately behind the position of the viewer of this sketch, is the canal feeder conduit to the Engine Arm in Smethwick). [2016].

Sadly, in 2020, the beautifully fashioned brick Canal Feeder Conduit from Edgbaston (Rotton Park) Reservoir is still present but no longer in use and in a poor state of repair. This runs along the high bank on the north side of the Birmingham Canal from Winson Green Bridge to Smethwick. It can easily be viewed by climbing the south bank by the Winson Green Stop (as seen in the photo to the left), where the ill-fated Sandwell Hospital under construction on the old GKN site is also visible.

Winson Green Stop looking south. The island functions as a santuary for wild life. The northern end of the Soho Loop comes in under the roving bridge on the left. Brindley's original route went left to right here and linked up with the Cape Hill Loop. Laden boats would be forced to stop here and be taxed according to their weight and other criteria. This was gauged using a measuring stick. It has always been accepted that the reason for blocking off the Cape Hill Loop was to prevent boaters trying to escape paying the tolls using the alternative side route.

Unkempt Edgbaston Reservoir feeder culvert to Engine Arm by Winson Green Stop 2010. In a poor state of repair.

--X--

The next part of the journey is as if the original route existed passing through the high bank bearing the conduit. The site of Sandwell Hospital rises monumentally (currently as a gigantic Meccano construction, 2020). It is being built on the vast site of the conglomerate of GKN factories that once resounded here. The GKN works straddled the crescent shaped Cape Arm loop and is still accessible from the north. For the sake of this narrative, the encompassing of the GKN site and straight finger-like projection to the Mitchells & Butler Brewery at Cape Hill is today purely virtual and for the next stage it is the latter that first is explored in this tangential shift of axis.

--X—

1.2 CAPE HILL BREWERY – MITCHELLS & BUTLERS LTD

Cape Arm Canal spikes in a south-westerly direction from the Birmingham Canal and has predominantly always been a waterway lined with heavy industry. A few hundred metres from its southern tip was one of the West Midland's largest breweries, although not dependant on the canal system, it does require mention in this context. Now a housing estate, its former function is well disguised. For many years the air of west Birmingham and the Black Country was filled with the aroma of roasting hops from the **Cape Hill Brewery**, or as most knew the name of **M & B, Mitchells & Butlers.**

On April 15 2006, Chris Upton wrote an article on the Cape Hill Brewery (Mitchells & Butlers Ltd) which started: *"It was practically the size of a small town. There were houses, sports club, garages, stables and even a fire station. It occupied more than 100 acres and 1,500 people were employed there. Now there are just the houses."* [REF: 108]

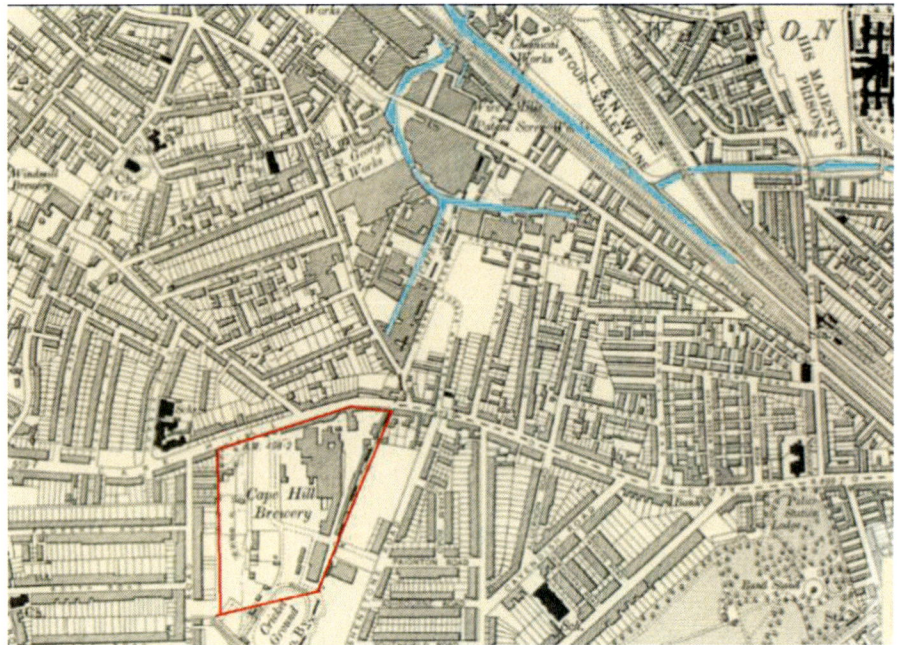

1902-3 surveyed O/S map showing the extensive site of the Cape Hill Brewery at the southern end of the Cape Arm

Two parallel families eventually came together with one common goal: - to make beer for Birmingham and the Black Country

1810   **Henry Mitchell Snr**. Was born at Bromyard, Worcestershire

1830s   Henry Mitchell was earning money as a hosier (a seller of hosiery)

1843   **William Butler** born

1850   Mitchell had moved to the Black Country and started working as a brewer

1854   Henry Mitchell was proprietor of the **Crown Inn, Oldbury Road,** Smethwick and had his young son, **Henry Mitchell Jnr.** working alongside him

1861   Henry Mitchell jnr. became sole proprietor of The Crown. Within a short space of time, he had bought the land alongside the pub and built a new brewery

1866   William Butler became landlord of the **London Works Tavern, Smethwick**. Also, he had a son, **William**

1870s Mitchell's brewery operated 24 hours a day except for Sundays. Expansion was so rapid, he ran out of space and needed to buy 7 acres of land wedged in between Birmingham and Smethwick.

1876   William Butler partnered his brother in law, **George Owen** who was running the **Crown, Broad Street, Birmingham**

1879   **Cape Hill Brewery brewed its first beer**. The business of making beer was changing from each publican having a cottage industry to large corporate businesses where breweries supplied several tied houses.

1881   Butler became sole owner of The Crown, Broad Street.

1888   300 employees at Cape Hill Brewery produced 90,000 barrels of beer/annum

1890   **Henry Mitchell Jnr**. owned 86 pubs in Birmingham

1897   Henry Mitchell joined up with William Butler, owner of 19 other city pubs to create the company of **MITCHELLS & BUTLERS LTD**. Butler, had also started his working life as a hosier. Butler's first pub had been the London Tavern, Smethwick and then he took on the Old Crown, Broad Street, Birmingham adjacent to Symphony Hall and the canal as it passes under Broad Street.

2020 A typical M&B pub; The Queens Arms, on the corner of Newhall Street and George Street, Birmingham

1898   All business of the amalgamated company moved to Cape Hill, which was on a vast site and had an inexhaustible artesian well. The successful pair bought up many smaller competitors in Birmingham and the Black Country.

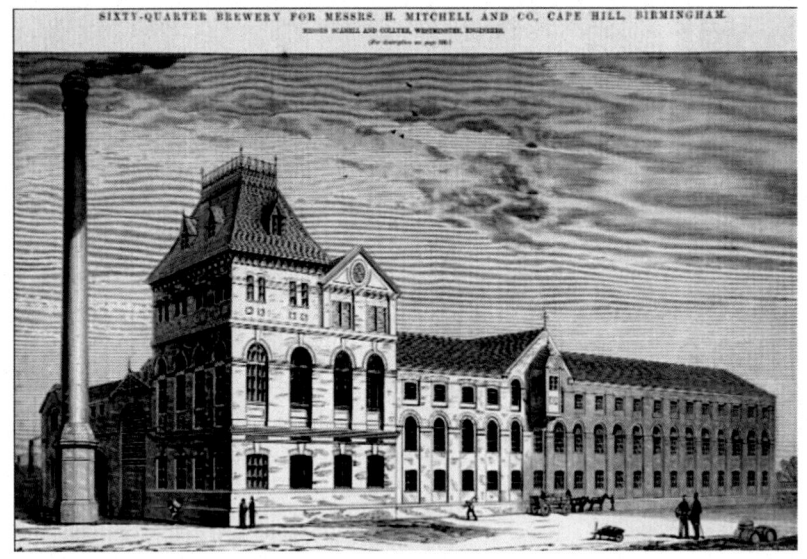

1907   William Butler died at a time when M&B was one of the largest breweries in the country, employing 1200

1914   Henry Mitchell died

1961   Mitchells & Butlers merged with Bass, Ratcliff & Gretton to form Bass, Mitchells & Butlers

1867   **Bass, Mitchells & Butlers merged with Charrington United Breweries** to form **Bass Charrington,** later shortened to **Bass PLC**

1989   **Bass PLC** formed separate brewing and retailing divisions: **Bass & Bass Taverns**

--X--

Now it is time to explore the second of the great sites in this southern quarter of Smethwick. GKN, now virtually razed from any semblance of its original size and dominance, had a phenomenal history in engineering terms and for giving mass occupation to the people of Smethwick.

--X—

1.3 GUEST, KEEN & NETTLEFOLDS
GUEST & CO., NETTLEFOLD & CHAMBERLAIN, PATENT IRON & BRASS TUBE CO., ARTHUR KEEN

*"of Birmingham, a British engineering company formerly known as **Guest, Keen and Nettlefolds** which can trace its origins back to 1759 and the birth of the industrial revolution."*
[REF: 16 Grace's Guide]

GKN has been one of the giants of industry in the West Midlands since the mid-18th century and was finally decapitated as recently as 2018, when it passed into the hands of the financial house, **Melrose** for an alleged £8.1 billion. The complexity of its development as three essential limbs is an extraordinary journey of historical heritage. At one time it was the holding company for 83 registered companies with a working population of 75,000 employees. The effect of its departure on Smethwick will be devastating to the town both in employment and financial terms; further compounded by the fact that the new **Sandwell Hospital** under construction at this time, is many years behind schedule due to the embarrassing collapse of overarching contractor, Carillion, who went into compulsory liquidation on 15th January 2018. It was probably "the largest ever trading liquidation in the UK"

To simplify the tortuous and complex history of how three major players, Guest, Keen and Nettlefold came together, this narrative has been split into five relevant channels, (not three), which have been explored chronologically. There is overlap in ownerships and changing partnerships as some prospered and others failed and it must be remembered that the large industries alongside the Birmingham Canal had a great deal of influence on each other. For example, there is interplay between the main **GKN** site and the **London Works**, although independence existed in each unit.

A. Guest & Co [REF: 23]

1759   The **Dowlais Ironworks** was established at Merthyr Tydfil and run by a partnership of nine members including **Thomas Lewis**, who had leased the land in 1747.

1767   **John Guest** was appointed manager of the works, having discovered coal on the land leased by Thomas Lewis.

1782   John Guest was made a partner with Lewis along with a salesman, **William Taitt**

1785   **John Josiah Guest** was born in Dowlais to **Thomas Guest**, manager and part owner of the Ironworks. Of this new and young Guest, Grace's Guide reports:

"Guest was educated at Bridgnorth Grammar School and Monmouth Grammar School before learning the trade of iron making in his father's foundry at the hands of works manager John Evans. He was renowned for his ability to roll a bar of steel or cut a tram of coal as well as any of his father's workmen."

1787   Thomas Guest succeeded his father, John

1795   **Thomas Guest Jnr.** Introduced steam power using a **James Watt engine,** (made in the Soho Foundry a few metres away on the other side of the Birmingham Canal).

1807   John Josiah inherited his father's share on the latter's demise and developed the firm in a positive manner.

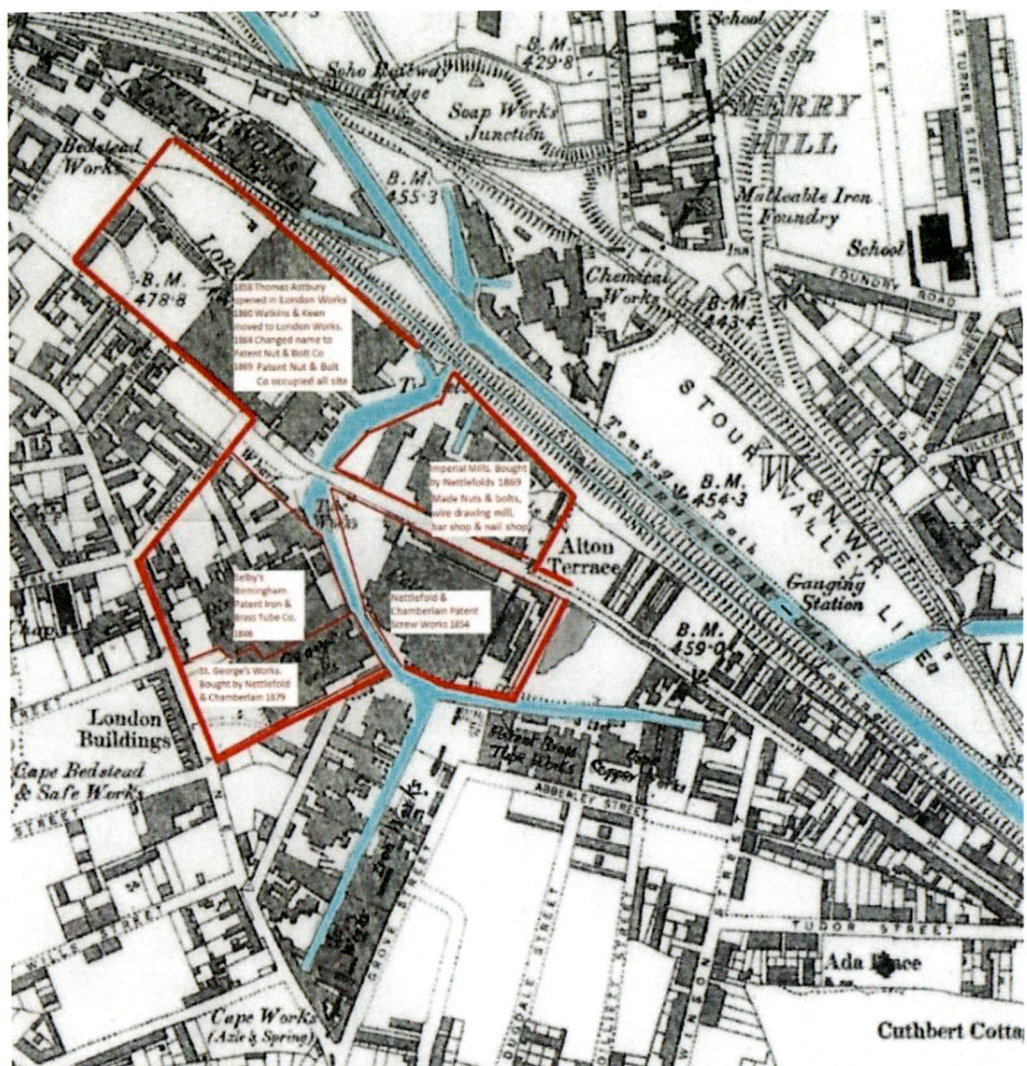

1888 O/S Map 6" : mile. The GKN site. Various references in the narrative relate to sites on this map.

1815   Guest was the sole manager of **Dowlais, the largest iron and steel producer in the world**

1819   John J. Guest became **Sheriff of Glamorgan**

1821   Great success came to the firm with the expansion of the railways requiring rails.

1824   **Guest Lewis & Co** were producing 15,000 tons per annum

1826   **John J. Guest was elected MP for Honiton, Devon**

1831   **Guest & Co bought up Dowlais Ironworks**, a major 19th century ironworks located near Merthyr Tydfil. [REF: 17]

1832   **John J. Guest was elected MP for Merthyr Tydfil**

1835   **Ivor Bertie Guest** born to **John J. & Lady Charlotte Guest** (titled by family connection). Ivor was educated at Harrow School and went on to graduate at Trinity College, Cambridge in 1856 in Master of Arts. He became **the 1st Baron Wimborne**.

An incidental finding under the Birmingham History website a contributor 'Wendy' [REF: 24] wrote:

"John Guest lived in Brosley, Shropshire then moved to Wales with his family, his grandson Ivor Bertie Guest 1835-1914 became 1st Baron Wimborne and was married to Lady Cornelia

B. Nettlefolds [REF: 16, 17, 18, 19 20, 21, 22]

1819   **John** Sutton Nettlefold (1792-1866), a British industrialist and entrepreneur married **Martha Chamberlain**, sister to **Joseph Chamberlain Snr**, (father of his more famous son) and between them, they had three sons Edward John, Joseph Henry and Frederick. They were Unitarian.

John Sutton Nettlefold (1792-1866)   Martha Nettlefold (née Chamberlain 1794-1866)

1823   J.S. Nettlefold opened a hardware shop at 54 High Holborn, London. He acquired a patent for *"certain improvements in the methods of making screws, brass, steel, or other metals for the use of all kinds of woodwork."* [From a mechanical watchmaker, John Gilbert of St. Marylebone.]

1826   J.S. Nettlefold set up a workshop to make screws in Sunbury-on-Thames powered by a water wheel.

1834   J.S. Nettlefold was in Birmingham, setting up a new factory **Nettlefold & Sons** at **Baskerville Place, Broad Street** using steam power. He presumably realised that this city was where steam power was so evident.

1851   **C/R** They lived in Hornsey, London and he was described as a General Merchant with his wife and seven children and three servants.

1851   At the **Great Exhibition at the Crystal Palace**, Nettlefold saw an American machine for the automated manufacture of wood screws

1854   Nettlefold purchased *'a licence to a U.S. patent for manufacture of a wood screw with a pointed end'*. This required heavy investment and he approached his brother in law, **Joseph Chamberlain Snr.**; they put in £30,000 (£2,326,000 in 2020) between them and a factory was established **Nettlefold & Chamberlain** in **Heath Street, Smethwick**, where John's sons. **Edward and Joseph Henry** ran with help from their nephew **Joseph Chamberlain**, who took on the firm's accountancy. It consisted of 20,000 sq. Ft. in two single-storey sheds.

Grace's Guide:
>   He *"expanded his small London business in iron and screws to Smethwick where he set up a factory to make screws using advanced, new machinery licensed from America. He was able to expand his enterprise partly because of an investment by his brother-in-law, Joseph Chamberlain. The partnership Nettlefold and Chamberlain in Birmingham became one of the*

Henrietta Maria Spencer-Churchill, daughter of John Spencer-Churchill. 7th Duke of Marlborough. There was a story in my family that we were related to G.K.N. but apart from an Ann Guest who married my G.G.Grandfather Samuel Peters at the Parish Church of Brosley in 1842 I have been unable to establish a link. if there is any substance to this story we were probably the poor relations. Wendy."

1838   **John J. Guest was made a Baronet**

1839   Guest Lewis & Co built the **Ifor Works** and owned 19 furnaces at Dowlais

1845   Employed 7,300 people and its 18 furnaces produced 89,000 tonnes of iron per year; "it was one of the largest steel and iron producers in the world" [REF: 25]

1851   The partnership between **Sir John Josiah Guest** and Edwin John Hutchins (little known of him) was dissolved

1891 Blast Furnaces at the Dowlais Steelworks. [Grace's Guide]

1852   **Lady Charlotte Guest** assisted (family title) **John J. Guest** in the management of the Dowlais Colliery but he died leaving her in control.

1865   The first **Bessemer steel** was rolled at Dowlais Works, being the first company licensed to use the technique

1867   A fatal accident occurred at a colliery belonging to Guest & Co

1868   **Ivor Bertie Guest was made High Sheriff of Glamorgan**

1869   Grace's Guide:
"*Monster Casting.— A casting of enormous proportions — a 70-ton block for a steam hammer — has just been successfully executed at the Dowlais Steel Works. The first charge of iron was tapped shortly after midnight, and successive charges followed from two cupolas throughout the day until 3 p.m., when the full weight of 70 tons had been poured into the mould, the metal keeping in a state of fusion for over 12 hours, and will not be cold enough to fix in position for some 12 or 14 days.*"

1899   **Sir Ivor Bertie Guest,(Lord Wimborne) sold Dowlais Ironworks to Arthur Keen** for £1.5 million (£118,000,000 in 2020). He died in 1914 at his home in Canford, Dorset

1900   **Dowlais Iron Co, Guest & Co and Patent Nut & Bolt Co. Chaired by Arthur Keen** merged to form **Guest, Keen & Co.** This enabled Arthur Keen to have his own coal to produce a remarkably diverse range of products.

1902   **Guest, Keen & Nettlefolds was created.**

> **THE BIRMINGHAM PATENT TUBE COMPANY.**
>
> FIRST CLASS MEDAL, LONDON, 1851.
> PARIS MEDALS, 1855 and 1867.
>
> MANUFACTURERS OF
> **IRON, BRASS, & COPPER TUBES,**
> FOR
> Marine and Locomotive Boilers and Condensers.
> **IRON, BRASS, AND COPPER TUBES AND FITTINGS,**
> **FOR GAS, STEAM, AND WATER PURPOSES.**
> *Solid Drawn & Brazed Brass & Copper Tubes.*
> **BRASS AND COPPER PLATES AND SHEETS,**
> For Condenser, and other purposes.
> BRASS AND COPPER WIRE, HYDRAULIC PRESS TUBES,
> **TUYERE AND OTHER COILS.**
> BEDSTEAD TUBES, CORE BARS, &c.
> Screwing Tackle and Gas Fitters' Tools of all Descriptions.
> COPPERSMITHS' WORK EXECUTED TO PLAN.
>
> **WORKS:**
> **SMETHWICK, near BIRMINGHAM.**
> London Office, 77, Cannon Street, E.C.

1874 [Grace's Guide]

1880s 'Lap-welded iron and steel boilers, solid-drawn brass and copper sheets, tubes and fittings for gas, steam and water', were being made from the site. But by the late 1880s, the company had ceased.

D. ARTHUR KEEN (1835-1915)

1835 **Arthur Keen** was born, the son of a Yeoman farmer and Inn Keeper in Cheshire. When young, he joined the London & North Western Railway at Crewe.

1855 Keen was appointed a goods agent for the railway and relocated to Smethwick where he met many industrialists among them was the wealthy iron founder, **Thomas Astbury,** his son **James** and daughter **Hannah** and an American inventor, **Francis Watkins** who had created a patent nut-making machine and was trying to sell it in the UK.

1856 **Thomas Astbury** funded **Watkins & Keen** at **Victoria Works**, Rolfe Street, Smethwick

1858 Arthur Keen married **Hannah Astbury**, they moved to Edgbaston and had 10 children

Keen realised the importance of Watkins's creation and they established the firm of Watkins & Keen with Thomas Astbury's money.

The same year Thomas Astbury & Sons took over part of and opened in **The London Works**

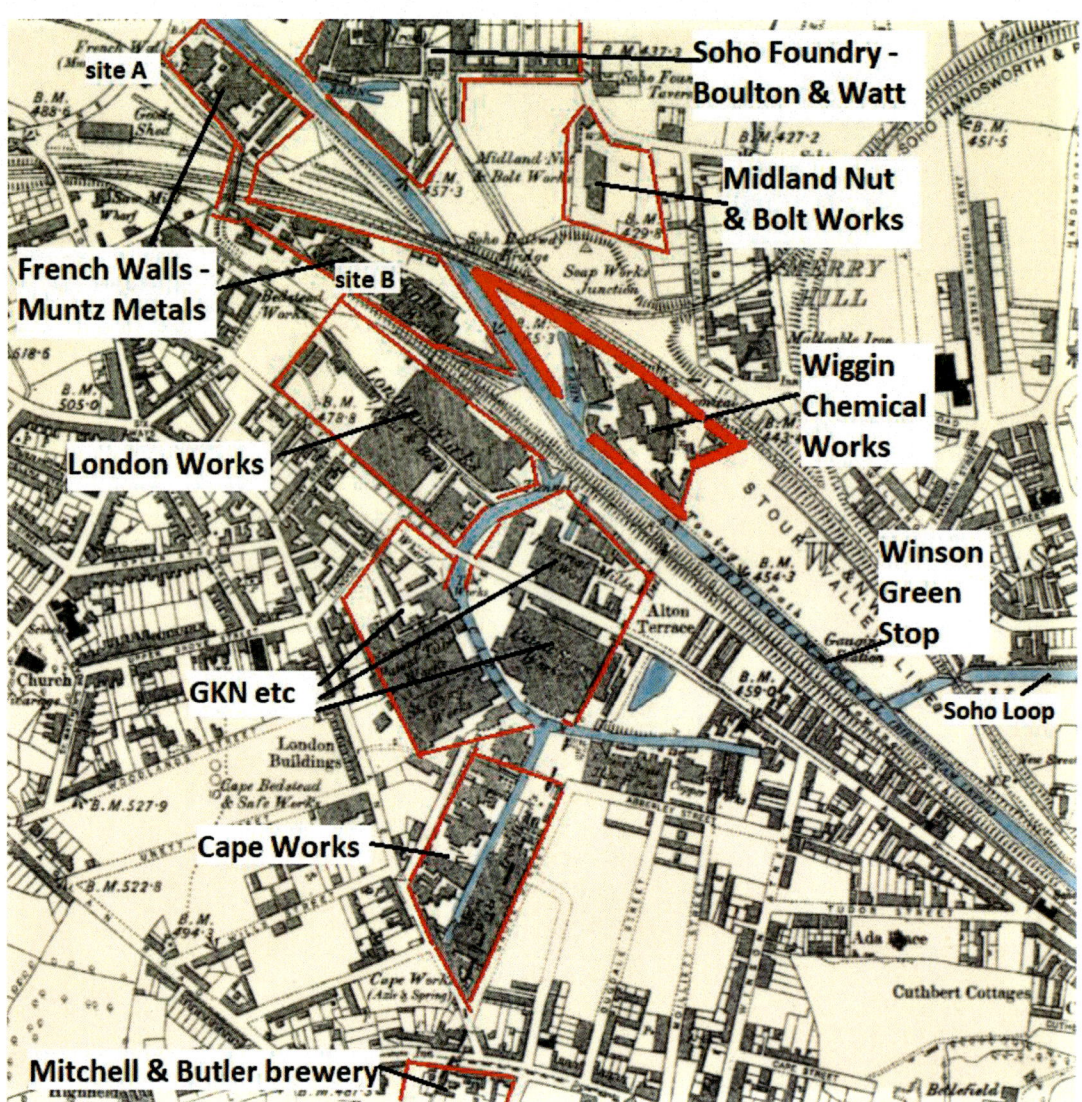

1888 O/S MAP (annotated) showing relationship of the various sites that amalgamated to become GKN and some of the neighbours that grew up alongside.

1860   **Watkins & Keen** with expansion, moved into **London Works**

1864   Watkins & Keen was floated as a limited company as the **Patent Nut & Bolt Co** and Watkins retired a few years later but the growing enterprise of Watkins & Keen as leading fastener manufacturers displaced **Astbury & Sons** from London Works. Keen then merged with a competitor, **Weston & Grice** of Stour Works, West Bromwich. By this time, Watkins & Keen were producing about a third of the nuts and bolts made in the Midlands. It is said that Arthur Keen tried to emulate his neighbouring company, Nettlefold & Chamberlain, but had less success. However, with the capital of the new company amounting to £400,000 (equivalent to £24,000,000 in 2020) and the site of the London Works, Smethwick, where the business was occurring, was considerably enlarged.

1869   Patent Nut & Bolt Co occupied all the **London Works** site

1870   Keen started to attempt purchase of Nettlefolds

1880   Arthur Keen became a Director of the **Birmingham & Midland Bank**

1898   The London & Midland Bank merged with the City Bank to become **London, City & Midland Bank** with leadership by Arthur Keen. He was elected Chairman of the newly formed bank and remained at its helm until 1908

1900   Arthur Keen bought the **Dowlais Ironworks** and **Guest & Co** for £1.5 million forming **Guest, Keen & Co**. and became the Chairman and Managing Director. It is said that the rapid and successful growth of Smethwick during this period was largely down to Arthur Keen. He was a major benefactor of the town and assisted with the provision of a **municipal gas works**, the construction of public baths, free libraries and laid out parks for the town. He was also a generous supporter and **Life Governor of Birmingham University.**

1902   The merger of Guest, Keen & Co with Nettlefolds occurred to form **Guest, Keen & Nettlefold**, of which Arthur Keen was the Chairman. This merger made GKN the largest employer in Smethwick.

Grace's Guide:

> *"These mergers heralded half a century in which the name Guest, Keen and Nettlefolds became synonymous with the manufacture of screws, nuts, bolts and other fasteners. The company reflected the vertical integration fashionable at the time embracing activities from coal and ore extraction, and iron and steel-making to manufacturing finished goods."*

> *"GKN was an enormously profitable business and Keen was held in high regard. Much of the business's profitability stemmed from a successful policy of price maintenance through the Birmingham Alliance that he forged with trade unionist Richard Juggins and which was realised in the midland iron and steel wages board."*

1903   **Birmingham Patent Iron & Brass Tube Co** was absorbed into **St. George's Works**. [REF: 5]

1909   Edward Nettlefold died

Edward Nettlefold (1856-1909)

E. MODERN TIMES

1914   GKN were producing over half the screws and a quarter of the nuts and bolts made in the UK.

1948   **Guest, Keen & Nettlefolds (Midlands) Ltd**, established: - The Bolt & Nut Division in Darlaston, Screw Division in Smethwick.

1950   The company amalgamated with **Mosers Ltd** to become Britain's leading wood screw manufacturer.

On a chat line in 2008, Master Brummie, Dave Rock described: *"St. Georges Mill was the main producer of self-tapping screws at GKN. Screws & Fasteners, Heath Street Mill produced woodscrews & the 'Bolt' Mill produced a variety of products including socket screws, (Seam assemblies?), push rods & many other automotive products."*

1960s   Black Country History:
In the late 1960s the headquarters of Guest, Keen & Nettlefolds Ltd., by then an investment company, adjoined the Heath Street Works, Smethwick, a 50-acre complex run by G.K.N. Screws and Fasteners Ltd. and employing some 4,500 people.

G.K.N. had several other subsidiaries in Smethwick:
- *G.K.N. Distributors Ltd. had its headquarters at the London Works,*
- *G.K.N. Group Services Ltd. was in Cranford Street,*
- *G.K.N. Reinforcements Ltd. in Alma Street,*
- *G.K.N. Fasteners Corrosion Laboratory in Abberley Street.*
- *Smethwick Drop Forgings Ltd. of Rolfe Street, acquired by G.K.N. in 1963, was run as a subsidiary of G.K.N. Forgings Ltd. [REF: 25]*

1861   GKN was a holding company of 83 subsidiaries and 75,000 employees.

1966   GKN had changed its name to **GKN plc**, acquired the **Birfield Group**, including **Hardy Spicer Ltd**, Birmingham to enter the automotive industry with automotive overdrive business and to be a competitor in prop shaft engineering and changing the name to **GKN Transmissions**.

1966   The business was reconfigured into 8 major sub-groups embracing over 60 separate industries

1980s   GKN were world leaders in powder metallurgy – diversified into military vehicles but left the steel industry, selling their interest to **British Steel**

1994   GKN took over **Westland Helicopters** and expanded into aerospace services and programmes including F/A-22 Raptor, Eurofighter, Airbus A380.

1998   GKN sold its armoured vehicle business to **Alvis plc**

2001   GKN plc and **Finmeccanica** of Italy merged with **Westland and Agusta** to create **AgustaWestland**, one of the two biggest helicopter companies in the world.

2003   GKN left the armoured vehicle business

2004   GKN sold 50% shareholding in AgustaWestland to Finmeccanica for £1,063 billion. The end of year turnover was £3.5 billion

2018   Wikipedia:

During January 2018, Melrose Industries announced its plans to purchase GKN as well as the firm's restructuring thereafter, that same month, GKN's management rejected the initial bid made. In March 2018, Melrose submitted a revised £8.1 billion bid for the company; this bid was controversial and was subject to criticism, being branded by some press agencies as a hostile takeover. Melrose's offer received shareholder support and was accepted. Following a formal review of the purchase, including of various objections put forward by GKN workers and trade unions, the UK Government allowed the transaction to proceed in April 2018 Melrose agreed to comply with several national security measures.

2019   In October 2019, **Melrose Industries** announced the appointment of Funmi Adegoke to its Board as an inaugural independent non-executive Director. [REF: 26]

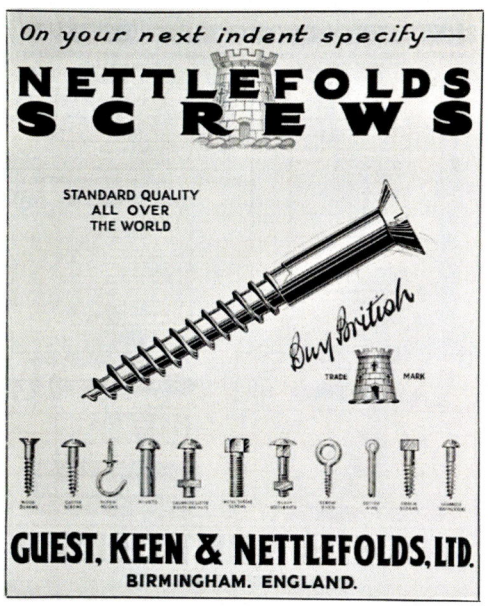
1927 [Grace's Guide]

2020 Remnants of GKN factory with the new Sandwell Hospital during its stoppage of construction through the bankruptcy of Carillion. Photo taken from the bank alongside the Birmingham Canal by the dual tunnel bridges.

--X--

As the Cape Arm emerges through one of a pair of dark and dingy short tunnel, the Brindley route would have gone diagonally opposite through another Horseley roving bridge, today further silted up and festooned with detritus of modern 21st century negligence and certainly not displaying the pride of an English Heritage Grade 2 Listing.

--X--

HISTORIC ENGLAND LISTING

LIST ENTRY NUMBER 1977155
DATE FIRST LISTED 1987
GRADE 2
TOWPATH BRIDGE AT SP 036 884 (APPROXIMATELY 640 METRES SOUTH EAST OF RABONE LANE). BIRMINGHAM CANAL BIRMINGHAM LEVEL
Bridge carrying northern towpath of Birmingham Canal over disused branch. Dates from widening of canal in 1827. Cast-iron. Brick abutments have stone dressings. Single elliptical arch. Sides each of two castings, bolted to central "keystone". Pierced in form of saltire crosses, with band of quatrefoils below handrail. Illegible inscription in south-west spandrel.

831. Foundry & Cape Arm branches (2020). Looking south towards Birmingham. The emerging Cape Arm branch was through the tunnel on the far right. The roving bridge on the left of this painting is Grade 2 listed and is the route followed by Brindley's original route on its way into Soho Foundry.

—X—

Once again, the journey must be virtual as already stated, this Horseley roving bridge passes over a vestige of Brindley's canal that would have passed the site of the Wiggins Soap and Chemical Works before threading neatly into the southern end of the vast Soho Foundry and W & T Avery site. The northern end of this track is still visible as another roving bridge. There is a piece of modern historical jigsaw that occurred here on the night of 28/29th October 1940, when during the thunderous and unrelenting bombing raids on the West Midlands a bomb did fall close to the railway line bridge where it crossed the canal. Damage to the stonework where shrapnel hit and a fire occurred can be seen. There is an unsubstantiated story that the bomb hit a boat passing beneath the bridge. [REF: 110].

—X—

1.4 THOMAS ADKINS, SOAP WORKS JUNCTION, HENRY WIGGIN & LUDWIG MOND

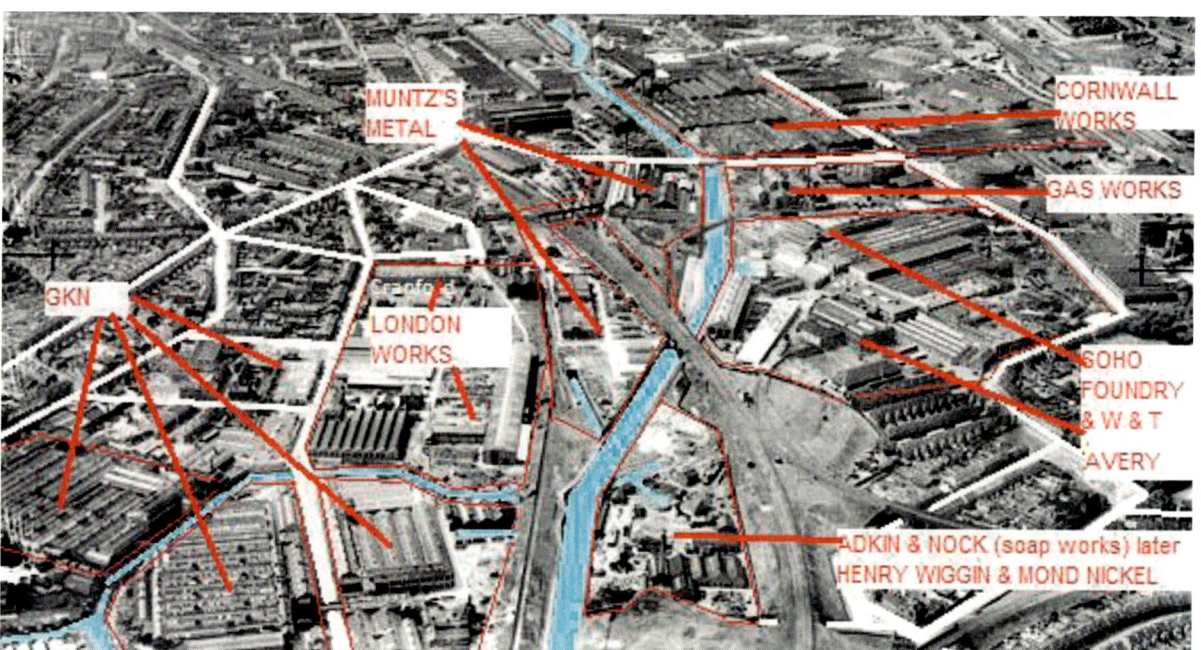

1947 GKN, Mond Nickel Co Ltd, London Works, Soho Foundry, Gas Works, Cornwall Works & Muntz's Metal Works from the south

1792   **Thomas Adkins Jnr.** was born to Thomas Adkins, a tallow chandler of Livery Street, Birmingham

1818   **Thomas Adkins Jnr** and **John Nock** built and owned a vast soap works on the north bank of the Birmingham Canal at Merry Hill. After a few years, a third partner joined by the name of **Boyle**, who had come to them from **Blair & Stephenson of Tipton**, the country's leading manufacturer of red lead and who recently had invented a new method of bleaching soap. The new business of **Adkins, Nock & Boyle** majored on its skill mix and wasted no time adding **red lead** to their list of manufactured items.

Thomas Adkins bought **The Grove**, (Smethwick) a large mansion house close to his factory) from **James Moilliet**, the son of a successful Birmingham banker, Jean-Louis Moilliet.

1841 Thomas Adkins of The Grove died. The business continued in the hands of Thomas's three sons; **George Caleb, Francis and Henry Adkins**.

1860s These three sons became important manufacturers of **red and white lead** and associated by-products and were the third largest manufacturers with the Midlands being the most important region for making this substance as well as being a successful producer of soap.

1865 **George Adkins** bought **Lightwoods Park & House, Bearwood**, and passed it to his son Caleb.

1866 **Henry Adkins** wrote two chapters in a book promoting Birmingham businesses, one of these chapters almost entirely devoted to the description of his own company's manufacturing process for soap, whilst the other concentrated on the production of red lead (the poisonous paint).

1887 George Caleb died.

1888 The business was sold to a successful industrialist relative of the Adkins, namely **Sir Henry Wiggin**, MP (1824-1905) already famous for his Nickel plant **Henry Wiggin & Co**, about a mile further south on the other side of the canal abutting the Icknield Loop and Wiggin Street. [REF: 85]. Wiggins used the site for the construction of a cupola and reverberatory furnaces for smelting Nickel and Cobalt ores.

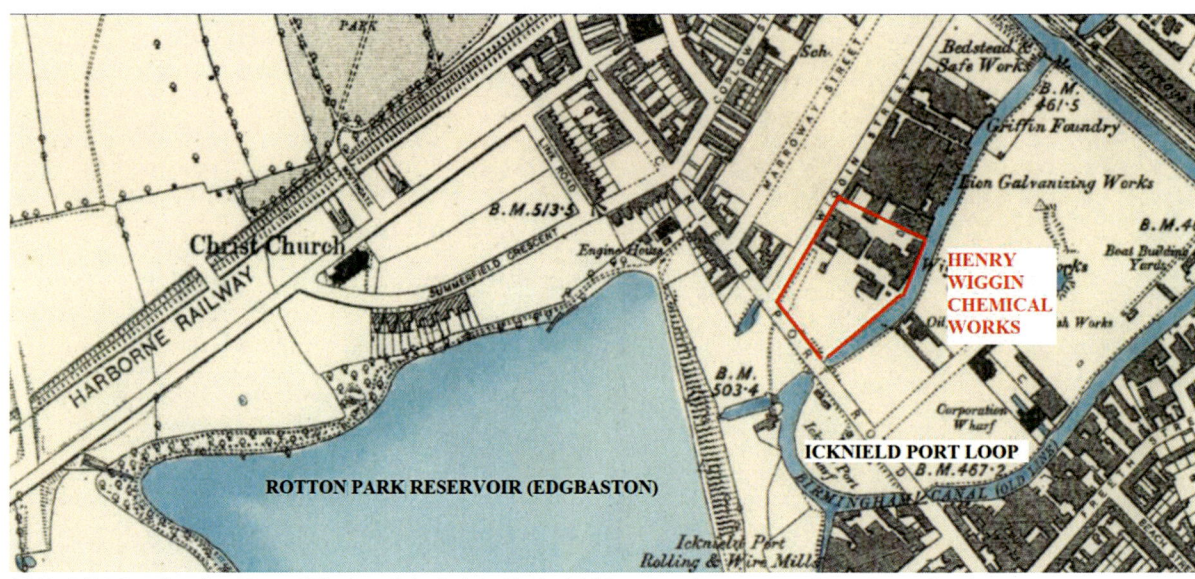

1888 O/S Map showing Henry Wiggin original site off Icknield Port Road, now part of Port Loop development

Wikipedia says of Henry Wiggin: [REF: 86]

> *He was also a Director of the Midland Railway, the Staffordshire Water Works Co., the Birmingham Joint Stock Bank, and Muntz's Metal Co. He was a governor of King Edward's School, Birmingham, a J.P. for Worcestershire and Birmingham, and Deputy Lieutenant of Staffordshire.*

1892 **Dr Ludwig Mond**, joined forces with Wiggin and built an experimental plant to produce the first carbonyl-refined Nickel. The same year Henry Wiggin was made 1st Baronet Wiggin/

1896   Wiggin started to make Tin Oxide at the Smethwick plant for the first time in Britain, with the production being supervised by German employees.

1902   Caleb Adkins died. Lightswood House was bought for Birmingham City by public subscription by a committee under the Chairmanship of a member of the Chance family; **Alexander M. Chance** chairman of the **Oldbury Alkali Co**.

1919   Wiggins was taken over by **Mond Nickel Co Ltd.**

1929   **International Nickel Co of Canada Ltd** took over Mond Nickel Co Ltd

1931   Production ceased at Smethwick [REF: 5]

1892 Sir Henry WIGGIN, MP – a caricature in Vanity Fair

[See also Hiscock: "Brindley Out Telford Home – A journey along the Birmingham Canal" p. 46 for more information on Henry Wiggin & Co]

--X—

The virtuality must continue as the original route into Soho Foundry is long gone and after the Rabone Lane Railway Bridge, on the towpath side travelling north, there is a footpath that moves between the railway and the Avery site. A few metres along here, a metal fence looms on the left, through which the original route can be imagined.

--X--

1.5 SOHO FOUNDRY
BOULTON & WATT, JAMES WATT & CO, W & T AVERY

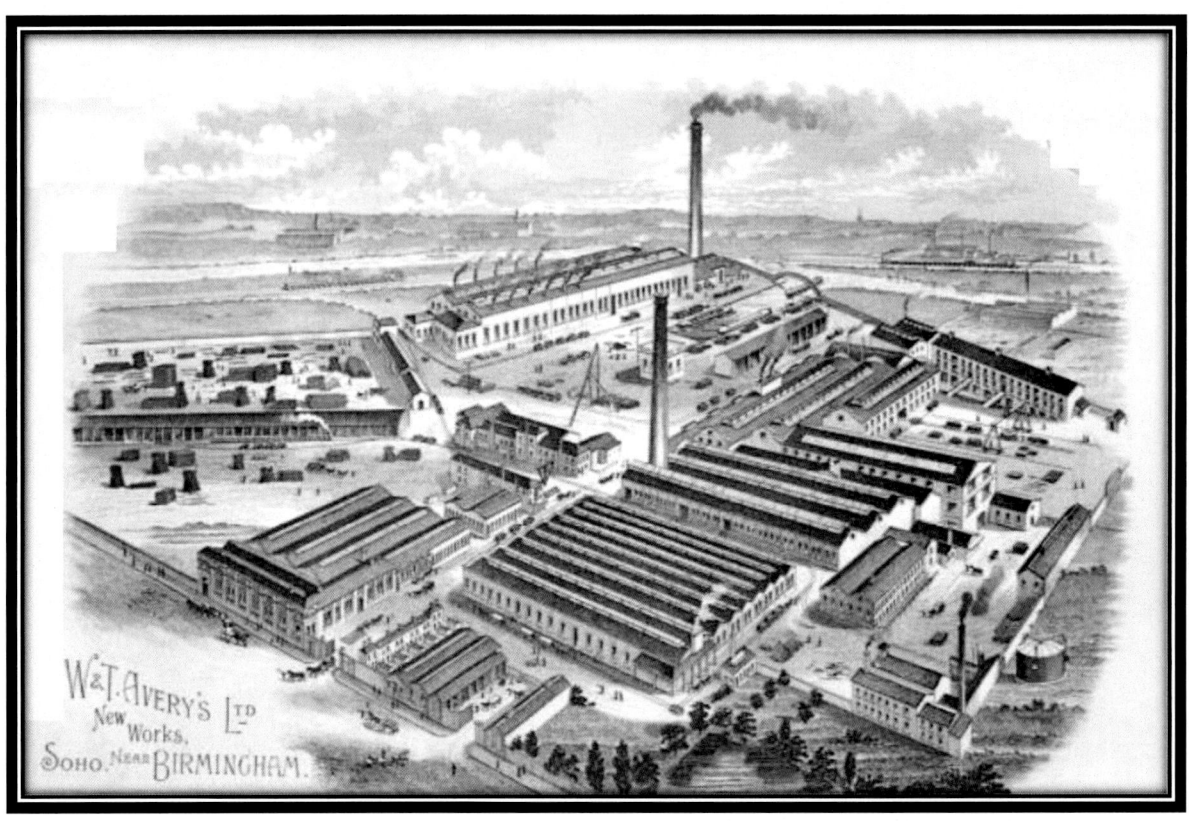

"When the Empress Catharine of Russia visited the famous Soho Works, she asked Matthew Boulton what was made there, and was answered "We make what monarchs are fond of – power!"

Sir Richard TANGYE – 1889

"This site is one of the world's most important sites relating to the industrial revolution"

Andrew LOUND (ex-Museum Archivist, Soho Foundry [REF: 33]

SOHO FOUNDRY - AN 'AT RISK' SCHEDULED MONUMENT

[Historic England terminology]

It was an urgent necessity; Boulton needed power for his Manufactory, the world needed power and with a meeting of genius, the two engineers came together and changed the way the world would behave for ever. Watt, the designer, Boulton, at that time, the financier. Between 1775 and 1895 two generations of Boulton & Watt families created engines beyond the wildest dreams of everyone in the world; Soho Foundry was at the heart of the Industrial Revolution, which was to alter the way the globe functioned for ever.

Today, the site is a dilapidated and neglected crumbling eyesore. It has one Historic England Grade II* and one Grade II listings within its perimeter and holds the accolade of being a Scheduled Monument but is also on the "At Risk" Register. Since 2008, charity funding was used to provide a protective roof over the most precious part of the site which has slowed the decay but not arrested it. Photographs taken from the canal in 1974, aerial photos in the series 'Britain from Above' and 'Google Earth' clearly demonstrate the alarming state of 'vandalism by neglect' this national monument suffers.

In 1896, W.& T. Avery acquired the site from the then defunct Boulton & Watt business which through a series of take-overs by a succession of overseas companies, since 2008 it has been in the ownership of Illinois Tool Works trading as Avery-Weigh-Tronix. Even the 90-year-old Avery Museum has been disbanded with dispersal of all exhibits and treasures of two centuries. The family names of Boulton, Watt and Avery have been synonymous with the power and money that made the very fabric of Birmingham and Smethwick. Today, these two communities have turned their backs on this icon of industrial creation. The family members of Avery, Boulton and Watt, who showed such altruism in the 18th and 19th centuries, would be turning in their graves to witness such lack of public and community responsibility.

Currently, this Foundry, could be argued to be as important historically as any in the country. Our Royal Family is part of our Sovereign Heritage whilst Soho is part of our Industrial Heritage but is an embarrassing national disgrace. If this site is not to disappear into a pile of rubble, something urgent needs to be done by central authority.

A. **HISTORIC ENGLAND – Scheduled Monument REMAINS OF BOULTON & WATT SOHO FOUNDRY [REF: 39]**

In 2008, Historic England (then called English Heritage) designated the Soho Foundry in Sandwell Metropolitan Authority to be a Scheduled Monument [List Entry 1268451].

Reasons for Designation The remains of the Soho foundry **provide a unique example of an early industrial Foundry. Soho was one of the first purpose-built steam engine manufactories in the world**, founded by the pioneering firm of **Boulton and Watt** and associated with other renowned engineers and new techniques. William Murdoch, John Southern and Peter Ewart all worked for Boulton and Watt.

In establishing this ground-breaking foundry and manufactory, Boulton and Watt established a format which was copied and developed by many later steam engine firms and general engineering concerns. At the date of its inception in 1795, the engineering industry had barely developed and the steam engine manufactory represented a pioneering venture of fundamental importance to the origins of an industry for which Britain became renowned.

- The site may be considered as one of the **founders of the great industrial lineage** in which Britain was pre-eminent in the world for much of the 19th century.

- In addition to steam engines, Boulton and Watt had important associations with the **development of steamships** from 1804 and the Boulton and Watt marine engine business was one of the most important in the country during the 19th century.

- Its most celebrated contract was the provision of the screw engines of Brunel's **Great Eastern**, which successfully laid the first transatlantic cables. Hardly a coincidence that Tangye Brothers, a neighbour of the Soho Foundry provided the pumps that assisted the ship's launch.

- In 1788 Boulton and Watt were the first to introduce **steam powered mint machinery**, which was then exported worldwide, for example to Mexico, Russia and India.

- The works were also the **first gas-lit factory building in the world** and responsible for pioneering the production of gas lighting equipment on a commercial basis. **The remains of the Boulton and Watt Soho foundry and mint survive well.**

- They helped to illuminate this **pioneering phase of industrial development in the West Midlands.**

- The significance of the site is enhanced by the exceptional archive associated with it which includes the **papers of the Boulton and Watt company** as well as the separate collections of the personal papers of James Watt and Matthew Boulton which are housed in the **Birmingham City Reference Library.**

834. Boulton & Watt Soho Foundry (2020)

B. BOULTON & THE SOHO MANUFACTORY

The story of **Soho Foundry** starts with that of the Soho Manufactory. These were two distinct buildings and sites but inextricably linked in function, purpose, design and ownership. Some authorities fail to appreciate that they were separate sites. The Manufactory has totally disappeared.

1761 **Matthew Boulton and John Fothergill** started toy manufacture from leased premises on Handsworth Heath containing 'a cottage and a water-driven metal-rolling mill'. [REF: 67]

1766 The mill was replaced by a new factory, designed and built by a rival of Robert Adam, **James Wyatt** (1746-1813). Wyatt had already become renowned for his exceptional neoclassical style of architecture and for his ability to amend stately homes. Meanwhile, the cottage was replaced by a grandiose home for Matthew Boulton in the construction of Soho House.

Belonging to Matthew Boulton & John Fothergill, built in 1766 under the design of James Wyatt.

The Hockley Brook was used to create a pool which powered the mill for the Soho Manufactory. This scene in 2020 is now a prefabricated industrial park of no particular architectural value. Soho House still sits at the top of the hill but surrounded by Victorian terraced streets a hundred years younger.

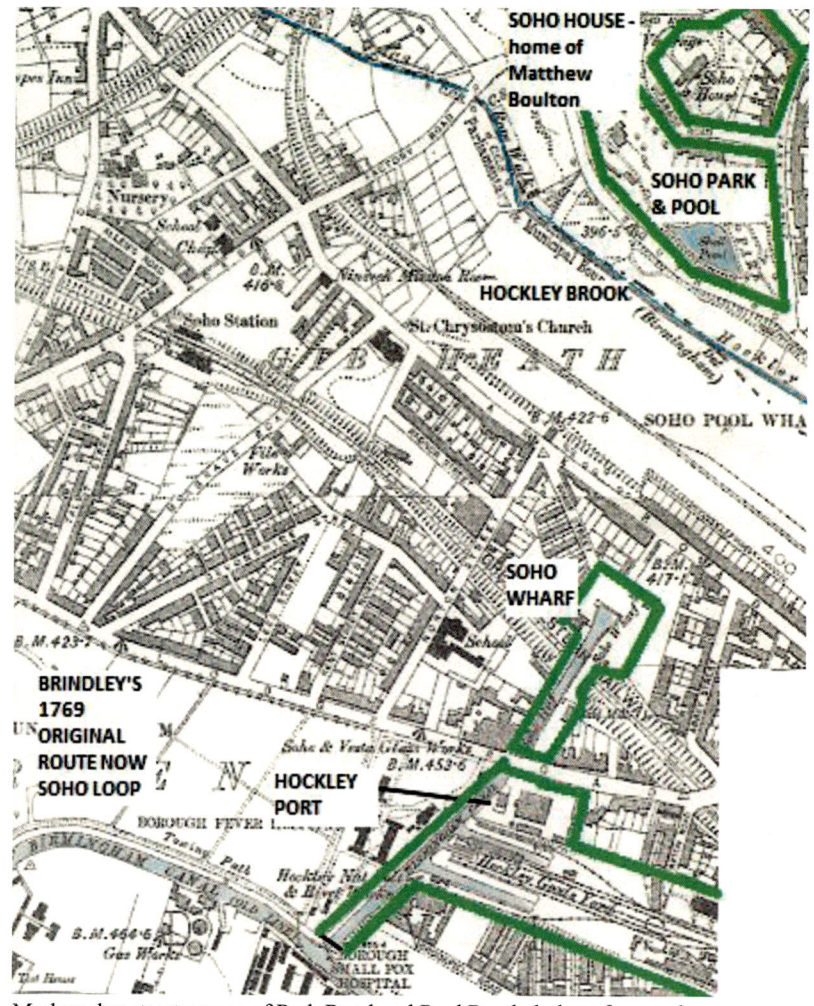

Modern day street names of Park Road and Pool Road elude to former days

C. THE UNIQUE HISTORY & HERITAGE OF MATTHEW BOULTON AND JAMES WATT IN THE CONTEXT OF THE SOHO FOUNDRY & THEIR IMPORTANT INDUSTRIAL RELEVANCE TO THE NATIONS OF THE WORLD

"Some of the inventors, notably James Watt, who first gave a decisive industrial value to the steam engine, were men of science." H.A.L. FISHER (1935) [REF: 45]

1736   **James Watt** was born.

1759   Watt worked on the power of steam as a source of motive power and gradually came to understand and define **latent heat**.

1765   Every school child brought up in the UK is aware of the legend that James Watt invented the steam engine because he saw a kettle boiling. Of course, this is not the whole truth but he was the first person to modify **Thomas Newcomen's atmospheric engine of 1712** by adding a 'separate condenser' and doubling the power. He further modified it to provide a rotary motion that enabled it to drive machinery. It was this major step in design that revolutionised power within factories that no longer had to use water and steam: suddenly the Industrial Revolution leapt in action.

1765-1813   The Lunar Society regularly met on nights of the Full Moon and had as its members, many of the eminent scientists, philosophers, industrialists, physicians, and intellectuals. Amongst its members were: Josiah Wedgewood, Matthew Boulton, Samuel Galton Jr, Erasmus Darwin, James Keir, Joseph Priestley, Dr. William Withering and James Watt

1775   After a previous partner, **Dr. John Roebuck** went bankrupt, Watt needed financial assistance and teamed up with **Matthew Boulton**, who had continued a highly successful precious jewels and gilt ware business at the **Soho Manufactory** since 1761. [REF: 44]

1777   **William Murdoch, the inventor of town gas**, at the age of 23 walked 300 miles to Birmingham from Scotland to ask for a job with James Watt. [REF: 60] He started work in the Pattern Shop making patterns for the casting of machine parts.

1776   Watt & Boulton designed and licensed other engineers to produce to Watt's design, **reciprocating motion pumps** which were extremely popular and successful at pumping out mines, particularly **in Cornwall.**

1779   Watt started the company **James Watt & Co**, (also with Matthew Boulton and a new partner, **James Keir**). They invented a crude **copying machine** for ink documents which lasted in service until the early years of the 20th century. The same year Murdoch was sent to Redruth, Cornwall as a senior engine erector for Boulton & Watt, where one of their engines was being installed to pump water out of Cornish Tin mines.

1779   Boulton & Watt made **2 steam beam-engines** which were brought into service about half a mile from where they were made. One was placed on the south side of the summit of Brindley's Canal as it passed over the high land between Smethwick and Sandwell and the other at Spon Lane, Smethwick. These two gigantic pumps were used to keep Brindley's Birmingham Canal topped up with water as it passed over this 150metre (491ft.) summit. Water supplies in this area were insufficient to enable effective use of the 6 locks on either side of the summit. The pump south of the hill was rescued by Birmingham City Council and is now housed in the **Thinktank Museum**, Millennium Centre, Birmingham and subject to some major replacement parts, is **the oldest working steam engine in the world.**

1781   **William Murdoch**, whilst employed with Boulton & Watt, designed a successful system called "**Sun & Planet Gear**", which gave motion to the wheels of mills or other machines". [REF: 60]. Apparently, *"one night after returning from his duties at the mine at Redruth, Murdock went out with his model locomotive to the avenue leading to the church, about a mile from the town."* The locomotive shot off into the distance when Murdock heard shouts and cries and on catching up with his invention, *"found the local vicar in great fear, thinking that the hissing, spitting demon was no other than the Evil One himself."* [REF: 4].

1782   Watt invented the notion of **Horsepower,** using a comparison with drafted horses, which was later adapted to include piston engines, electric motors etc. One mechanical horsepower (hp) was defined as 'one horse lifting 550 pounds (250kg) by 1 foot in 1 second'. Soho Manufactory was the first works to possess a Watt steam engine developed at the Soho Foundry by **James Watt** [REF: 55] and was the **first steam-powered mint in the world**, Subsequently, these presses were transferred to the **Birmingham Mint**

1783   Watt and Boulton standardised a definition that 'a brewery horsepower could produce 33,000 foot-pounds per minute'. [REF: 46, 47]

1784   Watt designed and patented the '**parallel motion' engine**; an especially important invention enabling straight line motion in cylinder rod and pump action.

1784   James Watt was made a Fellow of the Royal Society of Edinburgh.

1784   **Murdoch** designed the first model of a **steam carriage or road locomotive**. The same year, he devised an experiment to obtain ammonium chloride and iron filings. [REF: 60]

1785   James Watt designed the **Whitbread Engine**, which was one of the first rotative steam engines – (a type of beam engine where the reciprocating motion of the beam is converted to rotary motion); it is preserved in the Powerhouse Museum in Sydney, Australia. [REF: 57]

1787   JW was elected a Member of the Batavian Society for Experimental Philosophy, Rotterdam

1788   Watt developed a steam-powered **coining press** for his partner Matthew Boulton at the Soho Manufactory. [REF: 55, 56]

1789   James Watt was elected Member of the Smeatonian Society of Civil Engineers

1790   A Watt steam engine was running 8 presses at a rate of up to 150 coins per minute. [REF: 55]

1792   Murdoch invented **gas lighting as a replacement for oil and tallow produced light**. His house in Redruth was the first domestic residence to be lit by gas. [REF: 60]

1794   Watt was chosen by an English physician, **Dr Thomas Beddoes** to manufacture apparatus to produce and store gases for use in the gaseous treatment centre for disease, which he called his **Pneumatic Institution at Hotwells in Bristol**.

1795   Further land was bought to build the Soho Foundry by Boulton & Watt

1796   After a lengthy infringement of patent case, Watt was awarded massive damages in the courts at the same time the Soho Foundry started to manufacture steam engines. The British History on Line states:

"In 1795 Boulton, Watt & Sons, faced with difficulties in obtaining the components for their engines, decided to manufacture them themselves. James Watt bought 18½ a. by the canal at Merry Hill, about a mile from the firm's Soho Manufactory in Handsworth"

"in 1796 the firm opened Soho Foundry there 'for the purpose of casting everything relating to our steam engines'. Watt owned the land until 1801 but otherwise took no part in the new enterprise, its development being the work of Matthew Boulton's son M. R. Boulton and James Watt the younger. The site was carefully chosen, and the buildings were meticulously planned with the requirements of the various processes in mind. In 1799-1800 they comprised foundry stoves and furnaces, a boring mill, turning-, fitting-, carpenters', smiths', and pattern shops, a boiling-house, a magazine, a shed for sand, a drying-kiln, and 13 workers' houses. workers' houses. Stebbing Shaw [a notable 18th c. Staffordshire historian and topographer; 1762-1802)] noted "the extensive use of steam-power for 'whatever tends to abridge human labour and obtain accuracy' and was struck by 'the extraordinary regularity and neatness which pervades the whole". In 1800 the firm became Boulton, Watt & Co., with M. R. Boulton and James Watt the younger as the leading partners." [ref: 43]

"The Soho Foundry was planned with a degree of sophistication unprecedented for a factory of its time. Its products were produced out of standardised interchangeable parts, *reducing the need to supervise work as it was executed, simplifying stock control and enabling more efficient repair of faults for customers. The Soho Foundry stood out from other factories of the day in the sophistication of its planning, its production processes and its management techniques; practising concepts that wouldn't become commonplace until a century later"* [REF: 57]

1797   Boulton was permitted by the British government to make **a penny and two penny coins from copper**. They became known as "Cartwheels". They were only minted for a short period of 2 to 3 years and all one penny coins bore the date 1797. [REF: 54]

A bronzed two-pence of George III – 1797 Soho mint. Spink 3776; KM 619; 41 mm, 56.1 gm   [REF: 54]

1798   Murdoch returned from Cornwall to Soho Foundry to continue developing a system of gas lighting and **the Foundry was one of the earliest to be gas lit**. The first was Philips & Lee cotton mill in Manchester, which he designed and supervised.

1799   Murdoch invented a much simplified and more efficient steam wheel, which has been described as the **precursor of the turbine**.

1800   James Watt Snr retired to his home at **Heathfield Hall, Handsworth** (now demolished and the site part of a large Birmingham housing estate) but carried on designing and inventing from his **garret workshop**. (now in the Science Museum, South Kensington, London). During that year, Boulton & Watt made 41 engines. The partnership of **Boulton & Watt passed to the two men's sons.** James Watt designed and produced a 3-D copying machine that recreated sculptures and commemorative medallions.

1804   A third Boulton & Watt engine was put alongside the original one at the Engine Arm, Smethwick

1806   James Watt was conferred an Honorary Doctor of Laws, University of Glasgow

1807   Murdoch designed and built the **engine for a paddle steamer, 'The Caledonia'**, which sailed on the Hudson River, USA

1809   Boulton & Watt received licence from Parliament to produce lighting whilst successfully blocking a competitor from doing the same.

1813-1825   Marine engines of over 3,000 horsepower (2,200 kW) were made by Boulton and Watt and used in some 40 to 60 vessels.

1814   Watt was elected Corresponding Member & Foreign Associate of the French Academy

1814   Boulton & Watt abandoned gas lighting projects

1819   James Watt died at Heathfield Hall and is buried in Handsworth churchyard, Birmingham.

1849   **James Watt Jnr. Died. Boulton & Watt** name changed to **James Watt & Co** [REF: 50]

1851   The company received an Award at the 1851 Great Exhibition

SS Great Eastern was a vast ship designed by Isambard Kingdom Brunel. She was the largest ship ever built at the time of her launch in 1858, which was assisted by hydraulic jacks, designed by the Tangye Brothers, neighbours of James Watt & Co, on the Birmingham Canal, Smethwick. Her maiden journey was in 1859 and could carry 4000 passengers. [SS Great Eastern 1858. REF: 52]

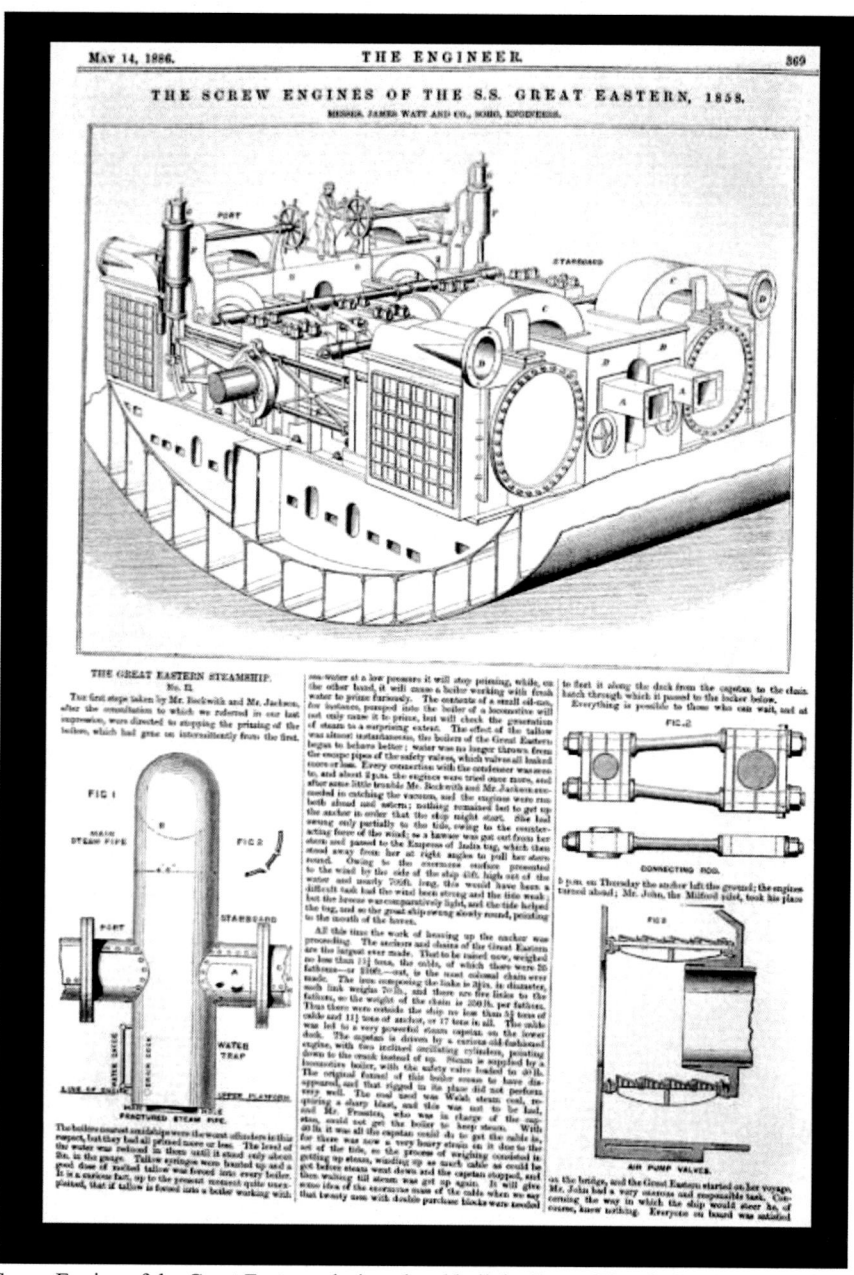

1858 The Screw Engine of the Great Eastern, designed and built by James Watt & Co. Courtesy of The Engineer

[Report from Birmingham Journal 2 April 1859 REF: 51]

"MONSTER CASTING. James Watt would have stared with astonishment had his eyes witnessed that which we had the privilege of seeing on Thursday afternoon at the steam-engine works of which he was the founder. What we then saw, **however, simply proved that the genius and energy which, three-quarters of century back, gave the Soho world-wide fame, are yet a living force** *; and that though the great engineer has been lying quietly in the chancel of Handsworth Church for forty years, the* **"James Watt and Co."** *to-day still maintains a foremost place in all that concerns the development of the mighty power with which the name of the firm is so indissolubly associated."*

The circumstance to which we are more particularly referring is the casting of some unusually enormous cylinders. They are intended for the engines of packets shortly to be placed, for purposes of postal communication, on the Holyhead and Dublin route. The vessels will be of 2,000 tons burden, and by the aid of the powerful engines now being constructed at the Soho Works, it is expected that a speed of from twenty-one to twenty-two miles an hour will be attained. This of course greatly exceeds anything now afloat, the rate at which the Queen's yacht goes being under eighteen miles hour. All who have ever crossed the Irish Channel will appreciate the change. The cylinders, as we have said, are of a size quite unprecedented for engines on the oscillating principle. Their diameter (internally, we may explain to the non-scientific reader,) is no less than ninety-six inches, and the piston will have seven-feet stroke. The Cylinders of the Great Eastern are only eighty four inches in diameter, and have four-feet stroke — the great power of the leviathan steam-vessels being obtained by the possession of two pairs of engines, one pair of which was made at Soho.

'A stroll through the works showed that they are in as fine a condition as ever. As can be expected, some of the buildings are low-roofed and old fashioned, but others are as spacious as can be seen anywhere. The great erecting shop has not its equal in Europe. All are filled with the most costly, elaborate, and powerful machinery for the execution of every kind of engineering work, and nearly a thousand men are kept constantly employed. Amongst the orders now in course of execution is one of great extent for the Indian Government.

The Soho was always famous for its coining machinery, and twenty-five years ago the present firm sent to Calcutta and Bombay all the presses, rolling mills, and other apparatus required for establishing a mint for each Presidency.

A number of marine engines for English frigates and men-of-war are also in course of construction at the works; and the firm appears now to have its hands full enough to keep the Soho in full swing for at least a couple of years

1864   James Watt & Co Supplied 4 beam engines for London Main Drainage

1877   Supplied two engines for The South Staffordshire Waterworks Co.

1883   Three engines for Hull Corporation Main Drainage Station & the same year, one more for Kingston-Upon-Hull Corporation. [The exhibit is in the Thinktank Museum, Birmingham]

1884   Beam Pumping Engine for Papplewick Pumping Station, Ravenshead, Nottingham

1889   The 2nd Congress of the British Association for the Advancement of Science adopted **the unit of power as a WATT.**

Sir Richard TANGYE of neighbouring Cornwall Works, in his autobiography of 1889 "One & All" [REF: 53]

> HEATHFIELD HALL—JAMES WATT. 179
>
> A few years since, my brother George went to reside at Heathfield Hall, near Birmingham, "where," writes Mr. Sam: Timmins, F.S.A., "one of the most remarkable and interesting relics of the great inventor of the steam engine has been reverently preserved, exactly as it was left by its owner nearly seventy years ago. It is a low-ceiled room over the kitchen of the house, and with the window overlooking the stable yard. It is reached by a narrow staircase, and it is practically separate from the rest of the house. It is known as the 'classic garret' or attic, or private workshop of James Watt, in which his later years of leisure were passed in various mechanical experiments as 'amusements' of his old age. It is now a 'relic room' of the machinery, apparatus, tools, and products of the old engineer after his fame and fortune had been made. On the

1895   **The firm had lasted 120 years** and still making steam engines but the Foundry was closed as much of the machinery and building were outdated and the site purchased **by W & T Avery,** a company like so many in this region, that was expanding at a phenomenal speed and needed more space outside the immediate confines of its city.

D. W. & T. AVERY

This company is described as one of the oldest in Birmingham dating back to 1731 and

'manufacturing by hand of steelyards (a straight-beam balance with arms of unequal length. It incorporates a counterweight which slides along the longer arm) and beam scales in a small workshop in Birmingham.' [REF: 67]

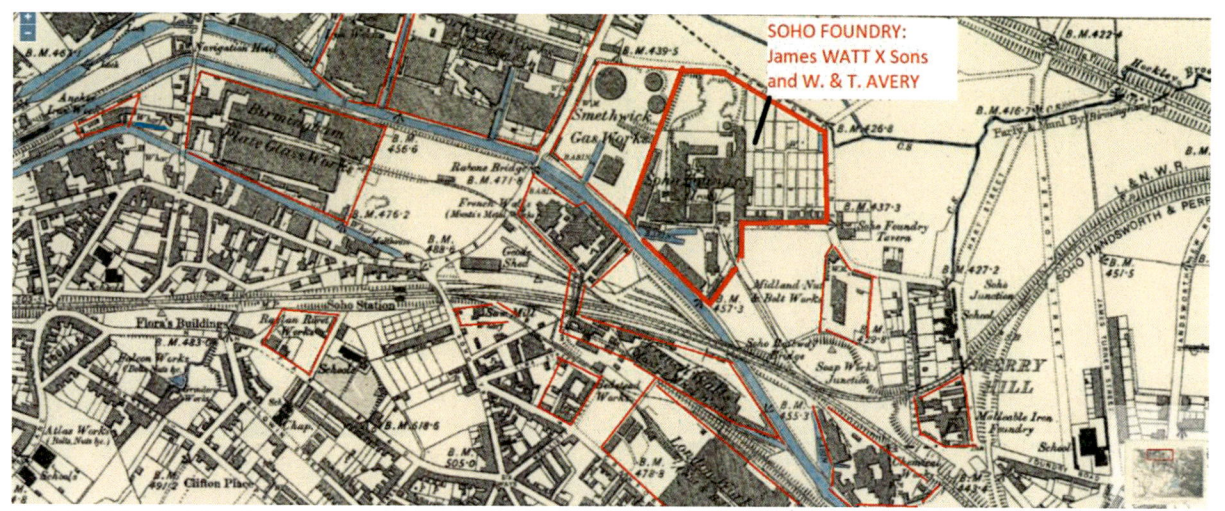

1888 O/S Map showing the large expanse of the Soho Foundry just before Avery took over the site in 1895

1731   A gent by the name of **James Ford** set up the company that manufactured weighing systems. At some stage, the company passed to **William Barton**.

1782   William Barton transferred the business to **Thomas Beach**, whose niece was **Mary Avery**.

1785   Mary Avery married **Joseph Balden**

1799   Thomas Beach handed his scale-making business to his niece's husband, **Joseph Balden**.

1811   **William Avery Snr**. (1789-1843), a draper of Birmingham, married **Elizabeth Balden**

1812   **William Henry Avery Jnr.** born

1813   Joseph Balden died intestate, leaving two sons.

'The elder son, failing to keep the business going, conveyed his estate to his cousin and brother-in-law, William Avery.'

1813   **Thomas Avery** born in Birmingham and baptized in St. Phillips, Birmingham

1814   **William Avery Jnr.** (1812-1874) inherited the scale-beam making business from his cousin **Joseph Balden**. With his brother, **Thomas Avery**, (1813-1894) injected energy into the company, trading as **William & Thomas Avery.** A fine example of inter marriage of Birmingham industrial families to secure industrial strength and wealth.

1842   Thomas Avery married Mary Anne Beilby

1843   **William Avery Snr**. died but already his two sons, **William Henry (b. 1812) Thomas (b. 1813)** were working in the company.

1851   The brothers employed 150 men

1853   William Jnr married a Scottish lady, Maria Richmond Beilby

1861   **Thomas & his wife Mary** were living in **Aston** but later moved to Edgbaston

1865 **William Jnr** took sole charge of **William & Thomas Avery**

1868 **Thomas Avery** became **Mayor of Birmingham**

1871 C/R William Avery Jnr was living in Norfolk Road, Edgbaston and employed '233 men, 71 boys and women'. He had four children living there at the time, one of whom was **William Beilby Avery** (1854-1908) and another **Henry J. Avery** (1861- ?). Presumably, his wife had died, as her sister was resident. There were 4 servants.

1874 Grace's Guide:

'Avery was largely responsible for the acquisition of a private waterworks, the development of which under town ownership brought potable water to the townsfolk, and the greater achievement of the provision of a sewage works. '

1874 William Avery Jnr. died

1877 Grace's Guide says of Thomas Avery:

'after a battle against the landowners concerned, a drainage board incorporating Birmingham and surrounding authorities was able to build a sewage farm which discharged purified water into the previously polluted River Tame.'

Alderman Thomas Avery (1813-18940 and his nephew, Sir William Beilby Avery (1854-1908)
[Courtesy Birmingham Museum Trust]

1881 **Thomas Avery** was elected **Mayor of Birmingham** for a second time

1881 **William Beilby Avery and Henry J Avery** took over control of W. & T. Avery, employing between 600 to 700 people.

1889 **Weights & Measures Act passed**, much influence in this Act came from William Beilby Avery

1891 The company was converted to a private company with **W.E Hipkins** as Managing Director.

1894 **W. & T. Avery** became a public company

1894 **Thomas Avery died at home in Edgbaston**

E. INTO THE TWENTIETH CENTURY WITH W. & T. AVERY

1895 Grace's Guide:

'The Soho Foundry at Smethwick was purchased and rebuilt as the company's main factory. Averys continued to repair some of the old James Watt and Co engines for several decades. All the other factories were closed, and the whole of the manufacturing was concentrated at Soho. Only the Digbeth premises were retained, as a Birmingham office, the head office being moved to Soho.'

1896 Avery, after having acquired the site, rebuilt much of it to house the **weighing manufacture**

1899 Royal Agricultural Show – massive weighing appliances were exhibited, railway weighbridges, shop counter scales

1900 A large 110-ton weighbridge was constructed for a large marine engineering company, in the North of England. Also, a hot-iron plate weighing machine was manufactured for the Dowlais Ironworks, *(Part of the neighbouring GKN works, see p. 18-19)*

Grace's Guide:
*'When legislation was introduced at the turn of the century requiring the stamping of all weighing machines used for trade **Avery** branches were set up in some 100 towns in the United Kingdom. This was the beginning of the sales and service organisation that expanded to cover not only every important town in the United Kingdom but was also established in many overseas countries.'*

1899 new automatic grain scale [REF; 66]

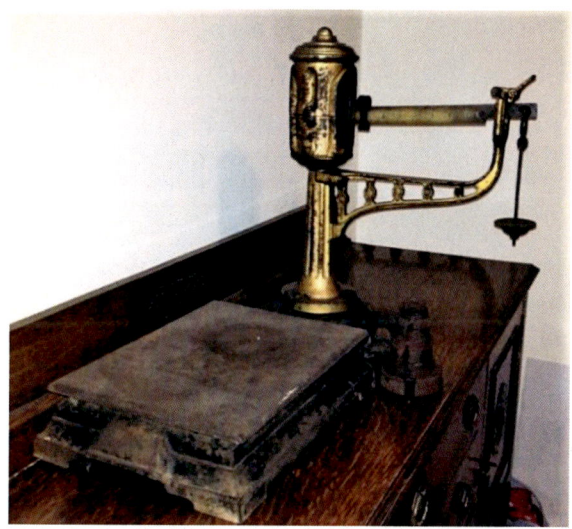

1900 c. Counter platform scales [REF: 66]

1905 William was created **Baronet as Sir William Beilby Avery, Bart**. He lived in Apsley House, Wellington Road, Birmingham, which still stands behind a high brick wall to the north of the wide thoroughfare in leafy Edgbaston.

1908 **Sir William Beilby Avery, Bart died** at the age of 54.

1911 **The archives of Boulton & Watt were given to Birmingham City**

1913 W & T Avery acquired **Henry Pooley & Sons** and **Parnall & Sons**, two substantial competitors

1914   Range of products included: weighbridges, testing machines, weighing apparatus of every description as required in works, collieries, railways, shops, etc and employing a workforce of 3000.

1914   the company occupied an area of 32,000m² and had some 3000 employees

1922   Avery's acquired by **De Grave, Short & Co**

1932   The company became licensed to produce metering petrol pumps

1937   Grace's Guide:

*Although **Averys'** business was, for many years, based primarily on high quality mechanical engineering, it also adopted developments in other fields of technology where they could contribute to its activities. It was the first in the United Kingdom to produce electrically operated weighing recorders in the 1930s. After the Second World War it employed such technologies as optical projection, digital encoding and, from 1963, electronic weighing.*

British Industries Fair *Advert for Weighing, Counting and Testing Machines for all purposes; Petrol Meter Pumps; Scientific Seating; Shop-fittings; Architectural Wood and Metal Work; Dairy Machinery. Recorder Weighing Machines (heavy capacity). Large Automatic Grain Weigher. New Continuous Liquid Weigher. Many new features. All Machines available for demonstrations.*

1937   In partnership with a French company Hardoll they created **Avery-Hardoll** and made petrol pumps

1953   Avery-Hardoll; Formation of JV by Avery-Hardoll with Beck & Co creating **Pump Maintenance Ltd**

1957   Made a private company

1958   **Averys Ltd**; a holding company was created

1961   **Avery-Hardoll** manufactured petrol pumps and products for the automobile, aviation and ancillary industries, employing 700 staff.

1971   Restructuring of the company **Avery-Hardoll** into three divisions:
            a. Weighing & Testing – b. General Products – c. International

1974   Developed automatic weighing machines for high volume free and non-free flowing products

1978   The net assets of the Avery Group amounted to £65.8 million for the year

1979   Avery Group acquired by **GEC** renaming **GEC-Avery**

1979   **W & T Avery was taken over by GEC**

1993   GEC took over the Dutch-based company Berkel and the Avery Berkel name was introduced. GEC Avery continued to operate as a part of the Avery Berkel Group. [REF: 58]

2000   **W & T Avery** was acquired by an American company to create **Avery-Weigh-Tronix**. The company is now a subsidiary of **Illinois Tool Works** specialising in industrial weighing machines and is one of the world's largest suppliers of weighing equipment. [REF: 58]

2008   Illinois Tool Works acquired Avery-Weigh-Tronix, whose headquarters are still sited in the Soho Foundry.

2009   Bank of England placed Boulton & Watt on the £50 note.

2015   There had been an **Avery Museum** for close on 90 years, which closed and exhibits dispersed.

An entry in Grace's Guide states:

> The Avery business is one of the oldest in the city, and began at Digbeth in 1730 ; its present locale is the famous Soho Works of Boulton, Watt & Murdoch, started by the first named in 1762. The original Avery firm set out primarily as manufacturers of steelyards, and in the course of years all types of weighing instruments, including testing .r and counting machines, have been added to their manufactures. They appear to have been the first to introduce agate bearings. In 1854 new buildings were started ; in 1894 the company became a 'public company under its present title ; in 1896 the Soho Works were acquired. The present works function in a living continuity with the old Soho. Many original workshops are still used : the erecting shop, Boulton's coining mint and strong-room, some workmen's cottages (in one of which William Murdoch dwelt), the old clock, James Watt's office, and some old plant, &c., are still used for various purposes. Growing out of all this is a modern works new and active. The present productions include weighbridges, capable of carrying loads up to 200 tons, automatic grain weighers, all types of ordinary weighing machines, scales, &c., down to finest balances ; testing machines for tension, compression, torsion, and shearing tests ; counting machines ; machines for weight and counting calculations ; machines for the use of inspectors of weights and measures, &c.

[Editorial: One wonders how long ago this was written and how true it is in 2020]

1907 Britain from Above   2020 GOOGLE EARTH COMPARISON note the 'temporary scaffold and roof which has been present for at least 10 years

1974 taken from the south side of the Birmingham Canal after demolition of the French Walls site of London Works. In 1974, the appearance of Soho Foundry seemed robust but since then, it has apparently deteriorated considerably.

2020 taken from about the same position

Bearing in mind that Soho Foundry is a Scheduled Monument and contains two specific features worthy of a Grade II* and Grade II Listing, the long list of Historic England's clear criteria of what makes a Scheduled Monument and the legislation that is there to enforce good care and maintenance are included on pages 167 to 170 of the Appendix.

The following few photographs show Soho Foundry to be anything but in good condition or cared for, nor being regularly inspected to remove any risk of deterioration.

2020 Viewed from the Birmingham Canal

2020 Courtesy of Google Earth Street View

F. COROLLARY

A lateral contemplation is to consider the stately homes of great industrial pioneers that have already disappeared from the West Midlands landscape:

1 SOHO MANUFACTORY - (Matthew Boulton's initial factory lost to Victorian terraced housing and the mill pool to a 20th century industrial estate.

2 HEATHFIELD HALL: (home of James WATT) & later, George TANGYE cleared away for suburban housing

3 SYCAMORE HILL (home of William MURDOCH) cleared away for suburban housing

4 James WATT GARRET WORKSHOP: (previously in Heathfield Hall) located in the Science Museum, South Kensington, London along with 6600 related exhibits [REF: 22]

5 SOHO HOUSE; home of Matthew Boulton, has been restored and open as a museum to the public by Birmingham City Council

6. SMETHWICK GROVE Home of **James Moilliet, later** Thomas Adkins and William SELBY [See p.22]

--X--

Adjacent to Soho Foundry on its northern flank is a large scrap metal yard, (2020) that abuts the prestigious site. Before scrap metal became such a normal part of modern-day language, the Smethwick Gas Works sat here in its heyday.

--X--

1.6 SMETHWICK GAS WORKS AT RABONE LANE

THE CARBURETTED WATER-GAS PLANT BUILDINGS.

The Boiler-House, the Machinery-Room, and the Generator-House, with a more distant view of the Coke-Feeding Plant.

1903. Rabone Lane passed behind this collection of buildings and Birmingham Canal is out of the picture, to the left
[Courtesy of Grace's Guide]

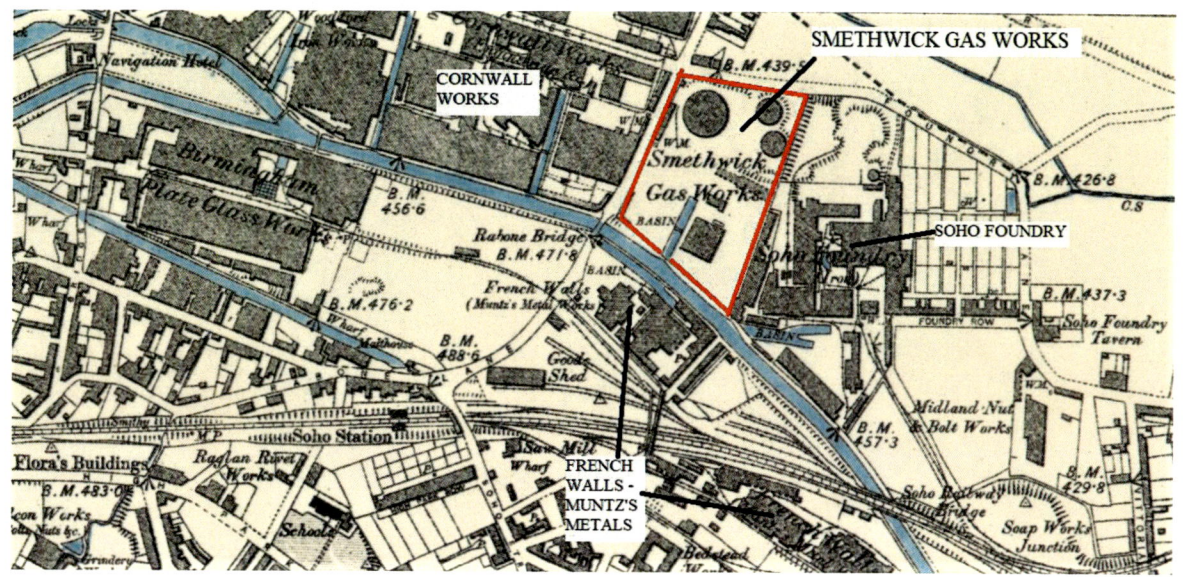

O/S 1888

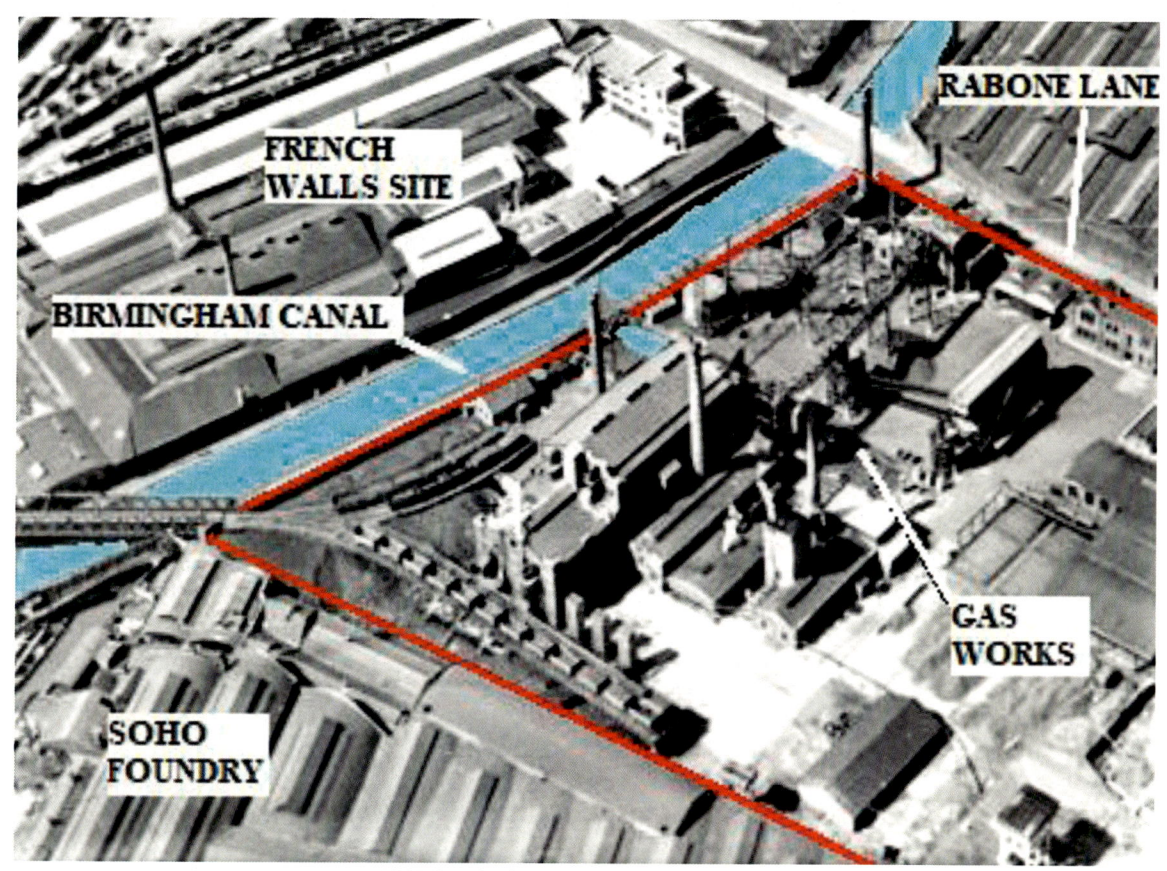

1937 Smethwick Gas Works from the East. [Britain from Above; Historic England]

1805   Amongst many inventions, **William Murdoch**, is credited with the manufacture of gas, which he delivered from the **Soho Foundry** site (next door), when he worked with **Boulton and Watt**.

1890c. Smethwick Corporation constructed **Smethwick Gas Works** with its own gas holders and coke-feeder with coal arriving by boat on the Birmingham Canal. It is not known when the site was cleared but it was certainly there in 1963, when **Graham Wigley** took this photo. In 2020 it is the site of a scrap metal company.

ABOVE: 1963. One of a fleet of tanker boats which carried tar (and certain other volatile liquids) from gasworks to tar distillers where the liquids were processed into various chemicals mainly for industrial purposes, sits in the branch arm of Smethwick Gas Works. The fleet was owned by Thomas Clayton (Oldbury) Ltd., and operated from about the 1870's until 1966, by which time practically all the gasworks had closed because of the discovery and distribution of North Sea gas.
[Courtesy of Graham Wigley]
BELOW: The Gas Works site in 2020 when used as a scrap metal works. Note the canopied Soho Foundry to the right

--X--

Twenty first century Smethwick alongside the banks of the Birmingham canal has a barrenness that lacks any architectural quality of mention. The history of these sites is exceptional, considering the grandiosity and importance of the one to the north of Rabone Lane Bridge on the right flank (East), which makes the destitution so much more real. The titanic pioneers of the late 18th and 19th centuries not only took pride in their jobs, their work forces but also the perceived permanence of their factories. They were vast edifices, not always a joy to work in but screamed contrast from the flimsy prefabricated featureless and temporary structures of today. Tangye Brothers bought up the land previously called Rabone Hall and Smethwick Hall before that and created a vast world famous works that changed the strength of hydraulic industrial power for ever.

--X--

1.7 CORNWALL WORKS
Tangye Brothers

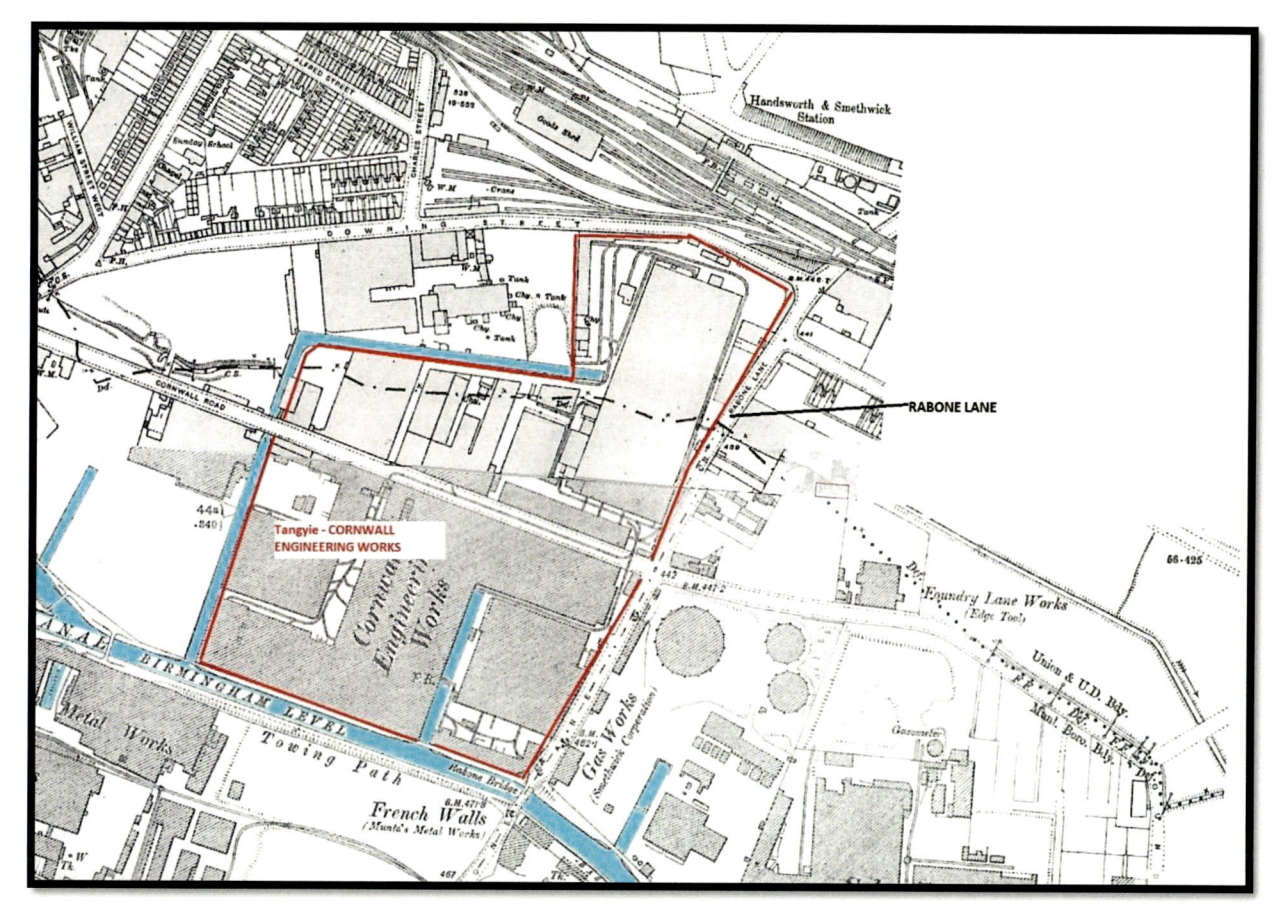

O/S Map 1904: 25 inches : mile [REF: 7]

James Tangye (1825-1913) lived at Hammel Hill, Ladywood & later Fairfield, Handsworth

Joseph Tangye (1826-1902)

Edward Tangye (1832-1909)

Sir Richard Tangye (1833-1906) lived at Gilbertstone from 1883. *"The house had extensive grounds which crossed into the area of Lyndon End and Bickenhill. It had a pool with a boathouse. On the side of the house was a 65-foot (20 m) tall tower."* [REF: 12]

George Tangye (1835-1920) lived at Heathfield Hall, previously the home of James Watt:
> *In 1881, when the firm was turned into a limited liability company, George Tangye was made vice-chairman and finally Chairman of the company when his brother — Sir Richard Tangye*

- died in 1906. For many years he lived at Heathfield Hall, which was formerly the home of James Watt. He carefully preserved, in the condition in which the great inventor had left it, the garret in which he had worked; and George Tangye was responsible for the fine collection of relics of Boulton and Watt, which he finally gave to the City of Birmingham. [REF: 11]

Richard Tangye wrote
"One great disadvantage which has been brought about by the great advance in the modern systems of manufacture, is the gradual extinction of the "All round" workman – the genuine "Jack-of-all-trades." 1889

One of the most amazing, repeated finding about the men who made Smethwick famous was that they were indeed self-made; the Tangye brothers were no exception. The five brothers, James, Joseph, Edward, Richard and George came from very humble origins in Cornwall, where their grandfather was an agricultural labourer, who worked until he could afford to buy some cheap land but in his own words it grew 'nothing but furze and stones' [REF: 4]. At night he 'obtained a situation as night-driver of a mine-pumping engine' and said, "I drove the engine for ten hours, worked on the farm seven hours, and wasted the rest." He lived to the age of 94 and never saw a doctor!

The brothers' father **Joseph Tangye**, was born at Redruth, Cornwall, which had become famous for being the town where the Scottish inventor, **William Murdock** lived when he invented gas-lighting and constructed the first locomotive ever made in England. Their father was a studious thoughtful teetotal Wesleyan Methodist, who worked in a local mine and their mother was *"a most excellent woman, clear-sighted and possessed of a vigorous intellect. She was quick to discern the bent of her children's minds and encouraged them in all their efforts at self-improvement."* On her deathbed she said to Richard Tangye, *"make straight paths to thyself."* Subsequently, both Richard and his wife became Quakers (REF: 4. One & All; p. 23)

1852   Richard Tangye always felt he was destined for a career in commerce, a desire which persisted during a period when he taught at a private Quaker School in Sidcot in the Mendips. He hated the exceptionally long hours from 05.30 – 21.00 and left there in 1852 to join a small business in Birmingham owned by **Thomas Worsdell**, the son of the first manufacturer of railway carriages for **the London & North Western Railway**. This was the opportunity these men needed to have the freedom of designing what they were naturally good at: engines.

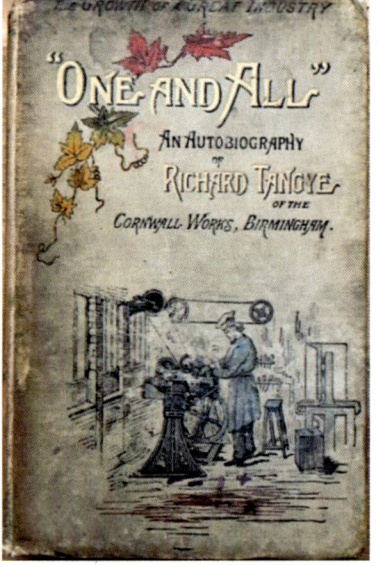

Sir Richard TANGYE (1833- 1906) and his autobiography "One and All" (1889)

What of the other brothers? **Richard** was the commercial genius in the making but the eldest, **James**, started life begrudgingly in a country wheelwright's shop; whilst the next one down, **Joseph**, was placed in a shoeing smith's shop. These men carried on jobs in the day that brought them a living but, in their hearts, they were engineers and, in the evenings, made model engines at home with their younger brothers turning the wheel. James's engineering brain became legendary and he was given a job designing a model of a bridge by a pupil of **Isambard Kingdom Brunel, Mr. Brunton**. **Edward** set out for USA but the ship went aground with the loss of 195 lives with Edward surviving. He was persuaded by Richard to join him as a junior clerk in Birmingham to be joined a year or two later by the two older brothers, James and Joseph, who were instantly given leading jobs in the works. Richard speaks little about **George**, but it was this one who in later years bought Heathfield Hall, from the family of **James Watt** and preserved the latter's garret workshop.

After having been in post for a few years, Richard had a personality clash with a new partner of Mr Brunton and he felt the time had come to leave. A good bookseller friend, **William White, (later Alderman & Mayor of Birmingham)** placed a desk for Richard Tangye to develop a business which was beginning to take off. After a period, the brothers started to work together as a team and took a portion of a factory, (a money-saving scheme that was commonplace in the 19th century). The proprietors possessed the central engines which provided tenants with the power to use their own tools for work. Brother Joseph was not only a very able tool designer but an exceptional artisan with a first-class lathe.

OUR FIRST WORKSHOP—"4s, A WEEK RENT."

REF: 4 Richard Tangye "One and All" 1889

Before James and Joseph came to Birmingham, they became noticed by **Brunel,** who had admired an **hydraulic press** they had made for a Cornish industry.

1856   Brunel's agent came to the Tangye small workshop and investigated this hydraulic jack and before leaving, had ordered several. This purchase was to assist Brunel launch his mighty ocean-going liner, the **Great Eastern**. Because of the enormous bulk of this liner, when it came to launching her, she had to be slid into the water broadside and the **hydraulic jacks** were to be engaged in the easing process.

1858   Unfortunately, at first the load was excessive and the number of jacks used had to be increased dramatically and with success, the **Great Eastern was launched** on 31st January 1858. Richard Tangye always said from that day forth: *"we launched the Great Eastern and she launched us"*. From that day, business never looked back, which could not be said about the unfortunate boat that after a very chequered life, ended up as scrap in 1888.

THE LAUNCH OF THE "GREAT EASTERN."

[REF: 4]

Richard Tangye with a hydraulic press by the Great Eastern during construction [REF: 2]

As business increased, so did the need for larger premises and the taking on of a work force. During these early years they met a fellow engineer, **T.A. Weston**, nephew to **Thomas Weston of Temple Row, Birmingham and Mayor of the city** when Prince Albert visited Birmingham. T.A. Weston had invented the **Differential Pulley Block** but could not find anyone to manufacture it for him until he met James Tangye who was able to oblige. Ultimately, it was younger brother, **George** who persisted with the design and succeeded in production one night by using a **differential pulley block**, enabling two men to raise and suspend a ton weight in the air. The patent was signed immediately and the Tangye brothers took over the care of this ingenious piece of apparatus.

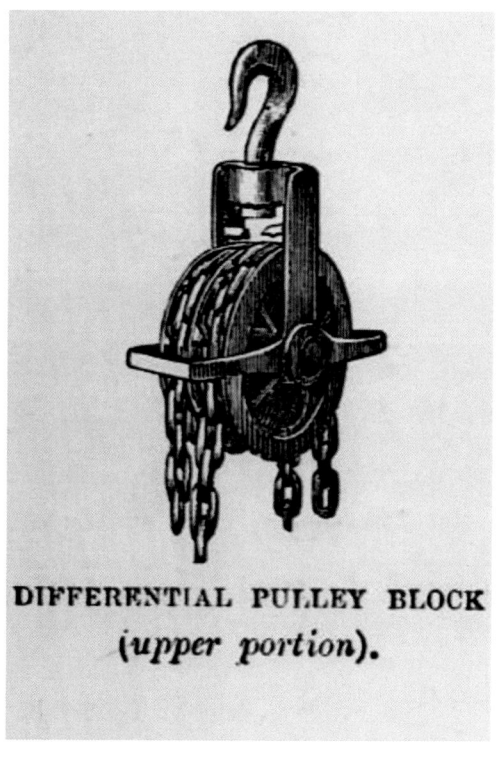

DIFFERENTIAL PULLEY BLOCK
(upper portion).

[REF: 4]

1859   demands increased and they moved their premises again, this time to Clement Street, Birmingham, (close to the Arena, Birmingham), and Richard married Miss Caroline Jesper.

During a public speech in Birmingham by the orator **John Bright**, (Birmingham City centre has a street named after him), Richard sat next to a man who turned out to be an eminent Australian, Mr. Way (later to become Chief Justice of the Supreme Court of South Australia, **Sir Samuel James Way, 1st Baronet, PC, KC**). During the speech, Bright eluded to a 'manufacturing company' anonymously, and Richard showed his new friend a letter from Bright to himself, corroborating the contact. Way asked if he could take the envelope addressed to Tangye in Bright's handwriting.

1862   The Tangye's outgrew the Clement Street works and a move was necessary to an out of town site. They bought **Rabone Hall** and its grounds, which had rested on the north side of the Birmingham Canal in Smethwick at least since the 17th century. Previously, it was called **Smethwick Hall** but by 1780, it was the home of a Birmingham merchant family, called **Rabone** who occupied it for about 80 years, during which time the name was changed to Rabone Hall. It is said that "A drive led south to what is now Rabone Lane, and the house was secluded from the road by trees." [REF: 9] After some years of tenancy, the Rabones sold the house to **Joseph Gillott**, (1799-1872), [REF: 8] the famous Birmingham steel-pen manufacturer, who sold it to the Tangye family in 1862. [REF: 5].

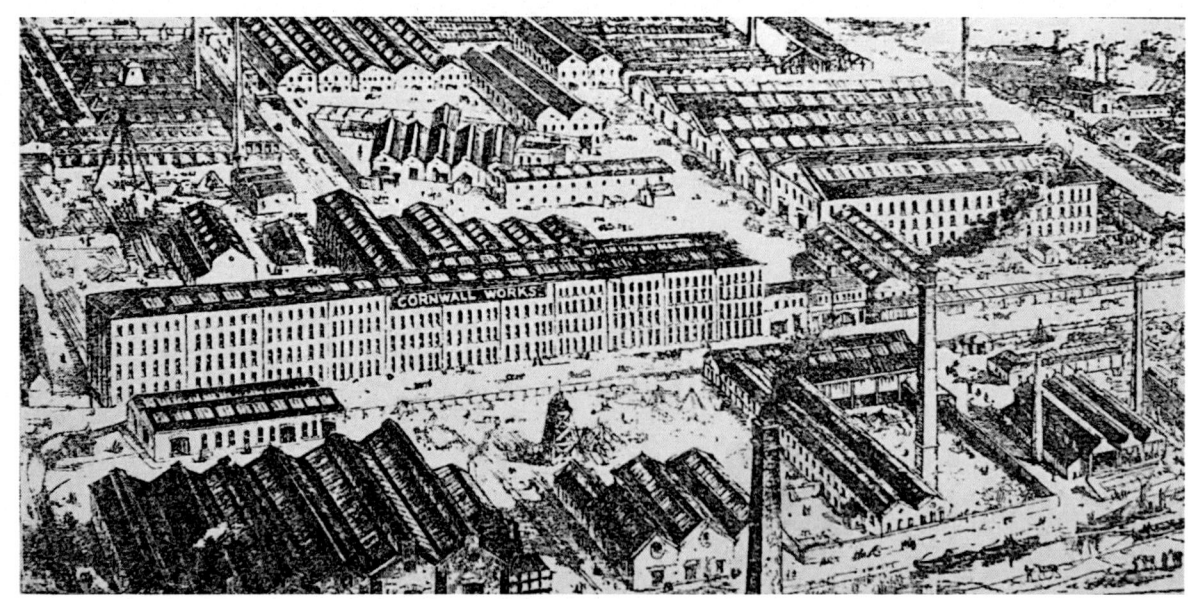

Cornwall Works, Smethwick. The Birmingham Canal can be seen in the bottom right corner. Rabone Lane runs diagonally across the upper right corner [REF: 4]

1866 The success of this family was dependant on two aspects: five brothers each with an individual skill, a dedication to perfection in the realms of engineering. The other was a degree of luck. In 1866, an American engineer had travelled all over the States and come to the UK to find a manufacturer who could make a 'direct-acting steam pump' for his client, the inventor, **A.S. Cameron of New York** and having travelled the country becoming more and more depressed as engineer after engineer shook their heads, he was returning by train to Liverpool to catch the boat back across the Atlantic and the train he was on, stopped at a nearby station where staring at him in massive bold letters he saw "CORNWALL WORKS" and was sufficiently tempted to leave the train with his luggage and prototype of the jack, made his way to the Tangye works, and the rest is history. He had thousands of them made and Sir Richard wrote " …. And during the continuance of the patent we paid the inventor about £35,000 (£2,191,000 in money of 2020) in royalties for the sole right of making it! One cannot help wondering how much Tangye's made on sales worldwide.

1875 In his autobiography, Sir Richard describes how in 1875 (aged 42 years), his health "having broken down", he was advised "to take long sea-voyage", so he went to Australia by boat, a journey of 56 days. It would seem he took this advice very seriously, for he lived until he was 73 and he managed about another 4 trips to that wonderful colony, the break down was soon repaired. He quotes:
"One voyage to Australia has become very much like another since the era of swift steamers commenced, the luxurious life on board, and the constant change of passengers at the various ports of call, closely resemble life in a busy hotel." This was an attitude far removed from the stories of the brothers' humble beginnings in Cornwall. Further he says: *" ... there is a wonderful variety amongst our fellow passengers. Here we see judges returning to their duties after a holiday all too short; Colonial statesmen, with sufficient time on their hands to allow their formulating a policy to meet every conceivable combination amongst their parliamentary opponents; and squatters and merchants returning to the Colonies to look after their property."*

1877 Another fascinating escapade in which they had influence was the collection and erection of **Cleopatra's Needle in London**. It is worth reproducing Richard Tangye's account of what happened. [REF: 4]

I have already given an account of the use of our hydraulic jacks in the launch of the *Great Eastern;* and it may be interesting here to give some particulars, of a more or less remarkable character, in which they were employed. An interesting illustration of the great power of these machines was seen when the Cleopatra Needle was being brought to London. In 1820 Mehemet Ali offered the Obelisk to the English Government, but the cost and difficulty of removing it were so great, with the appliances then available, that no vigorous efforts were made, and the Obelisk still remained prostrate in the sand. In 1877 Professor Erasmus Wilson and Mr. John Dixon, C.E., generously undertook to bring it to England, and set it up in London at their own expense. This involved the building in England of a wrought-iron cylindrical vessel, which was shipped to Alexandria in sections. The actual work of removal then commenced, and Mr. Dixon's previous experience with our hydraulic jacks naturally suggested their employment in this novel undertaking, for they were as much in advance of the power of an ordinary screw, as that was in advance of the unaided power of man. It was an easy matter to place a jack under one end of the Obelisk, and for one man to raise it sufficiently to enable it to be swivelled round broadside on to the beach. Then the cylindrical vessel was built round it, after which the whole was rolled down the beach into the sea.

The "Cleopatra" was in charge of Captain Carter and a crew of seven or eight men, and was towed by the s.s. *Olga*, behaving remarkably well on her voyage along the Mediterranean until the 14th of October, 1877, when a fearful storm arose in the Bay of Biscay. As long as the wind was from the South, although very high, it involved no serious danger, as the course was northward; in the evening, however, the wind veered round to the west, and a heavy sea struck the "Cleopatra" on her side. Captain Carter's last entry in his log is as under :—

> "5 p.m. This is a most unpleasant night. The swell of the sea is very high, and the *Olga* seems determined to tow us through or under the water. Almost wish she would break down; the great pitching (16 pitches per minute) is almost unbearable, the water is rolling over us fore and aft."

The Captain then decided that it would be necessary to "lie to" for the night, and signalled to the *Olga* accordingly; another sea, however, struck the "Cleopatra," causing her to roll, which she had only done once before. Feeling something moving under him, the Captain knew that his ballast had shifted; this ballast of old iron bars had been put into the ship at Alexandria, and although not secured so well as it might have been, was considered quite satisfactory, not having previously shown any signs of moving. The little ship was at once thrown on her side, and every wave washed clean over her, causing the deck-house to disappear entirely each time. The Captain now signalled to the *Olga* to cast off, as he would be utterly unable to show any lights during the night; while the weight of 400 yards of steel-wire rope between the vessels would certainly cause them to come together. The "Cleopatra" had nothing to fear from a collision, but the fate of the *Olga* would be certain.

Hoping to right the vessel the mast and rigging were cut away, but without much effect. A boat's crew of six brave men volunteered to leave the *Olga* to rescue the crew of the "Cleopatra;" and when they approached her they caught the rope that was thrown to them, but unfortunately were unable to hold to it, and were blown away, nothing more ever being heard of them or their boat. The life-boat of the "Needle" ship was then got out, but was instantly smashed by the sea. At great risk the *Olga* subsequently approached the "Cleopatra," and passed her a rope by which a boat was drawn to and fro, and the crew of that strange little ship were safely brought to the steamer. The *Olga* then steamed away in search of the missing boat, but failed to find any trace of her. She then made for her consort again, but could not meet with her; and assuming that she had gone down, sailed for Falmouth. But on the following day she was picked up by the steamer *Fitz-Maurice*, and towed to Ferrol. It is easy to say,

after the misfortune happened, that a little more care in stowing the ballast would have prevented its shifting, and that the use of a hemp rope instead of a steel one would have allowed the vessels to lie to for the night without being cut adrift; and that in that case there probably would not have been the loss of those six brave men, nor any necessity for Mr. Dixon

CLEOPATRA'S NEEDLE.

to pay to the owners of the *Fitz-Maurice* £2,000 for the salvage of the "Needle."

On arriving in London four of Tangye's hydraulic jacks were used in raising the Obelisk, each jack being worked by one man. The time required for this operation was without doubt far less than that occupied by Thothmes III. when he originally set up the Obelisk at Heliopolis (perhaps in the presence of

Once the Tangye brothers had accrued vast fortunes, and vast they were, they became extraordinary benefactors of the city of Birmingham, particularly in the realms of education at every level. They set about ensuring the city inhabitants benefited from their prosperity. In a community that was supposedly strictly Church of England in its religious denomination, Quakers were often scorned because of their teetotal views. However, Birmingham was rife with wealthy Unitarianism, Wesleyanism and Quakerism with families like Lloyd, Cadbury and Tangye.

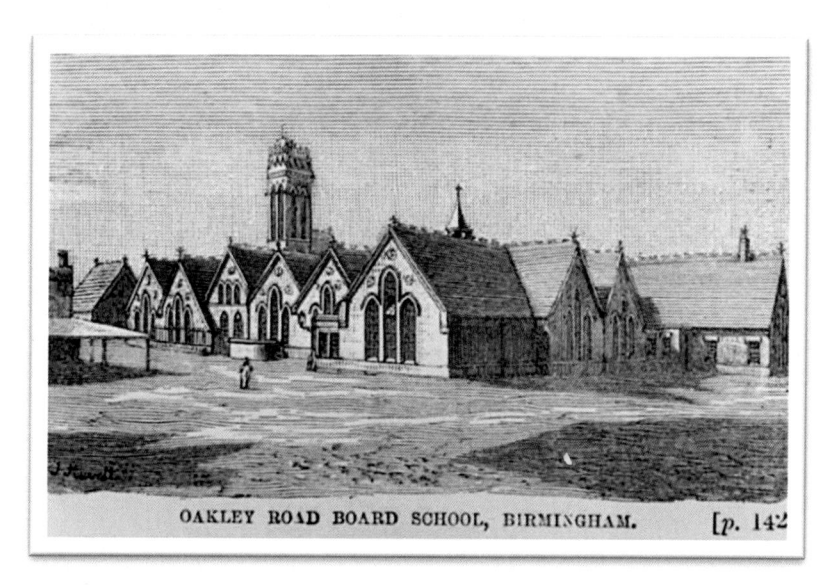

OAKLEY ROAD BOARD SCHOOL, BIRMINGHAM. [p. 142]

This school still exists today as Barford Primary School on Barford Road, near Summerfield Park. [One suspects it is incorrectly named in the book of 1889]

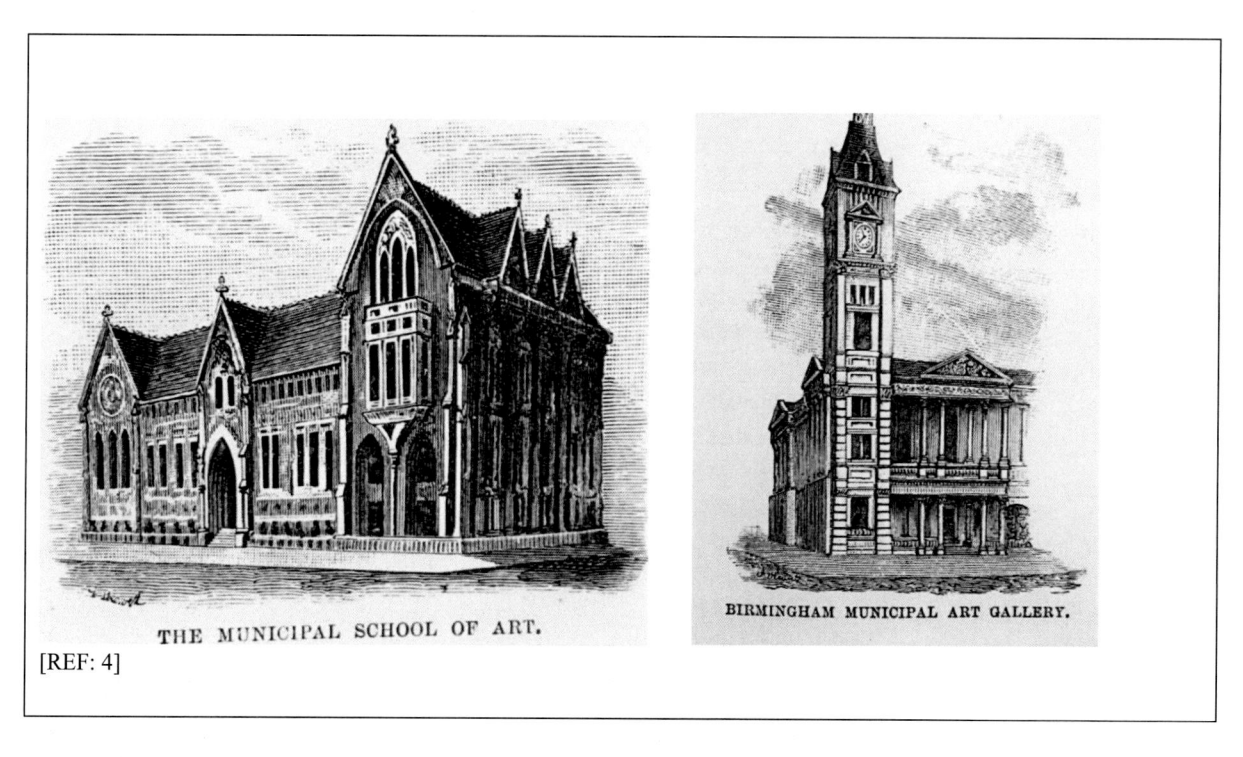

THE MUNICIPAL SCHOOL OF ART.
[REF: 4]

BIRMINGHAM MUNICIPAL ART GALLERY.

According to the Wikipedia account of the **Birmingham Museum & Art Gallery**, *"A £10,000 gift by Sir Richard and George Tangye started a new drive for an art gallery and in 1885, following other donations and £40,000 from the council, the Prince of Wales officially opened the new gallery on Saturday 28 November 1885." [REF:10]*

A few paragraphs from Richard Tangye's autobiography of 1889. [REF: 4]

During my frequent visits to the Continent I had been much impressed with the advantages afforded the artisans of almost every manufacturing town by the facilities possessed by them for studying the highest examples of Art in Municipal Museums and other public collections.

The lack of such facilities for the artisans of Birmingham had long been recognised and deeply deplored, but it was not until a few years since that an opportunity occurred to supply this deficiency. The Corporation possessed a small collection of objects of Art which were exhibited in a building inconveniently situated at a distance from the centre of the town, and in 1880 it was proposed to transfer these to a temporary building to be erected in a more

148   THE BIRMINGHAM ART GALLERY.

convenient position. I felt that if this course were adopted, the result would be the postponement for an indefinite period of the provision of an Art Gallery commensurate with the requirements of the town, and in conjunction with my brother I made the Council an offer, which they accepted, and which involved the erection by them of the present noble Art Gallery, at a cost of £100,000.

[In 2020, £100,000 would equilibrate to about £8.5 million & the figure below for the School of Art, a further £840,000]

There now remained but one thing to be done to complete the circle of Educational institutions in the town, and that was the provision of suitable buildings for the School of Art. On the 9th of November, 1881, the Mayor read three letters to the Council containing offers of a site for the School of Art, and of the needful funds for its erection, whereupon the following resolution was adopted :

"That the munificent offers of Messrs. Tangye to contribute the sum of £10,000 (afterwards increased to £11,000) and of an Anonymous Donor (the late Miss Ryland) of a further sum of £10,000 towards the erection of a School of Art, and Mr. Cregoe Colmore, to present a valuable piece of land as a site for a School of Art for this borough, be, and they are hereby, gratefully accepted."[1]

Towards the end of his account, Tangye refers specifically to the previous home of **James Watt**, whom it seems he respected immensely. His brother, **George**, had bought **Heathfield Hall**, (no longer there but a housing estate to the north of Lozells Road) where Watt had lived between 1790 until his death in 1819 and he found in its entirety, James Watts' garret. The collection of over 6600 items is now an exhibit in the Science Museum, Exhibition Road, South Kensington SW7 2DD. [REF: 14]

The sad state today of the Soho Foundry, (a listed National Scheduled Monument at risk combined with the total loss of Soho Manufactory) makes one realise that deference to genius has all but passed away from our society and that if a popular person is not famous for being a TV celebrity, there is no position in contemporary life for fame.

HEATHFIELD HALL—JAMES WATT.   179

A few years since, my brother George went to reside at Heathfield Hall, near Birmingham, "where," writes Mr. Sam: Timmins, F.S.A., "one of the most remarkable and interesting relics of the great inventor of the steam engine has been reverently preserved, exactly as it was left by its owner nearly seventy years ago. It is a low-ceiled room over the kitchen of the house, and with the window overlooking the stable yard. It is reached by a narrow staircase, and it is practically separate from the rest of the house. It is known as the 'classic garret' or attic, or private workshop of James Watt, in which his later years of leisure were passed in various mechanical experiments as 'amusements' of his old age. It is now a 'relic room' of the machinery, apparatus, tools, and products of the old engineer after his fame and fortune had been made. On the left of the illustration a series of drawers is shown, in which numerous and various tools were methodically arranged; also a stove with coal-scuttle and fire-irons; and a Dutch-oven in which he could cook his own meals without being disturbed is seen over the stove. Under the window stands his lathe, with its lamp and tools left untouched as he himself placed them, and with the stool on which he sat. His old leathern apron remains as he left it. Round the walls are shelves containing fossils, minerals, gallipots, bottles, crucibles, and many small drawers carefully labelled, in which are lenses, scales, mathematical instruments, sketch books, pocket books, and countless memorials of his long and busy life. On the right hand are busts and figures, his old chair, a bench on which lie many varied tools, and underneath a sad memorial, an old hair trunk, in which the school books and sketches and copy books of the early childhood of his brilliant son Gregory were kept for long years after his lamented death by his mourning father. Among other relics are those of the early machine, now universally used for copying letters, with packets of the powder sold by 'James Watt and Co.' to make the necessary ink for securing the copy on the damped paper.

"The two most prominent objects in the centre and on the left require more detailed description. The one in the centre is the first 'medallion,' or 'copying machine,' which Watt invented, on the principle of the pantograph, now popularly known for copying drawings, by means of a pointer at one end of a bar and a pencil at the other, the copy being larger or smaller than the original according to the relative length of the parts of the bar from the fulcrum. Watt's invention added a cutting tool, rotated by a simple action, which, in his own words, 'ate its way' into the material to be carved exactly as the other end of the bar (or pointer) was raised or lowered. A perfect copy of any medal or disc was thus secured, and many very beautiful examples remain, carved in wood, ivory, plaster, or metal. The other and more complex machine (on the left) was a further development of the ingenious process, and was devised to make complete copies of busts or figures. This was accomplished by placing the original in a sort of lathe, in which it was rotated slowly, and the 'pointer,' travelling over its revolving cutter, thus produced an exact copy, but generally on a smaller scale. The finest examples were those

WATT'S INVENTIONS. 181

of the bust of Watt, by Chantrey, most beautiful and delicate copies of which Watt gave to his friends as the 'works of a young artist in his eighty-first year.'

"The machinery was slowly improved from the 'medallion' of 1810 (his seventy-sixth year), to his death in 1819, when the 'bust carving' machine

JAMES WATT'S ROOM.

had been perfected to reproduce copies in wood, ivory, jet, alabaster, and metals of various kinds. Some of the finest examples were those of Locke (a large example in ivory), of De Luc, of Dr. Black, and of Dr. Priestley. Although only an amusement 'for mind and body,' the same arrangements have in later years been largely used for automatic copying

182   JOSEPH STURGE AND THE RUSSIAN WAR.

of 'models' or 'patterns,' such as complete gun-stocks, in which every detail is produced by machinery only, without any touch from a workman's hand.

"The 'classic garret' contains innumerable examples of the inventions and productions of James Watt, from his earliest to his latest days, and even the books and papers of his father, as well as many of his own. Its interest is unique, its relics are priceless as personal memorials; and to enter the room and look around is to stand in the presence of genius at work, although the busy brain and skilful hand have been at rest for nearly seventy years."

Richard Tangye 1889.

Courtesy of the Black Country Living Museum [REF: 13]

—x—

Immediately adjacent to Tangye Brothers' Cornwall Works is a site that has gone under a few titles at different times: British Tube Works, Woodford Iron Works and the home of the Incandescent Heat Works. Today, the intervening canal branch that passed due North between the two sites and then turned east, has been infilled and there is no hint of recognition that anything other than prefabricated modern factory units has ever rested on this soil, with the exception that into the wall by the first Smethwick Roving bridge [described as "Footbridge at Junction with Wolverhampton Level (approximately 230 metres east of Bridge Street) Birmingham Canal] are about twenty large iron rivets driven into the adjacent Graffiti festooned wall. The two Roving Bridges at Smethwick Junction are Grade 2 Listed.

HISTORIC ENGLAND LISTING

LIST ENTRY NUMBER 1214908
DATE FIRST LISTED 1987
GRADE 2
FOOTBRIDGE AT JUNCTION WITH WOLVERHAMPTON LEVEL (APPROXIMATELY 230 METRES EAST OF BRIDGE STREET) BIRMINGHAM CANAL BIRMINGHAM LEVEL
Canal footbridge. 1828. Cast-iron. Brick abutments have sandstone dressings. Single elliptical arch. Sides each of two castings, bolted to central "keystone". Pierced in form of saltire crosses, with band of quatrefoils below handrail. Spandrel inscribed: "HORSELEY IRON WORKS STAFFORDSHIRE 1828". Southern abutment partly repaired with C20 brick and concrete.

800.74 Smethwick Junction during industrial heyday" c. 1938, looking North-west. The bridge and overflow still exist. The cooling towers on the right, were made of timber and formed part of the intricate processes carried on by the Incandescent Heat Company during the 20th century. Just beyond the moored boat is the canal branch into the works. Previously in 1888, the northern part of this site was occupied by the Etna Iron Works. This is the point where Telford's 1827 canal (left) split from Brindley's 1769 canal that veers to the right

67

LIST ENTRY NUMBER 1342672
DATE FIRST LISTED 1987
GRADE 2
FOOTBRIDGE AT JUNCTION WITH BIRMINGHAM CANAL,SMETHWICK JUNTION (APROXIMATELY 190 METRES EAST OF BRIDGE STREET) BIRMINGHAM LEVEL
WOLVERHAMPTON LEVEL
Canal footbridge. 1828. Cast-iron. Brick abutments have sandstone dressings. Single elliptical arch. Sides each of two castings, bolted to central "keystone". Pierced in form of saltire crosses, with band of quatrefoils below handrail. Spandrel inscribed: "HORSELEY IRON WORKS STAFFORDSHIRE 1828".

--x--

1.8 BRITISH TUBE MILLS

Woodford Iron Works, Incandescent heat Company

A. BRITISH TUBE WORKS

There is not much written about this site except that **British Tube Mills** of Cornwall Road and adjacent to the Cornwall Works of the Tangye Brothers, was absorbed into Tube Investments. It is interesting that on the 1888 O/S map, the site is shown as **Woodford Iron Works** but by 1913 survey, it had changed to British Tube Mills.

Francis Henry Griffiths (1867-1922) was born and bred Birmingham boy, who, in 1892, at the age of 25, became manager of the British Tube Mills. [REF: 2; Grace's Guide].

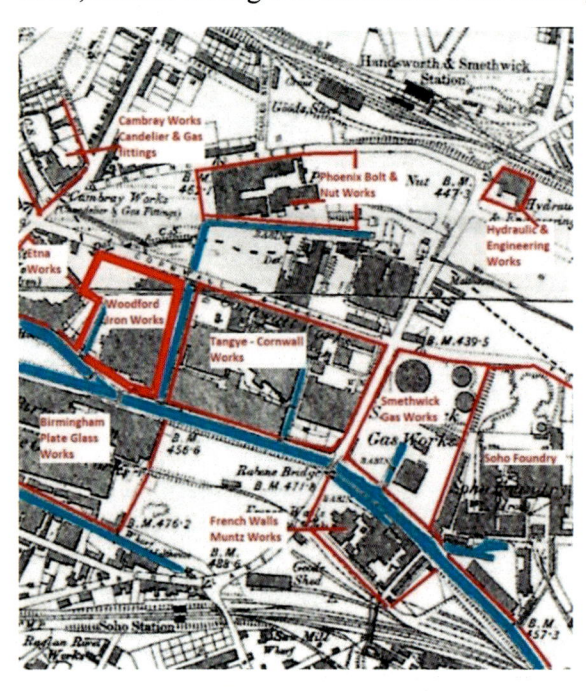

1888 O/S Map

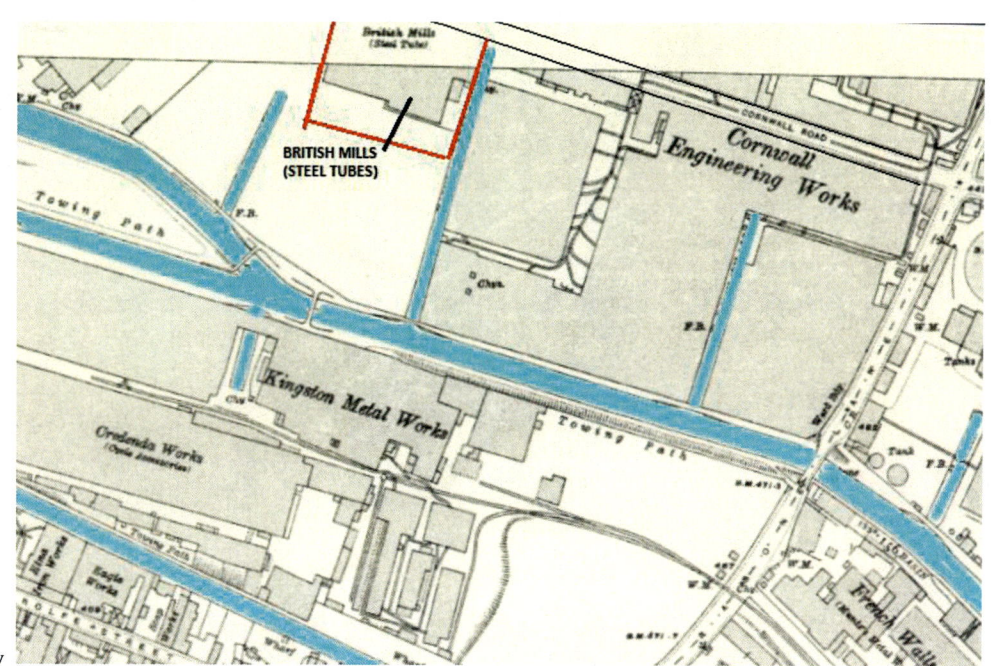

1913 O/S survey

1925

1927

ANOTHER "BRITISH" VICTORY!

THE production of a new butting machine whose many operating advantages enable us to increase output and to offer butted steering tubes of outstanding quality and finish at reduced prices.

There is nothing better on the market.

Enquiries for butted steering tubes with plain finish, or turned, screwed and slotted, or screwed and slotted, or screwed only, will receive our immediate attention.

BRITISH TUBE MILLS Limited
CORNWALL ROAD, SMETHWICK, BIRMINGHAM.

1927

69

B. INCANDESCENT HEAT COMPANY WORKS

Incandescent *"becoming white ... candidus; luminous, glowing with heat. Glowing, brilliantly luminous"* [Shorter Oxford Dictionary]. These days it seems to be reserved for public rage at some offending action, often by a politician. The company's details are a bit obscure.

1904   A public company was created with the intention of **"exploiting important patents in connection with furnaces for the metallurgical and other industries."**

1908   Demonstration of patent core for furnace development by Alfred Smallwood. Several major industrial users of these furnaces testified as to their efficiency.

1830   Grace's Guide:

> "**The Incandescent Heat Company, Ltd.** whose Works and Head Office are situated at **British Mills**, Cornwall Road, Smethwick, Birmingham, was incorporated in 1904, the object of the Company being to exploit important patents in connection with Furnaces for the metallurgical and other industries. The Company have extensive foreign business, and their furnaces and equipment are covered by patents in the leading industrial countries throughout the world."

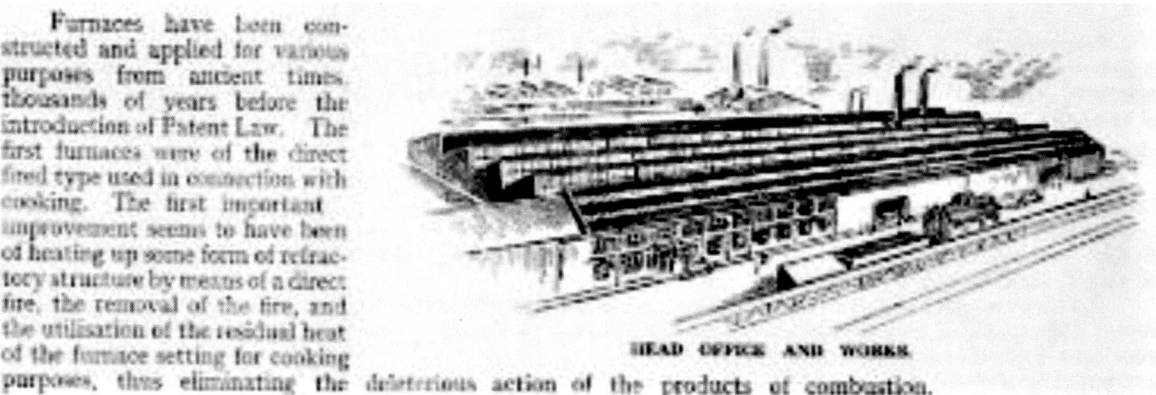

"Furnaces have been constructed and applied for various purposes from ancient times, thousands of years before the introduction of Patent Law. The first furnaces were of the direct fired type used in connection with cooking. The first important improvement seems to have been of heating up some forms of refractory structure by means of the fire, and the utilisation of the residual heat of the furnace setting for cooking purposes, thus eliminating the deleterious action of the products of combustion."

1937-1961 Furnace producers & specialists

1952   Patented improvements in reciprocating ram pumps

1957   A further patent for improved suspension device for use in the heat treatment of crankshafts

1961   Acquired by **Wellman, Smith, Owen Engineering Corporation**

1967   **Wellman Incandescent Natural Gas Systems** formed

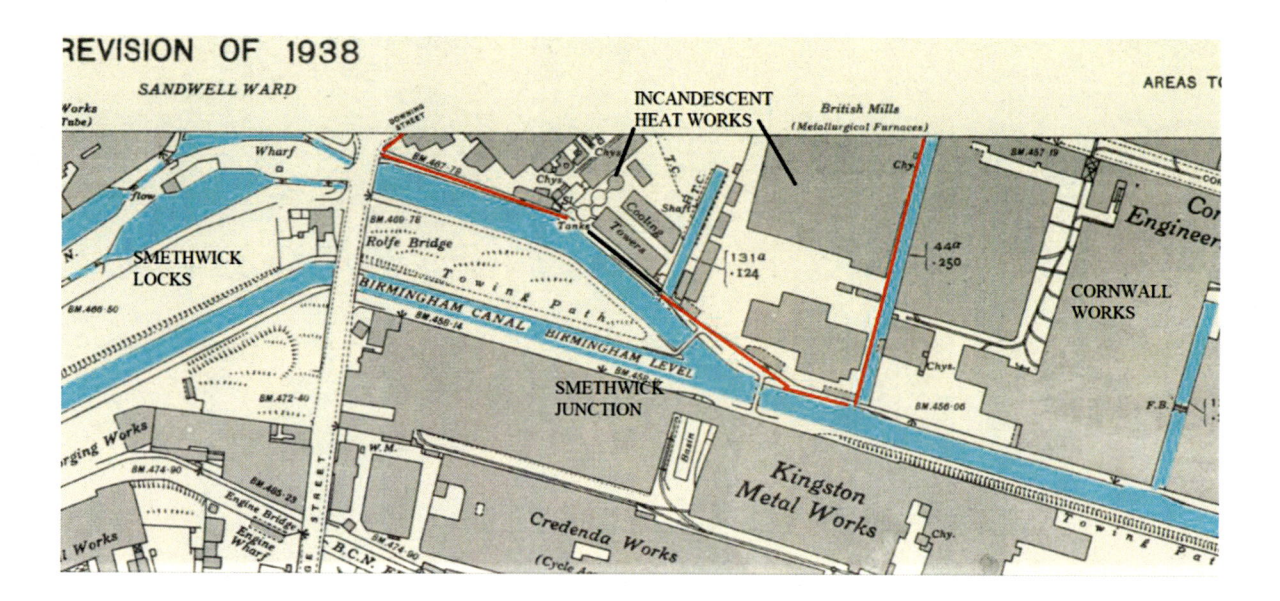

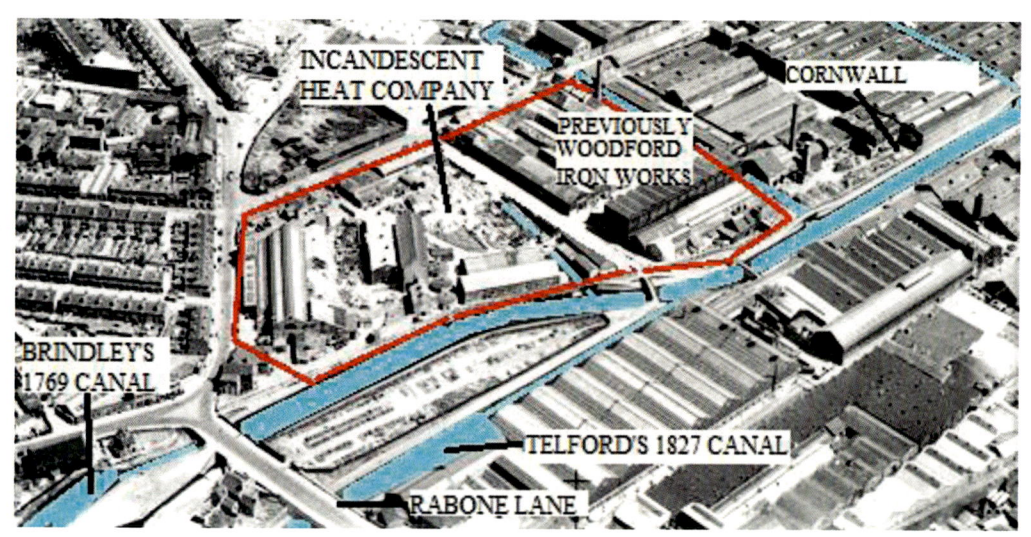

1946 The Incandescent Heat Works [Britain from Above]

--X—

It is at this convenient point that the first part of this journey is curtailed. Part 2 continues the journey along the unique waters of Brindley's 1769 canal. It passes up the locks at Smethwick, past the junction with the Grade 2* Engine Arm Aqueduct, (which is explored later), follows beyond the 'New' Smethwick Pumping Station and Museum, through Smeaton's Summit Tunnel past the vestigial Sandwell Colliery Wharf and after some exploration in the Spon Lane vicinity, ultimately to the Stewart Aqueduct. For some many metres, the canal formed the boundaries between Smethwick and West Bromwich and therefore some of the more important industries that lined the northern bank that fall into West Bromwich and thus Sandwell are equally explored as being important in the context of this canal journey.

Soon Rabone Lane is reached, with a remnant of the Incandescent Heat Company's long elegant Victorian workshop immediately by the bridge on the right and adjacent to that is a powerhouse of the Tramways, looking like an M&B pub. The original Brindley tunnel was bricked up in the 1960s and its now brick is clear as it emerged into the canal

--X--

PART 2.

SMETHWICK TO STEWART AQUEDUCT

234. A storm closes on bottom lock (2006)

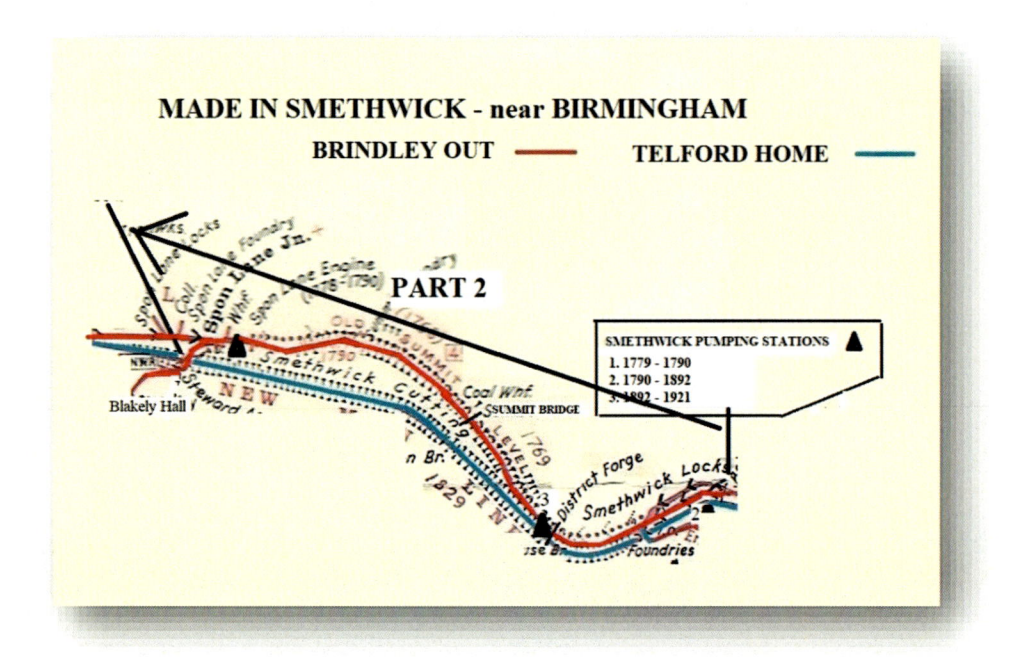

2020

--X--

When Brindley approached Smethwick, there was a summit of about 1 km of high flat land to cross. Originally, he proposed a tunnel but the ground was not stable enough to follow this plan through and six locks were therefore constructed at each end. Very quickly, it became apparent that congestion of heavy traffic led to traffic jams which combined with the extreme difficulty finding a system that produced sufficient water to go up the hill, the route failed. In 1778, a pumping engine was installed at Spon Lane and a second at Bridge Street, Smethwick in 1779, (later referred to as The Smethwick Engine Site) which simply returned water from the bottom to the top. When John Smeaton solved the engineering problem of the Summit in 1789, the canal route was lowered by 5.5 metres (18ft), half the locks could be dispensed and traffic flowed again. Also, to improve the congestion, a further parallel set of locks was added at Smethwick Locks. The three additional locks remain today, each being Grade 2 Listed, whilst the original ones (to the north) were infilled in the 1960s. Graham Wigley remembers travelling these locks in 1958.

--X—

From Canal & River Trust display board at Smethwick Locks

In the centre of the photo above, heavy industry that existed along both sides of the canal is very evident. To the left, the Sandwell Iron & Axle Works occupied the lockside vista with the lock keeper's hut and roving bridge in the centre. The massive chimneys and distant factories behind the Iron Works all belonged to Richard Evered's Surrey Works, all now gone in favour of modern-day housing. The buildings on the far right have also been cleared and the canal to the left of the hut infilled and landscaped. A modern reconstruction of the hut sits as a vandalised burnt-out shell on the site of the original. The three locks are Grade 2 Listed [1077129, 1215330, 1077162]

--x--

2.1 SURREY WORKS
RICHARD EVERED & CO LTD

1809 **Richard Evered** established his metal tube manufacturing company **Richard Evered & Sons**, in London.

1851 Evered & Co exhibited at the **Great Exhibition at Crystal Palace**

1860 Evered moved to Birmingham

1866 He came to Smethwick from Birmingham.

1869 A London office was established in Drury Lane

1874 As the company expanded, Evered had need of a third site, the **Manchester Works**, alongside the Birmingham Canal Old Main Line banded to the north by Lewisham Road. Later, the building was further adapted and renamed the **Surrey Works**, where brass tubes and fittings of all varieties were made but with a speciality for brass bedsteads.

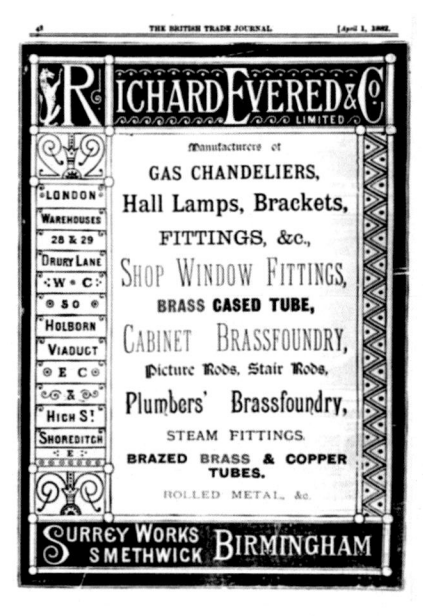

1882

1884   Richard Evered & Co became **Evered & Co**

1894   Evered was making cots

1900   Evered & Co had a workforce of over 1000 employees in Birmingham and Smethwick

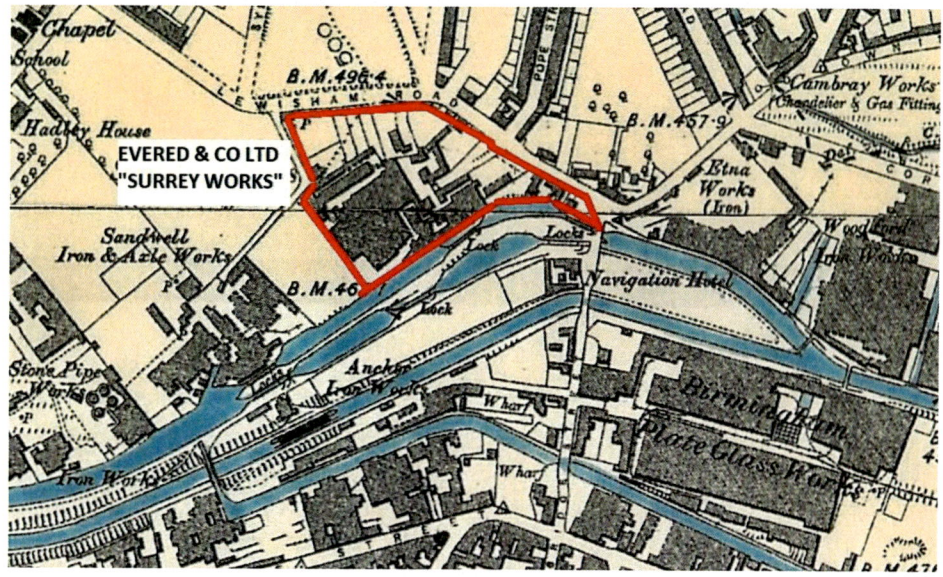

1904 O/S MAP

1908   the company had diversified into fittings for water, gas and electrics alongside the staple manufacture of brass and copper tubes.

1914   Grace's Guide quotes:

"Brassfounders, Bedstead Makers and Tube Drawers. Specialities: Gas Light and Water Fittings, Electric Light Fittings and Electric Bells, Cabinet Brassfoundry of every description, Metallic Bedsteads, Cots and Wire Mattresses, Brass and Copper Tubes, Rolled Metals etc."

Between the two World Wars, the Surrey Works were significantly enlarged to accommodate the growth in the company's output.

1916 [Grace's Guide [Ref. 76]

1937 The company was made public and exhibited at the British Industries Fair making:
"Temperature Measuring Instruments, including Indicating Pyrometers, Temperature Recorders, Automatic Temperature Controllers for Gas, Oil, Electric Furnaces, Molten Metal Pyrometers, Surface Contact Pyrometers, Optical Radiation Pyrometers, Moving-Coil Galvanometers, Thermometers."

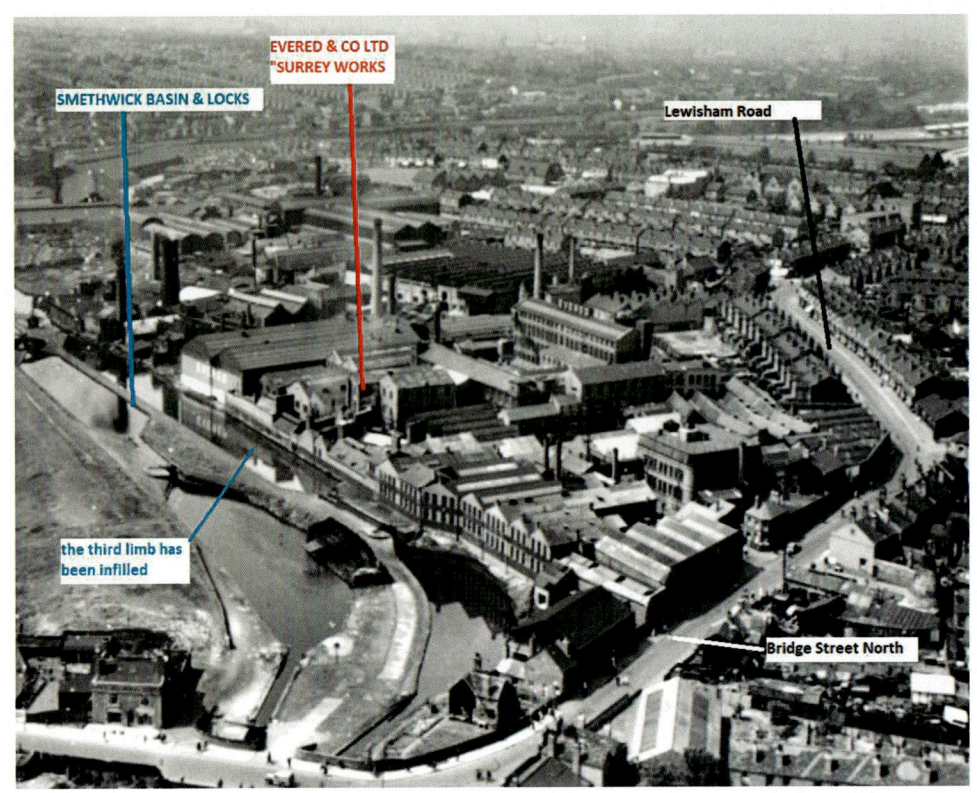

1948 Britain from Above: Smethwick Basin showing the Surrey Works (Richard Evered's third factory) [Ref 1]

1961 *"Manufacturers of brass and copper tubes, rolled metals, gas and water fittings, plastic mouldings, metal bedsteads and hot brass stampings." [REF: 76]*

1970 Renamed to **Evered & Co Holdings**

1980 Most of the production was non-ferrous strip, tube and extrusions, castors and wheels for furniture and locks for security systems.

1983 Acquired **Hawkins & Tipson** (ropemakers)

1984 Acquired **Brockhouse Group** [see District Iron Works p.82]

1991 Formation of **Evered Industrial Products EIP**

2005 **EIP absorbed into PRYMETALL GMBH & CO.** moved location to Rabone Lane, Smethwick, which is no longer visible as an enterprise.

Maker's emblem for Evered & Sons

ABOLISH THE POLISH
LESSEN THE LABOUR

THE

"CROBRITE"

SMILE THAT WON'T COME OFF!

Bath and Lavatory Fittings Plated in the New "CROBRITE" (Regd.) Untarnishable Finish are Never Affected by Heat, Steam, Grease, Soap or Soda, and Retain a Brilliant Appearance.

Sole Manufacturers:
EVERED AND COMPANY, LTD., SURREY WORKS, SMETHWICK.
Write for descriptive Folder No. 236.

1928

A FEW SPECIALITIES FROM OUR EXTENSIVE RANGE OF BUILDERS' HARDWARE

No. S.174 MORTICE DOOR BOLT
No. 1109R. AUTOMATIC CUPBOARD CATCH
No. 735 FLUSH HANDLE
No. 1152 ADJUSTABLE ROLLER BOLT
No. 988 BRONZE SPRING DOOR FASTENER
No. 989 & 1090 TRACK AND RUNNER FOR SLIDING DOORS
The "CYCLONE" SPRINGLESS DOOR BELL
No. 14333 BRASS CHANNEL RUNNERS FOR GLASS DOORS

Manufactured by
EVERED & COMPANY LTD.
SURREY WORKS, SMETHWICK, 40, ENGLAND
London Office: 23 Albemarle Street, W.1

1951

—X—

A deviation to the north and away from the canal is now made, for although not abutting it, the works featured were an important employer for the town. They were conveniently located adjacent to the main GWR railway line which passed only a few hundred metres to the north. In view of their national importance, they are included here in the historical record.

--X--

2.2 BIRMINGHAM CARRIAGE & WAGON COMPANY
BIRMINGHAM RAILWAY CARRIAGE & WAGON CO., BIRMINGHAM WAGON CO.

The Birmingham Wagon Company Ltd, launched in 1854 at Saltley, Birmingham, by a forward-sighted group of Birmingham businessmen who came to Smethwick in 1864 to become a vital employer for the town. They found a conveniently placed 10 acre site astride the Great Western Railway line as it passed through the area in what is now the Middlemore Estate. The site was set a bit away from the canal and was dependant on easy access to the rapidly growing railway network.

Aerial view of the Birmingham Railway Carriage & Wagon Company Ltd works showing the Great Western Railway cutting through the middle of the site. The main line connection is on the extreme right. The private railway bridge connecting the two halves of the works is on the left. Transversers stretched the full width of the north site works.

Robert Ferris

The company made carriages and wagons for railways but also a wide range of vehicles, including aeroplanes, gliders, buses, trolleybuses, and tanks. Its prime function was to supply rolling stock to the major UK railway companies (GWR, LNER, SR and LMS), British Rail, Pullman and overseas railways, e.g. Wagons Lits, Egypt, India, South Africa.

1854   Company formed

1855   Public company formed

1864   Moved from Saltley, Birmingham to 10 acre site on Middlemore Road, Smethwick

1892 – 1902 During the Second Boer War, the company **designed and built hospital trains** to carry injured serviceman from the front lines.

1939-45 The Second World War saw the production of A10 Cruiser, Valentine, Churchill, Cromwell and Challenger Tanks as well as Hamilcar gliders. [REF: 2, 5, 68]

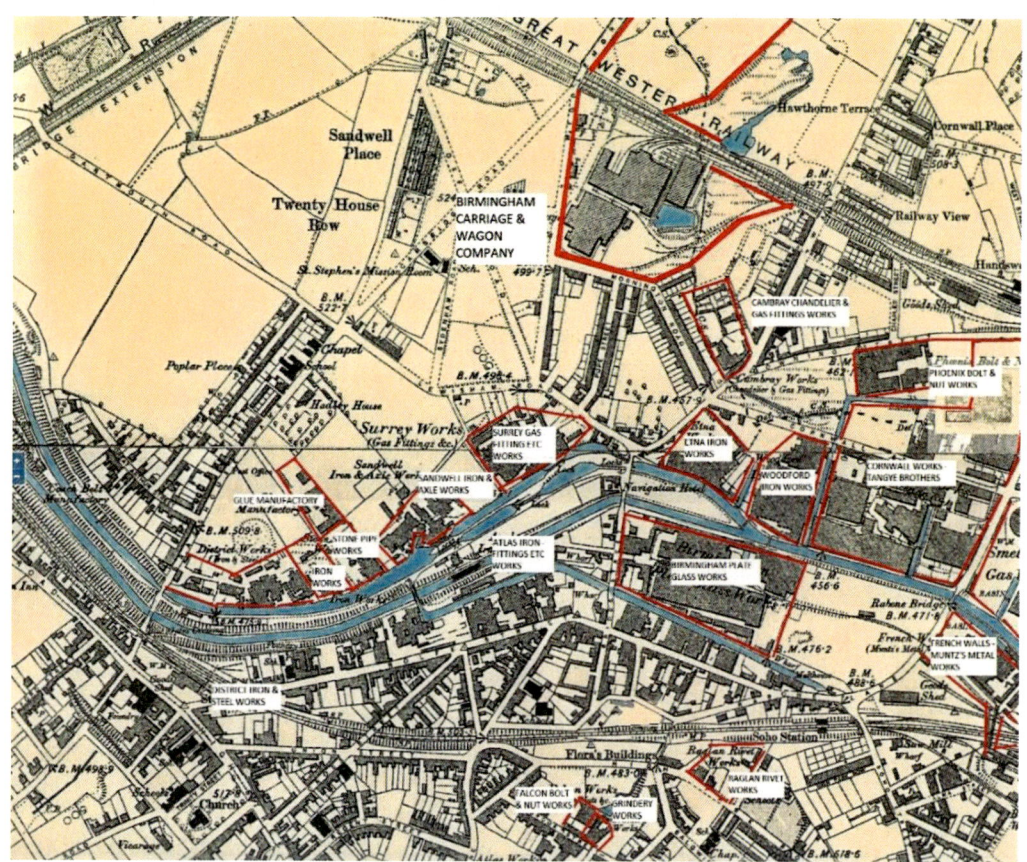

1888 Survey; O/S map 6" : mile. The vicinity of Smethwick Locks, showing the heavily industrialised water edge

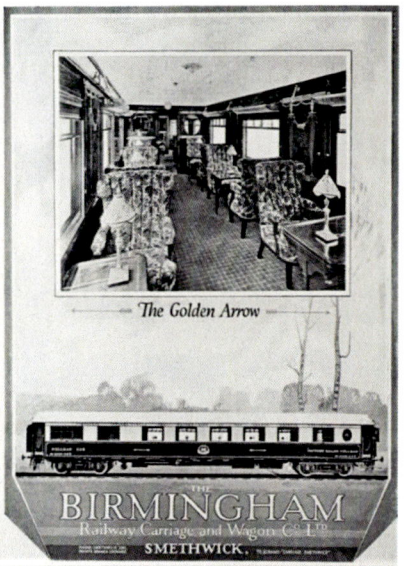

1900 Hospital train   1929 The Golden Arrow ran between London and Dover, where customers crossed the Channel on The Canterbury by First Class and then boarded the Fleche d'Or to Paris [REF: 2. Grace's Guide; & REF. 69].

"Before World War II, the company had built steam-, petrol- and diesel-powered railcars for overseas customers, not to mention bus bodies for Midland Red, and afterwards developed more motive power products, including BR's Class 26, Class 33 (both diesel) and Class 81 (electric) locomotives." [REF: 70 Science Museum Group]

East Coast Dining & Corridor Trains – The Kitchen Car [REF: 2]

"In the years before 1963, the company had built an extensive number of locomotives, diesel multiple unit trains, and Underground cars, but it then became apparent that fewer rolling stock orders were to be expected, and the company restructured itself as an industrial landlord and financing business.[4] The self-funded main line locomotive prototype Lion was a particular disappointment. Powered by a Sulzer 2,750 hp (2,050 kW) diesel engine, it was pitted against another self-funded prototype, Falcon, built by Brush at Loughborough, which had twin 1,400 hp (1,000 kW) Maybach engines. After trials, British Railways preferred the BRCW approach, but ordered them to be built by Brush Traction, and they became British Rail Class 47.

In June 2014, the company was reformed as a not-for-profit organisation, to reconstruct locomotives from the 1960s that had been lost to scrap, including D0260 Lion." [REF: 68]

[REF: 68]

--X--

Returning to the canal route and to the edges of the Smethwick Lock pounds.

--X--

2.3 SANDWELL IRON & AXLE WORKS

Little is written about this engineering site on the north bank of Smethwick Locks of Brindley's canal to the west of Evered, Surrey Works

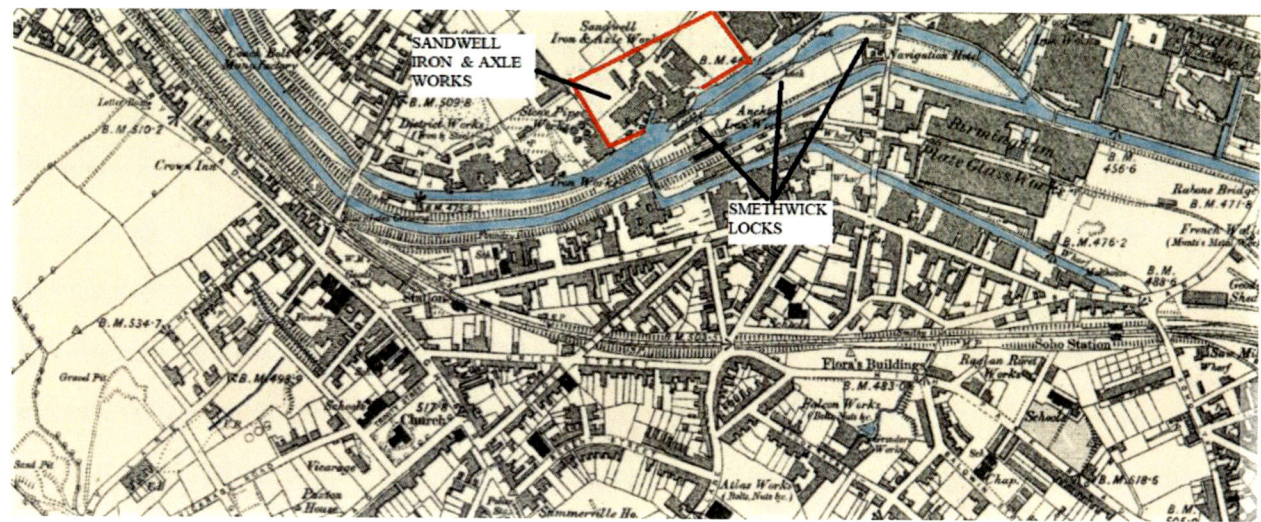

O/S Map 1888

1870   A company was established as **Lones, Raybould & Vernon** of Rolfe Street, Smethwick

1872   The company changed its name to **Lones, Vernon & Holden**

1876   Opened the **Sandwell Iron & Axle Works**

1919   **John Brockhouse & Co Ltd** took control of the company [see District Iron & Steel Works page 82-83]

1939 c. A further merger occurred

1958   All production ceased

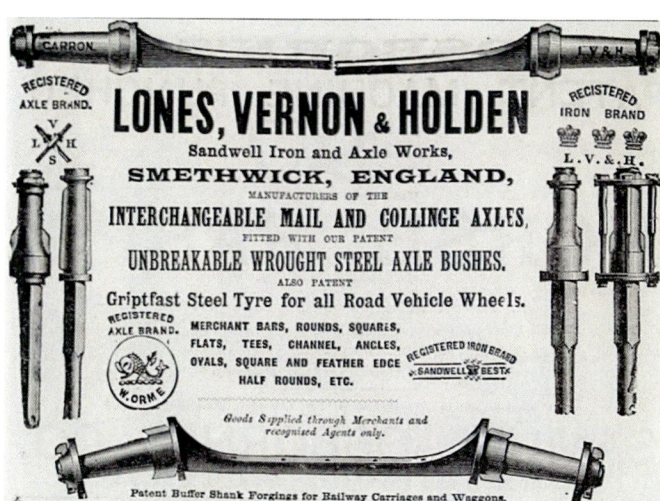

1896

2.4 DISTRICT IRON WORKS
J Brockhouse & Co, Evered & Co Holdings

1867 Company established

1892 Incorporated as a Limited Company

1894 **Commenced manufacturing close joint tubes**

1898 Fencing manufacture commence

1914 The company was now described as a **steel rolling mill** and close joint & electric welded tube mill, employing 350

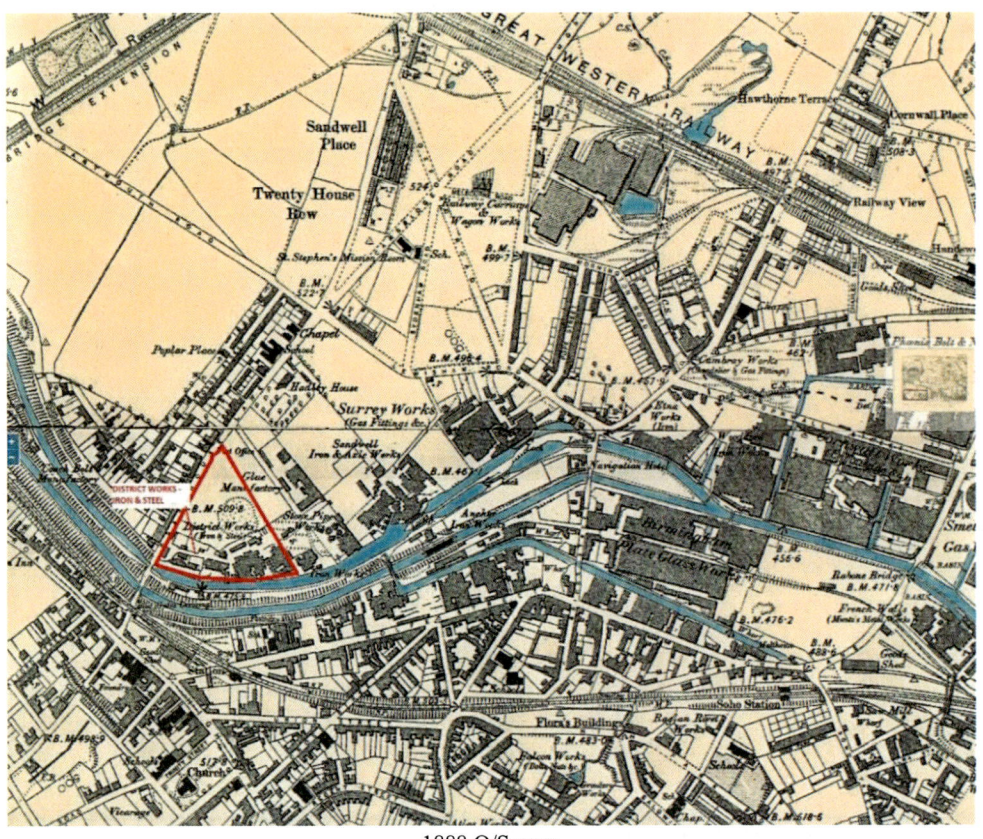

1888 O/S map

A. J. BROCKHOUSE & CO (West Bromwich)

John Brockhouse was a manufacturer of **vehicle axles and springs**. industry working from Victoria Works, West Bromwich with offices in Australia House, London

1844 John Brockhouse was born in Wednesbury to a coach smith, also John

1857 John Jnr. was orphaned at the age of 12 years and became an apprentice to **R Disturnal & Co,** Wednesbury who made axles

1859 Brockhouse left Disturnal and joined **John Rigby & Sons**, spring and axle makers. Later in the 20th century, J Brockhouse & Co took over Disturnal amongst many others.

1864   He moved to **Richard Berry & Sons**, Alma Street, Birmingham, making laminated springs

1865   He returned to John Rigby & Sons as Manager

1871   C/R   A coach smith

1881   C/R   Coach spring maker

1886   John Brockhouse started a company called **Brockhouse & Co**, on the death of Rigby from where he manufactured springs and axles

1891   C/R   Still described as a coach spring manufacturer

1893   John's son, **John Thomas BROCKHOUSE** entered the business

1897   Axles were added to the repertoire. The same year he built new premises Victoria Works, West Bromwich

1909   John Brockhouse became **Mayor of West Bromwich**

1911   John's sons were: John Thomas (managing director in waiting), Henry (Company Secretary). Frederick (Works Manager), Arthur (coach spring fitter), Frank (Foreman of Works)

1914   John Brockhouse & Co employed 700 workers making axles, ironwork including motor carriage & van springs. They were very buoyant during WW1.

1822   **John Brockhouse died** and **John Thomas** took over

1934

1936   **District Iron Works, Smethwick** was acquired by **J Brockhouse & Co** who had acquired the next-door premises, where laminated springs and railway equipment were made

1944   **John Thomas died**

1951   **Nationalization** led to the company being part of the Iron & Steel Corporation of Great Britain

1953   Sold back to **J. Brockhouse & Co**

1967   Company described as one of the larger independent steel-rollers

1984   Acquired by **Evered & Co Holdings**, Smethwick [see Richard Evered & Co, 'Surrey Works' p. 74-77]

—x—

The journey now passes a modern housing estate on the right bank as the canal turns northward and soon approaches a road bridge over the canal. Through the mature archway, a majestic brick pumping house comes into view. This was the third of those built on the Birmingham side of the Summit Tunnel.

—x—

2.5 SMETHWICK PUMPING STATION NO. 3

800.73 New Smethwick Pumping Station

HISTORIC ENGLAND GRADE TWO LISTED

LIST ENTRY NUMBER 1077154
DATE FIRST LISTED 1978
GRADE 2
SMETHWICK NEW PUMPING HOUSE APPROXIMATELY 50 METRES NORTH OF BRASSHOUSE LANE BIRMINGHAM CANAL BIRMINGHAM LEVEL

Pumping house between Smeaton's Old Main Line on the Wolverhampton Level and Telford's New Main Line on the Birmingham Level. 1892. Brick with slate roof. One storey to Old Main Line and two storeys to New Main Line. Lower storey has four-bay blind arcade with impost band, and a smaller doorway within right-hand arch. The upper storey has four windows with segmental heads, the two right-hand ones blocked, and a drip course. Miniature false machicolation to the eaves; adjoining to the left is the ashes hole with a doorway for removing the ash. Hipped slate roof in two spans, with louvred ridge ventilators. Right- hand return wall of three bays, with blocked windows. North-east wall, facing upper level, has two wide elliptical arches with smaller inner segmental arches. The right-hand one is blocked, the left-hand one is a doorway. In front of the right-hand archway are the foundation walls of the coal hole. Interior: steel roof trusses. History: This pumping house replaced two earlier pumping stations on the Engine Arm of the Birmingham Canal. It was the last to be erected on this section of the canal and housed two vertical compound engines driving centrifugal pumps capable of lifting 200 locks per day. In 1905 one engine was removed for use at Bentley, the remaining one being in use until the early 1920s. The pumphouse is a prominent feature of the canalside landscape.

1891   The need for improvements on the original **Boulton & Watt pump of 1779** became apparent, when a canal engineer called G.R. Jebb realised the pump had worn out. He built the engine house and proposed the new engine would pump:

"200 lockfuls of water per day rather than the 160 lockfuls per day of the Boulton & Watt engine." The design consisted of two Lancashire boilers being fed with water by two sets of Duplex feed pumps and supplied steam to two vertical Z crank compound engines. These were fitted with Korting Bros. injector condensers and drove centrifugal pumps." [REF: 111]

1892   This classical industrial pumping station therefore replaced James Watt's original old Engine Arm Pump and was designed to restore water content between the two levels pumping water from Telford's much lower canal up to the sometimes-parched Brindley Canal.

1905   One of the two engines was removed to the Walsall Canal.

1920   The traffic on the old Brindley limb had dropped and it became unnecessary to pump water back up to it

1921   The boilers were removed.

1930   All the remaining plant was sold to Messrs. J. Cashmore for scrap and the building became void.

1940   During WW2, a diesel submarine engine was installed as a precaution against enemy action breaching the canal bank. Fortunately, this was never required to work.

1946   Once again, the contents of the building were removed and decay continued for many years

1978   The building was designated Grade 2 Listed

1982   Restoration commenced

2000   The building was restored to its current magnificence.

2003. The parallel routes of mainline railway, Telford's deep cutting and the more raised Brindley Canal on the far right with the restored Smethwick Pumping Station No, 3 just disappearing on the right

Smethwick's New Pumping Station is also the home of the Galton Valley Canal Museum

https://www.sandwell.gov.uk/info/200265/museums_and_art_gallery/10/our_museums_and_sites/2

—X—

It is only a few metres to **John Smeaton's** remarkable engineering feat of levelling the course of Brindley's original canal with the construction of the Summit Tunnel in 1788-9. This engineer solved the problem of insufficient water supply by driving a tunnel through the hillside over which Brindley had constructed a series of locks. It is also this point the two canals diverge for a while and the housing estate is left behind. On the left side is the remnant site of one of the Galton family estates with Galton House being positioned between the two waterways.

—X—

2.6 JOHN SMEATON & SUMMIT BRIDGE (1788/9)

1769   The Brindley Canal was opened

1772   The canal opened for traffic but there was a water shortage on top of the hill in Smethwick and despite the use of engines at both sides of the summit being used to pump water to the top, a height above sea level of 150m (491ft.) unlike the proverbial 'Jack & Jill', there was little point climbing 'up the hill to fetch a pail of water' for frequently with busy traffic the canal became unnavigable.

1787   the Birmingham Canal Company decided to drop the summit at Smethwick by just over 5 metres (18ft.) and John Smeaton, [see p. 148-9] who name had become synonymous with water engineering successes, was asked to design and supervise the project.

1789   **Smeaton** opened the revised scheme by not only dropping the highest point of water, but also removing now redundant locks and driving the canal course through the hillside by constructing a vast and sturdy bridge to carry Roebuck Lane across the deep cutting.

Summit Bridge, Smethwick. Grade 2* & SCHEDULED MONUMENT [Courtesy of Historic England]. Alongside and within the arch is the tunnel bearing busy Telford Way.

Today, the aesthetic of this Grade 2* Listed monument is clouded by modern worship of travel all around it. Roebuck Lane has been widened, Telford Way, a busy dual carriageway link to the M5, is a roar of conurbation traffic and a railway line crosses to Galton Bridge station leaving this one of the West Midlands' best kept secrets.

HISTORIC ENGLAND LISTED BUILDING
Grade 2* listing: [1391875]
Road bridge over the cutting of the summit of the Birmingham Canal, Old Main Line Wolverhampton Level. Constructed between 1788-9 by John Smeaton when he improved the canal by reducing the summit level from 491ft to 472ft.

Grade 2 listing: [1215275] Railway Bridge 15 metres north of Summit Bridge/Roebuck Lane, Birmingham Canal Wolverhampton Level.

MATERIALS: Constructed of red brick with brick copings and a sandstone keystone.
PLAN: It is a massive single span bridge with segmental arch. The towpath passes under the south western side.
EXTERIOR: There are protruding brick pilasters, a double string course, and curving flanking abutments with short protruding end piers. On the north western face there is a cast iron date plaque bearing the legend 'MDCCXC'.
SOURCES: `Smethwick: Communications', A History of the County of Staffordshire: Volume 17 (1976), 96-8; http://www.british-history.ac.uk/report.asp?compid=36174. Date accessed: 25 September 2006; AM7 Scheduling, WM12, Smeaton's Summit Bridge, 9 May 1972.
SUMMARY OF IMPORTANCE: Smeaton's Summit Bridge, survives as an un-altered example of engineering prowess from the height of the industrial revolution. Designed by the leading civil engineer of the time, its massive proportions demonstrate technical innovation, providing an elegant solution to the requirement for a road crossing at this difficult site. The scale of the project can be seen as a precursor to later engineering projects of the railway era and ably demonstrates the technical excellence of John Smeaton. As part of the improvement scheme to the Birmingham mainline canal the Summit Bridge also provides reference to the high level of investment in, and importance of, canal navigations to the industrial development of Georgian England.

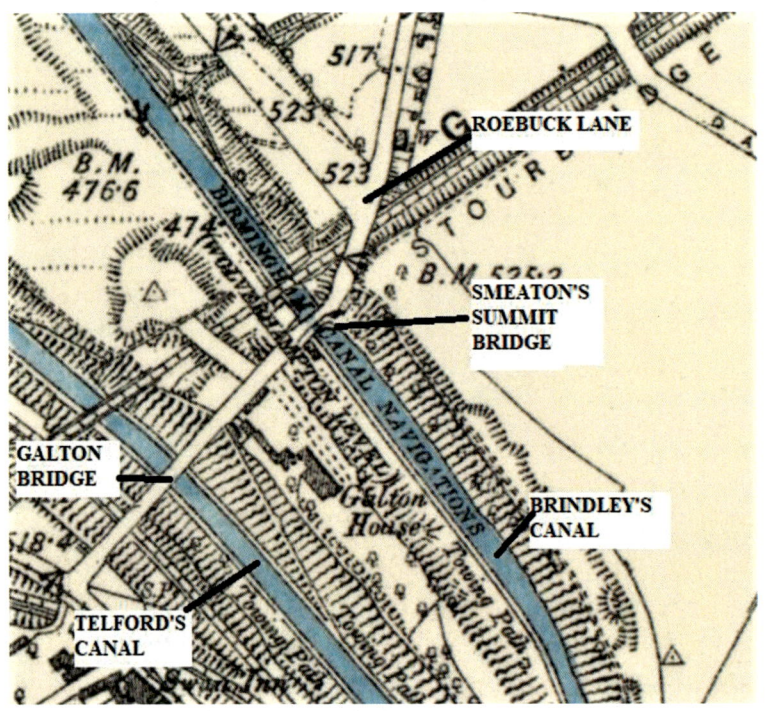

1888 O/S MAP

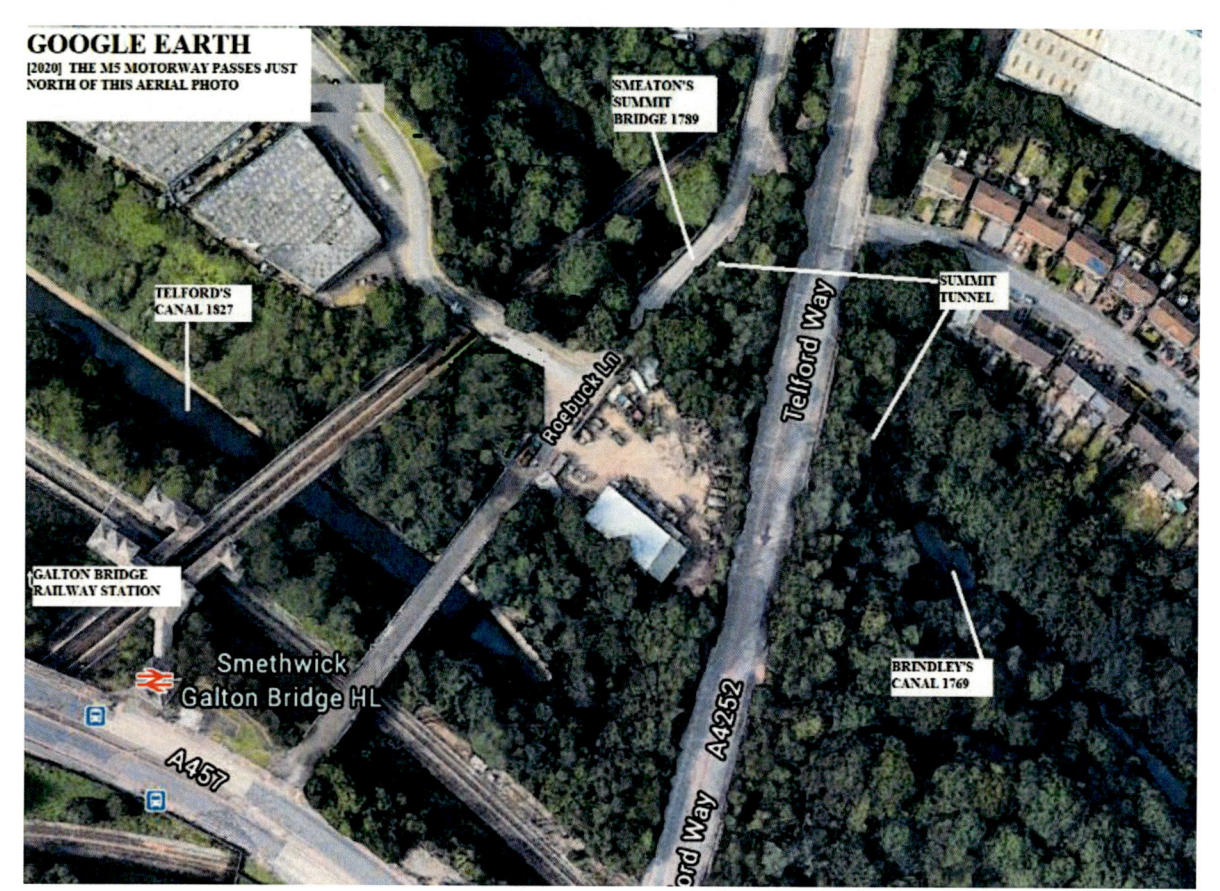

2020 Google Earth

560. Underneath the Arches. 2012. A painting by the author of the three bridges from the north west. In the foreground is the Grade 2 Listed railway bridge partially obscuring John Smeaton's Summit Bridge and beyond is a narrow boat coming through the Summit Tunnel bearing 20th century Telford Way.

--x--

A few metres to the west of Summit Tunnel in an area now respectably reclaimed by the wildness of nature, an incongruous concrete remnant on the opposite bank to the towpath seems a random memorabilia to an industrial past belied by the current rural setting.

--x--

2.7 SANDWELL PARK COLLIERY CO.
SANDWELL PRIORY, SANDWELL HALL & THE EARLS OF DARTMOUTH

"Although the Thick Coal underlies Smethwick, the district is situated beyond the fault which formed the eastern limit of early working in the South Staffordshire coalfield." [REF: 5].

A. **SANDWELL HALL & THE EARLS OF DARTMOUTH**

1531   **Sandwell Priory** was taken on by **Dame Lucy Clifford** after the Dissolution of the Monasteries

1569   The grandson of Lady Lucy, **Robert Whorwood** purchased the Priory

1611   The Priory was then called **Sandwell Hall** when Thomas Whorwood lived there

1624   **Thomas Whorwood** (son of above) was Knighted by King James I

1701   After the Civil War, **Sandwell Hall** was purchased by the **1st Earl of Dartmouth**

1st Earl of Dartmouth (Godfrey Kneller)

1711   The rebuild was completed.

1750   The **2nd Earl of Dartmouth** took possession of the estate. This gent became a famous politician during the **War of American Independence** and Sandwell hall was his favourite residence of the several he possessed.

1753   During the early 19th century, as the industrial revolution accelerated it would seem the **5th Earl of Dartmouth**, a Conservative politician, chose to move his residence to Patshull Hall, Staffordshire.

George Frederick Muntz of **London Works** [see p. 135-8] fame rented it for a while. [REF: 109].

B. SANDWELL PARK COLLIERY CO

1870   **SANDWELL PARK COLLIERY CO** was formed and a consortium under the engineering leadership of **Henry Johnson**, who sank **a shaft to the east of Roebuck Lane** on land belonging to Lord Dartmouth of Sandwell Hall. The house was rebuilt using the skills of West Midlands architect **William Smith** from Tettenhall,.

1874   **Thick Coal was reached at a depth of 383m.** (1254ft) This was followed by a **second shaft** being started later that year in Sandwell Valley called the Jubilee.

1883   **A third shaft** was drilled reaching coal at 385m. (1263ft). Johnson's success was down to his courage, leadership and the use of dynamite, which was still considered risky at that time.

1896   483 men were employed below ground and 162 above. The workings were mainly in a south-easterly direction towards Handsworth, with none extending beneath the Birmingham Canal.

1914   **Production ceased** because the company had opened a new colliery in West Bromwich to reach the coal seams to the north. [REF: 5]

1930s   Sandwell Park Colliery was bought by the **Warwickshire Coal Company**, who modernised the plant extensively. This included erecting the concrete loading bunker alongside Brindley's original canal (see below).

The concrete loading wharf built after Warwickshire Coal Company took over Sandwell Park Colliery in the 1930s. In 2020, there remains only the lower wall. [REF: 75]

Sandwell Park has now been developed into a fine **Nature Reserve**, with considerable public amenities or lakes, wildlife conservation, a renovated farm and centre, a gold course and is dissected by the north south route of the M5.

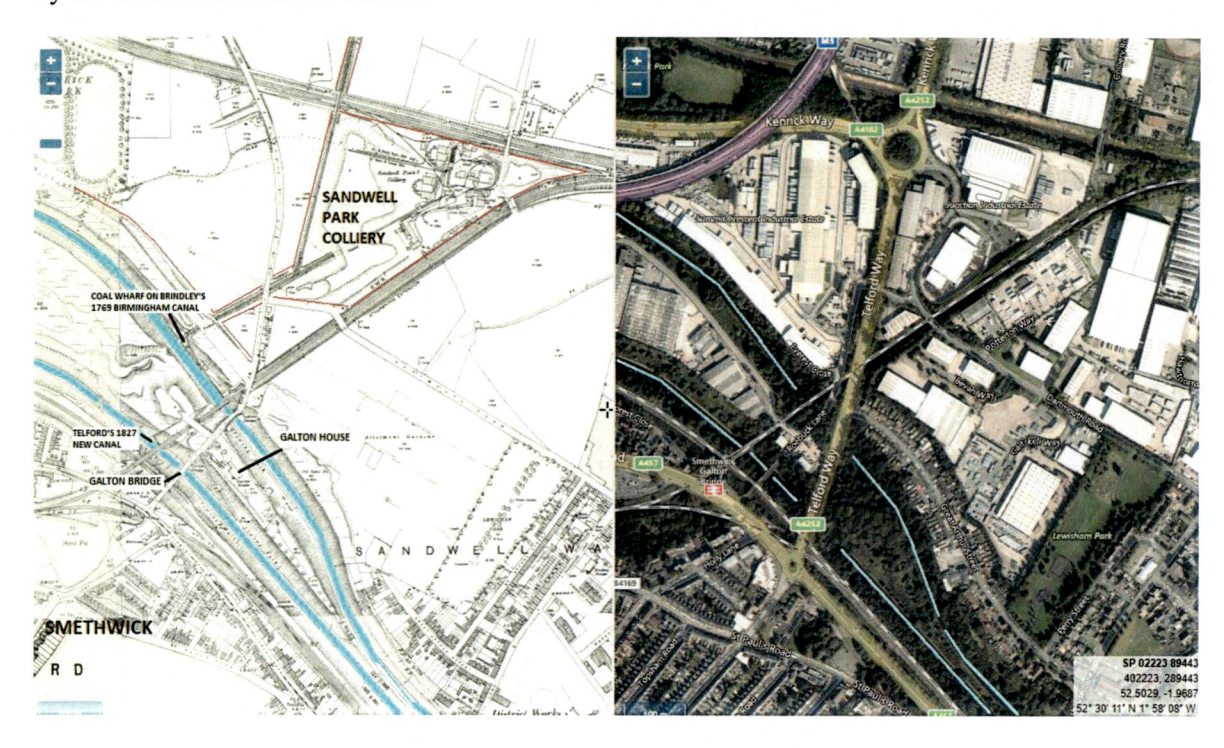

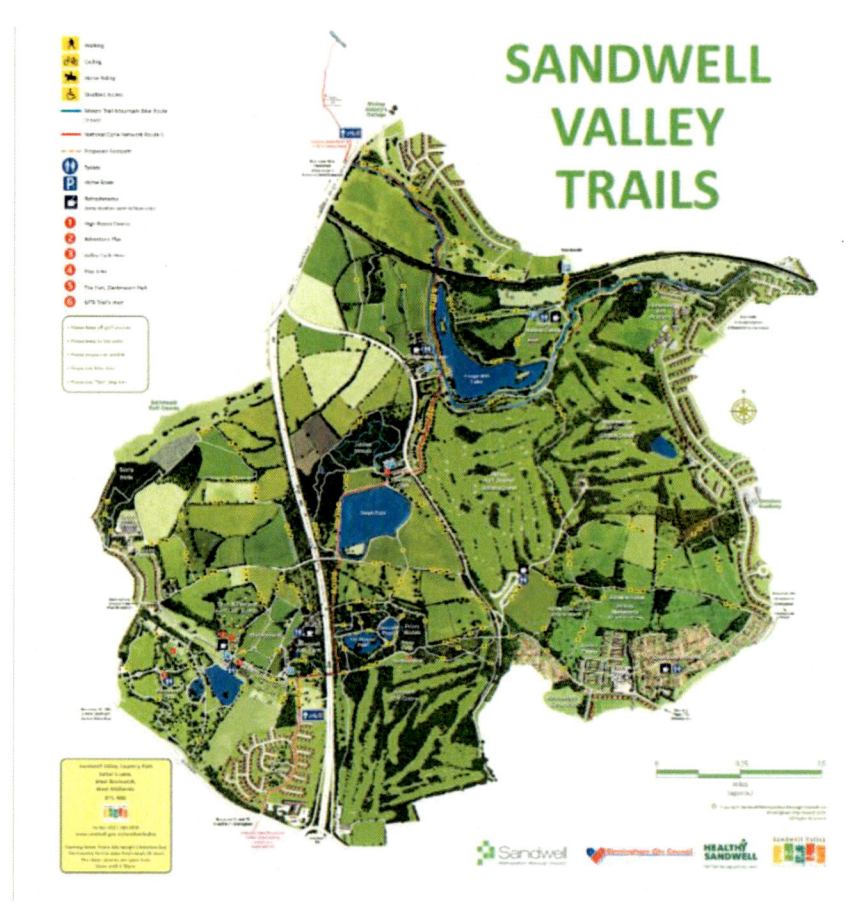

The site of the old colliery is now a well designed nature reserve with living farm, parkland, lakes, an educational centre and many wild trails

--X--

After the site of the old colliery, the canal turns westwards but already the roar of the M5, high on stilts and disturbingly visible, dominates the now otherwise verdant landscape. Very soon, the canal is hidden beneath the concrete Leviathon as if now totally without significance. Visible through the gaps of the gigantic pillars on the other bank a few metres distant is an imposing red brick Victorian factory. Strictly speaking, not in Smethwick, but Sandwell, this historic centre of industrial heritage cannot be ignored because of arbitrary clerical boundaries.

--X--

2.8 ARCHIBALD KENRICK WORKS

Despite not being in Smethwick but West Bromwich; this establishment was close to Brindley's Old Main Line. Today, it is still visible from the M5 northbound carriageway on the left as it passes over the canal and divides old West Bromwich from Smethwick.

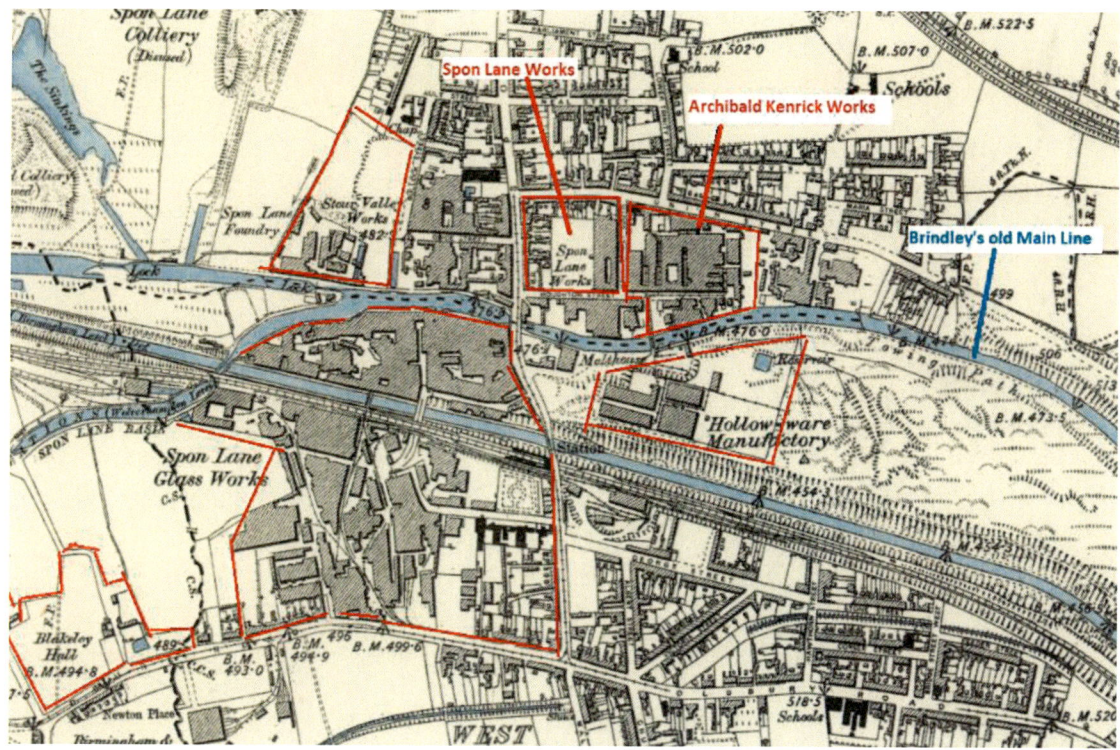

O/S 1888 survey 6"/mile

Grace's Guide [REF: 2] quotes:

"Archibald Kenrick (1760-1835) of Archibald Kenrick and Co and Archibald Kenrick and Sons 1760 November 12th. Born at Wrexham the son of John Kenrick (1725-1803) and his wife Mary Quarrell (1718-1801)

1780   **Moved to Birmingham.** Went into business in the **buckle trade** with a distant relation who, like him, was a Unitarian.

1787   After acquiring a knowledge of plating, and with financial support from his father, Archibald went into partnership with another buckle maker, Thomas Boulton

1790   December 1st. Married Rebecca Smith (1770-1809)

1791   **Archibald Kenrick** set up an **iron foundry** in West Bromwich.

"Kenrick's tinned hollow-ware gained a reputation for being lightweight, attractive, and hygienic cooking utensils, of a quality and at a price to mostly replace "black" hollow-ware and to compete with similar vessels made from copper or brass."

1812   Archibald's nephew **Samuel Kenrick** joined the company when it was named Archibald Kenrick & Co. At the same time, they expanded on to the adjacent land of **Spon Lane Works.** In that same year, he married his second wife, Mary Eddowes (1763–1854). There were four sons and three daughters from his two marriages.

1815   records show they employed numbers of workers that "could be counted in tens"

1835   Archibald Kenrick died but by this time the company employed "several hundred" workers

2020   After many years of neglect, the building is undergoing extensive renovation

Archibald Kenrick & Co, West Bromwich    Archibald Kenrick (1760-1835) REF: 3]

--X--

Whilst still lurking beneath the cacophony of the motorway above, there is a divergence a few metres further on where the **Spon Lane Locks** peel off to the right to follow one of the most direct routes to Wolverhampton. There is another limb of the original canal to the west, that winds towards Wednesbury. They meet again further north. This area is nearing the most northern point of the remit of this journey but the industry that spanned the area is worthy of mention, starting with Historic England's numerous listed items at Spon Lane Locks.

HISTORIC ENGLAND LISTINGS AT SPON LANE
List Entry No. 1215249 [1987] GRADE 2
TOP LOCK, SPON LANE LOCKS, WITH ATTACHED FOOTBRIDGE BIRMINGHAM CANAL WOLVERHAMPTON LEVEL
One of flight of three locks on Wolverhampton Level of Birmingham Canal, with attached lock bridge. Probably 1790, when Brindley's original flight of six locks built in 1769 was reduced to the present three: some C20 repairs. Brick, with sandstone kerbstones [coping] partly replaced by concrete. Cast-iron sluice [paddle] gear. Upper gate single, lower gate double. Across the lower entrance to the lock chamber is a footbridge, of cast iron and having brick abutments with sandstone dressings. The bridge was originally in two halves, with one cantilevered from each bank, allowing a rope to pass through a central slot. The walkway is now concreted and the cast-iron railings remain only on the downstream side. The Old Main Line, on the Wolverhampton Level, was by-passed by Telford's New Main Line on the Birmingham Level in 1829. (Paget-Tomlinson, E W. "The Complete Book of Canal and River Navigations", 1978, p 950.

List Entry No. 1342651 [1987]
MIDDLE LOCK, SPON LANE LOCKS BIRMINGHAM CANAL WOLVERHAMPTON LEVEL

List Entry No. 1288230 [1987]
BOTTOM LOCK, SPON LANE LOCKS BIRMINGHAM CANAL WOLVERHAMPTON LEVEL

List Entry No. 1077160 [1987]
FOOTBRIDGE OVER OLD MAIN LINE AT BROMFORD JUNCTION, (APPROXIMATELY 40 METRES) WEST OF SPON LANE LOCKS BIRMINGHAM CANAL WOLVERHAMPTON LEVEL
Footbridge over the Old Main Line (Wolverhampton Level) of the Birmingham Canal at its junction with Telford's New Main Line. 1829. Cast-iron with brick abutments having some sandstone dressings. Single elliptical arch. Each side formed from two castings, bolted to central "keystone". Sides pierced to form pattern of saltire crosses, with a band of quatrefoils under the handrail. Spandrel inscribed: "HORSELEY IRON WORKS 1829".

List Entry No. 13342645 [1987]
FOOTBRIDGE OVER NEW MAIN LINE AT BROMFORD JUNCTION, 20 METRES SOUTH OF BOTTOM LOCK, SPON LANE LOCKS BIRMINGHAM CANAL BIRMINGHAM LEVEL
Footbridge over the New Main Line (Birmingham Level) of the Birmingham Canal at its junction with the Old Main Line (Wolverhampton Level). 1848. Cast-iron with brick abutments. Single segmental arch. Lattice sides bolted together in three sections. The central section is inscribed: "THE HORSELEY COMPANY TIPTON 1848".

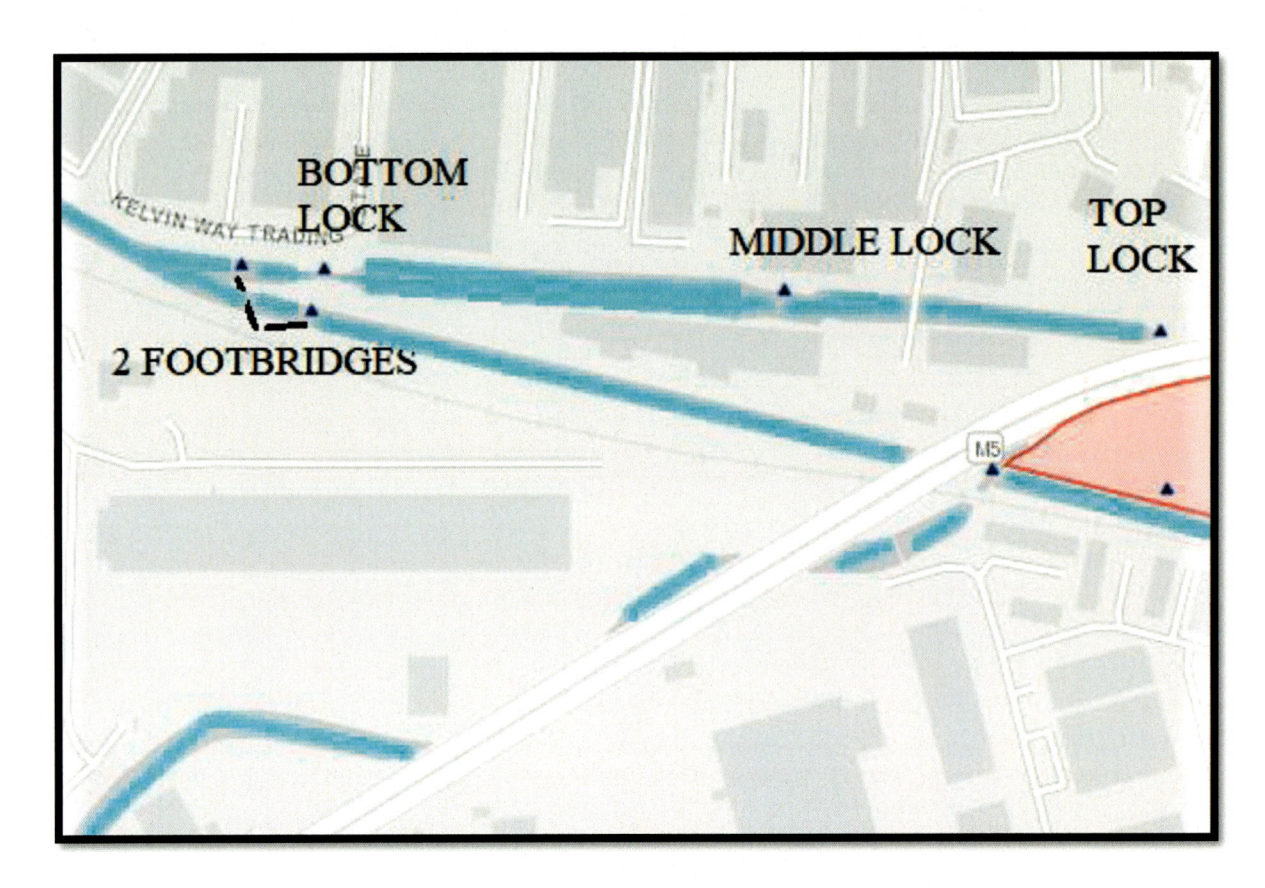

Courtesy of Historic England https://historicengland.org.uk/listing/the-list/map-search?clearresults=True#?search

The view of the Spon Lane Locks in 2020 is very different from Brindley's day and this area has seen dramatic changes in function both above and below ground. First, it is necessary to drift away from the prescribed route and to consider a manufacturer operating a few miles away at Tipton, whose work is highly relevant to the success of Brindley's canal.

--x--

2.9 SPON LANE FOUNDRY & HORSELEY IRON WORKS

A. HORSELEY IRON CO.

1813 **Aaron Manby,** was born in Albrighton, Shrewsbury but came back to the West Midlands from having been a banker in the Isle of Wight**,** to join a partnership with a local Tipton man, **Joseph Smith,** who took control of the **Horseley Iron Company.** It was during this year that **Manby** took out **a patent for making bricks** from furnace slag and **built a retort to produce coal gas.** [REF: 95]

1815 An iron works was built near the **Toll End Communication Canal** by **Aaron Manby called Horseley Iron Company.**

1817 Some enormous castings were made at Horseley; in the case of one cylinder, it was possible to drive a wagon and team of horses through its bore, literally.

Aaron Manby (1776-1850)

1821 Horseley was famous for constructing the first iron steamer "**PS Aaron Manby**"

1822 The first iron vessel propelled by steam was built at Tipton and assembled in London at Rotherhithe, which sailed to France and worked the River Seine between Paris and Le Havre.

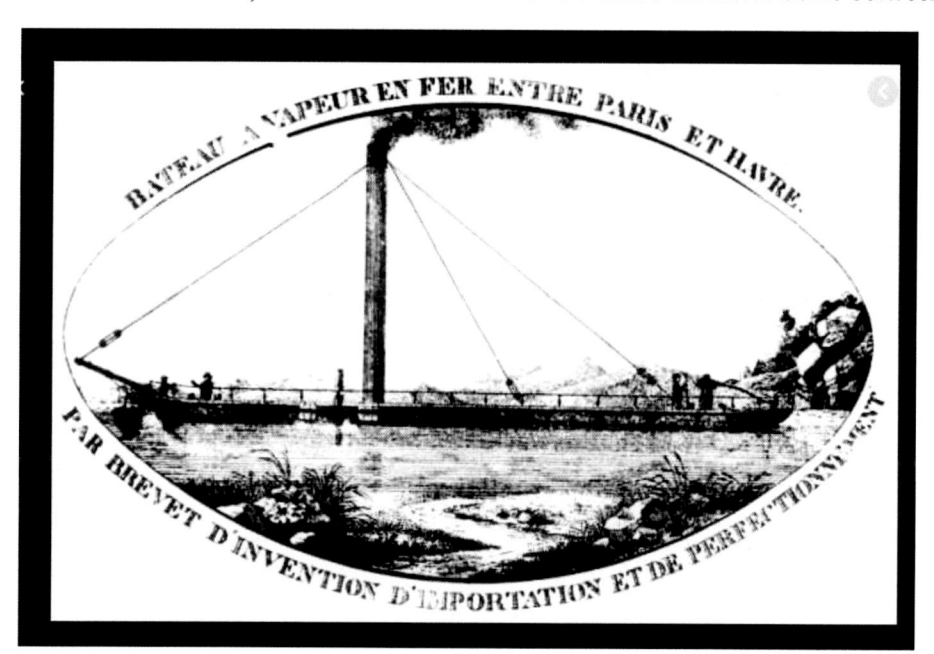

1829 **Galton Bridge** was built by Horseley Works and constructed for Telford's new canal in Smethwick [see p. 120-22]

1832 Several Railway engines rolled out of this iron works

1834 Manby supervised the construction of a **30HP non-condensing engine** for the East Boston Sugar Refinery, Boston, Mass.

1843 According to Grace's Guide, an advertisement for sale appeared in the **Wolverhampton Chronicle** [REF 96] :

'TO CAPITALISTS. THE HORSELEY IRON WORKS, STEAM ENGINE & BOILER MANUFACTORY ATTACHED, TIPTON, near Birmingham. THE ASSIGNEES of the HORSELEY ESTATE are desirous of DISPOSING OF, in one lot, the Intirety of the MACHINERY and BUILDINGS connected with the above celebrated Works, of which a lease may be obtained from the Proprietors on very liberal advantageous terms.

'The Mines of Coal and Ironstone may be worked with them, if required, at Royalties, which would enable the holder to make Pig Iron at profit, and to compete with the productions of Wales and Scotland.

'The Works consist of two Cold Blast Furnaces, worked by a powerful Engine manufactured by Boulton and Watt, which blows, in addition, two Refineries, three Cupolas, and all the Smiths' Fires, which are numerous.

'There are also three Air Furnaces. The Stoves are of various sizes, and the Cranes so arranged to command the range of the whole Foundry, which is on a large scale, and capable of turning out from 100 to 150 tons of Castings per week.

'The Pattern Shop and Storerooms are large and commodious, and the Fitting up Shops, Lathe, and Planing Machine Shops and Erecting Sheds are very conveniently arranged.

'The Smiths' Shop is large and airy, and the Boiler Yard is everything that could be desired. All the Premises are lighted with Gas, the House containing eight Retorts, and the Purifiers, Gasholder, and Fittings being quite complete.

'The Wharfs, Sheds, Cranes, Weighing Machines, Stables, Drawing Offices, Clerks' Offices, &c. are conveniently placed among the Works.

'The Machinery, which is of the very best description consists of a Water-wheel, with a good supply to which Steam Engine is attached in case of need. This power drives the Boring Bars, Roll-turning Slide Lathes, Drilling Machines, and Planing Machines, one of which is capable of planing a surface of about 20 feet by ten. In the Boiler Yard there is a small Engine, which drives the Punching, Shearing, and Remering Machines. There is also a good Horizontal Steam Engine the new Lathe Shop, which works a large and magnificent Lathe, also other Lathes, Slotting Machines, &c.

'And there is a large and commodious House, with suitable Out-offices, for Partner or Manager. In fact, the Horseley Works are too well known to need any comment, and being now disencumbered of a heavy and unprofitable stock, a most favourable opportunity presents itself for the employment of capital, with every prospect of realizing a good income.

'For all further particulars and terms of treaty for the Works and Machinery, apply to John Williams, Esq., the Friery, Handsworth, or to Messrs. Jonah and George Davies, Albion Foundry, Tipton, the latter of whom will show the Machinery; and for further particulars and terms of treaty, in regard to the Colliery, apply to Mr. Benjamin Shorthouse, of Horseley Heath, Tipton. There may be an arrangement for the Machine and Works to be let together for a term of years, if thought more desirable, without sustaining the outlay of purchasing the Machinery."

1844 & 5   Two similar advertisements appeared and the whole stock was sold to **John Joseph Bramah of London Works,** [see p. 141] who lived at Ashwood House

1846   **Bramah** died and Horseley Works went into liquidation

1847   **Robert Broad** became proprietor of Horseley Ironworks and changed the name to **Horseley Co.**

1865   The firm moved to a site on **Dixon's Branch** near the South Staffordshire Railway line

1874   Robert Broad died and **Peter Duckworth Bennett became Chairman**

B.   SPON LANE FOUNDRY

1825   **Peter Duckworth Bennett** (1825-1885) born as the fourth son to William Bennett in the village of Hawarden, Cheshire

1839   Bennett was articled to the **Oak Farm Company**, Dudley

1846   He became Manager of the Constructive Department of Oak Farm Company

1847   Bennett became employed by **Cochrane & Co**, Woodside, Dudley

1859   He was elevated to the Chief of Draftsman ship, Estimating & Constructing Department of Cochrane & Co

1852   Peter D Bennett joined **Fox, Henderson & Co** [see p.141-2] as Chief Engineer and is arguably reputed to have supervised the preparation of ironwork for the Great Exhibition of 1851. [*Conflicting dates in the timeline*]

1853   He started his own business in **Spon Lane** as a Mechanical Engineer, where his work was chiefly associated with engineering on railways and gas companies

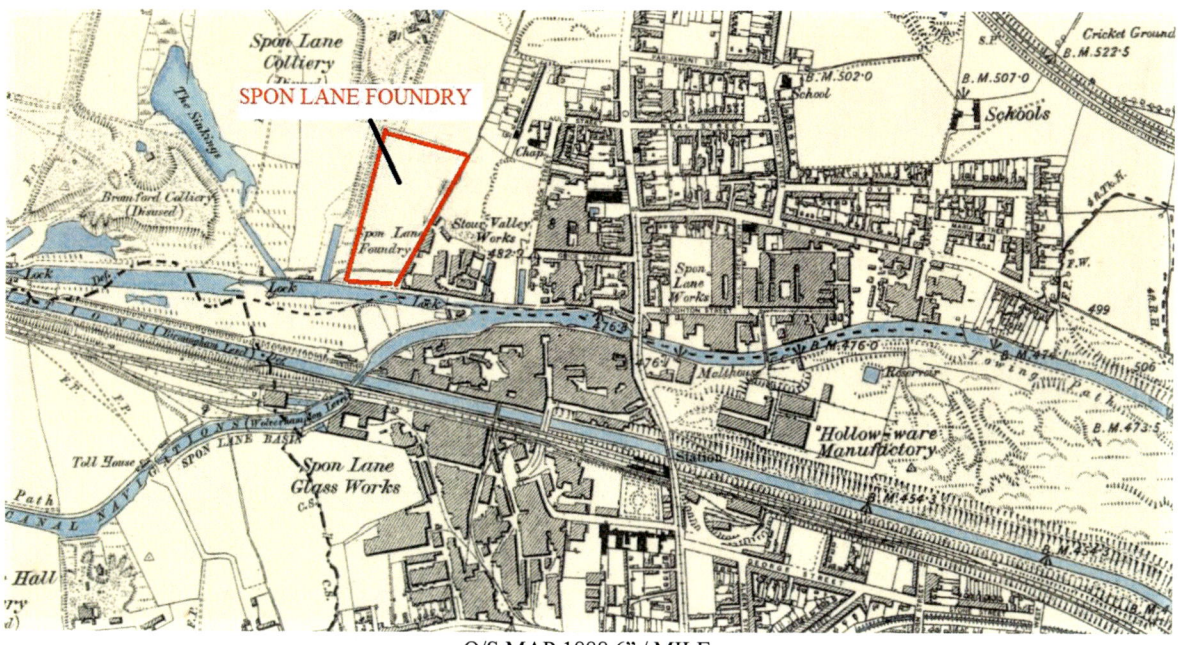

O/S MAP 1888 6" / MILE

1869   Member of the Iron & Steel Institute

1874   In the Annals of Tipton Industries, [REF 95] **Horseley Engineering Works** recorded events that lead to Bennett's rise into this prestigious company run by the eminent engineer of the day, **Aaron Manby**:

> "Thanks to Aaron Manby, the engineering business {Horseley Engineering Works] quickly developed. Some of the earliest products were marine steam engines. On the 9th July, 1821, Manby took out a patent for an **oscillating marine steam engine** and for the use of oil to get-up steam. He also took out a French patent for the design for an iron ship. He formed a company in France with Charles Napier to operate steamboats on the Seine between Rouen and Paris. Their first iron boat was built at Horseley and registered on the 30th April, 1822 as **'Manby'**, although it was

> *generally known as the 'Aaron Manby'. After successful trials, the ship crossed the channel and **became the first iron ship to put to sea**. It successfully operated on the Seine for about thirty years."*

A bit later:

> *On 2nd January, 1874, **Robert Broad** died.[Chairman] He was replaced as Chairman by **John Cochrane**. **Thomas Short became Vice Chairman**. A new steam riveting machine was installed in the boiler shop in 1876, and in 1877 John Cochrane resigned. He was replaced by **Peter Duckworth Bennett**, a West Bromwich ironfounder. The firm acquired his business and decided to sell his loss-making Spon Lane Foundry in 1880.*

1877   Bennett became **Chairman of Horseley Iron Works**

1878   He amalgamated his business with Horseley Co. Ltd of Tipton, where he was Managing Engineer and supervised work on the widening of Charing Cross Railway Bridge, London.

A further sobering entry in the Annals of Tipton Industries concerning Horseley – not an employer with a good track record:

> *"Working in an ironworks could be a dangerous business. In October 1878 two men lost an arm when a girder slipped, and two men were seriously injured at the Ryde Pier site. In May 1879 a man was killed in the works when a bar of iron fell from a wagon, a man was also killed on the Manchester Gas Works site, and another man was killed at the Commercial Gas Works site at Poplar, Tower Hamlets, London, followed by a second fatality in 1881. Between 1877 and 1881 there were 23 accidents at the factory. There were also fatal accidents at the Liverpool Alexandra Dock Warehouse and Dudley Gas Works."*

1880   **Spon Lane Foundry sold**

1885   **Peter Duckworth Bennett** was killed during an accident during a visit to Birmingham by the Prince of Wales (later King Edward VII). He fell through a glass roof while witnessing the departure of the Prince from the Birmingham Council House.

After his untimely death at 60 years, a letter to the Editor of the Daily Post read:

"1885 'THE LATE MR. P. D. BENNETT.
To the Editor of the DAILY POST.
Sir,-In your notice yesterday of the sad case of the late Mr. P. D. Bennett, there is a slight mistake with regard to his having been connected with the well-known firm of Fox, Henderson, and Co. It is well known to many persons living around Dudley and elsewhere that his introduction into and early training in the engineering world was due to an uncle of his, Mr. Glover, at that time head of the engineering department of an establishment known as the "Oak Farm Works," near Kingswinford, about 1848. Mr. Bennett then became connected with the eminent firm of Cochrane and Co., Woodside Works, near Dudley, who, as sub-contractors, had much to do with the Great Exhibition building in 1851, and possibly with New Street Station. He remained there until he commenced business on his own account-first at the Albion Foundry, near Oldbury, and afterwards at Spon Lane; so that, directly, his name was never identified with the firm of Fox, Henderson, and Co.
Birmingham, December 1. J. WOODWARD"

{Oh Dear! Who was correct? [REF: 94] }

Other eminent activities of Peter Duckworth Bennett.

- Chairman of the Sandwell Park Colliery [see p.91] and chief instigator of the 1869 trial-sinking when coal was reached at 366 m. (400 yds)
- Member of the Institution of Mechanical Engineers
- Director of the Birmingham Stock Bank
- A Justice of the Peace for Staffordshire
- Member of the Council of the Birmingham & Midland Institute
- Chairman of the West Bromwich Commissioners
- Supporter of the building of the new Birmingham Art Gallery and lent a collection of ivory carvings and damascene work

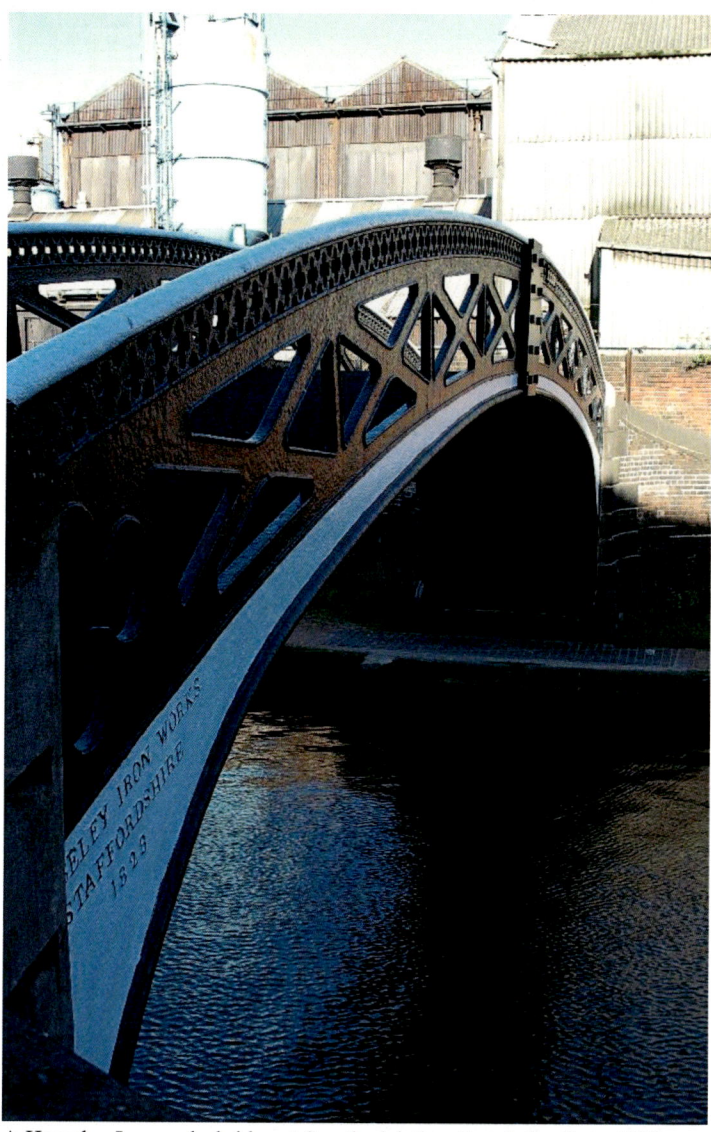

A Horseley Ironworks bridge at Smethwick Junction dating from 1828

--X—

Still in the same vicinity and keeping to matters above and below ground.
--X--

2.10 BLAKELEY HALL, BROMFORD & SPON LANE COLLIERIES, JENSEN MOTOR LTD

A. BLAKELEY HALL, BROMFORD & SPON LANE COLLIERIES

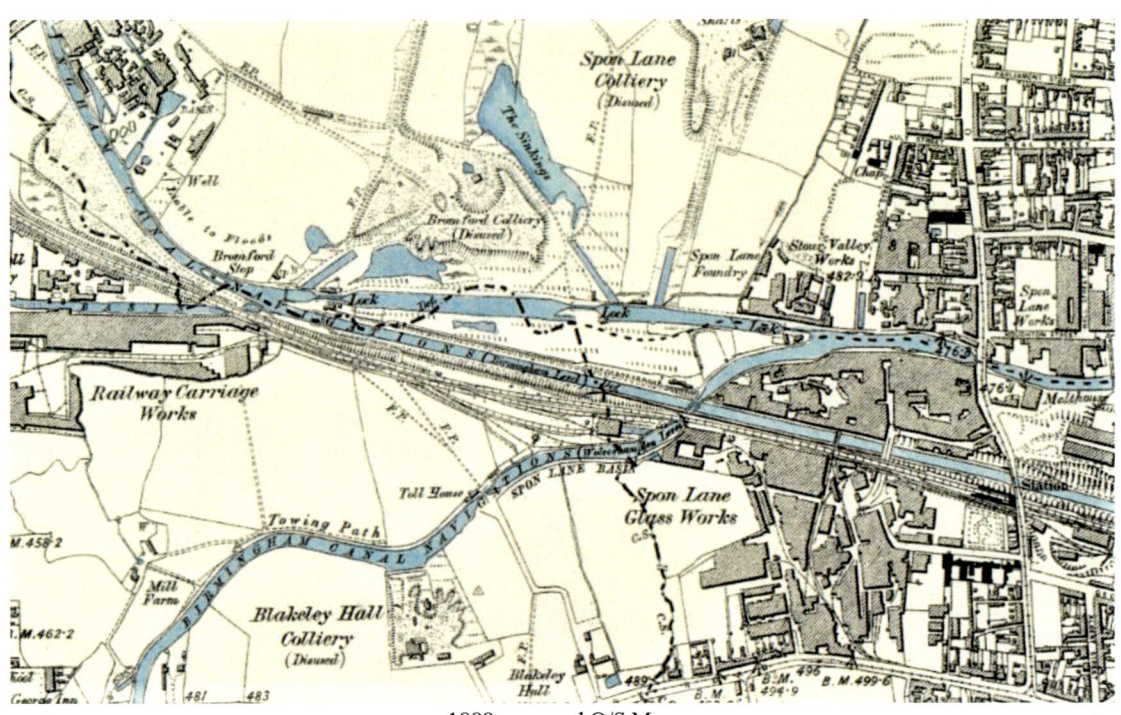

1888 surveyed O/S Map

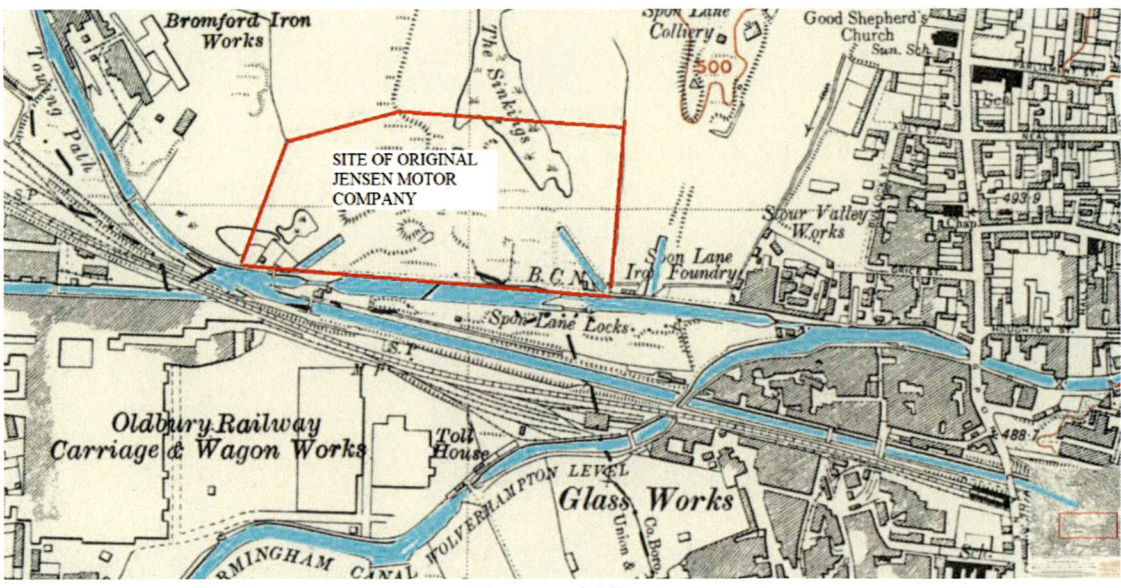

1938 surveyed O/S map

The 1888 map shows the disused sites of the **Bromford and Spon Lane collieries,** whilst the O/S survey of 1938, demonstrates how the land had fallen into disuse. It was this northern bank of

Brindley's Spon Lane Locks close to the Telford reunion of 1827 where the Jensen Brothers set their works for their short-lived life.

Extraordinarily little can be found about these two colliery sites adjacent to the **Spon Lane Locks**. As with virtually all the sixty collieries in the West Bromwich area that attempted start-up, they failed within a few years for a variety of reasons; insufficient financial investment, insufficient coal, poor knowledge of processing the coal, poor management.

1835   **William Henry Dawes** worked the two-shaft Bromford Colliery.

1855   A mining company started up under the directorship of a group named as **Davis & Sons, Samuel J. Dawes and Bullock Brothers.** Samuel James Dawes, iron master of adjacent Bromford Iron Works, lived at Woodvill, Handsworth, Birmingham

1873   **Bromford Colliery Company** floated. The British Mining No 57 Memoirs records about the Bromford Colliery:

> Bromford Colliery would, according to a report, be capable of producing 4000 tons per week with double deck cages. This would give a profit of eight shillings per ton or, over twelve months, a profit after expenses of £42,000. The prospectus also mentioned that the estate was estimated to contain over five million tons of coal, so a rosy picture was painted of a company which could not fail to produce profits for the shareholders.

1875   The company ran into difficulties with directors resigning and considerable intrigue occurring as investors lost money and major promises of investment failed to materialise. **Bromford and Blakeley Hall collieries** were put up for sale when a wholesale draper from Birmingham bought both for £17,200 *[in 2020 = £1,140,000]* at auction. [REF: 101]

1875   **Spon Lane Colliery Co** was started. The Spon Lane Colliery Company Ltd sold start up shares of £10 in 1875 [REF 99]

1876   The failing success of the company cannot have been helped by a recorded pit accident when a flywheel broke [REF: 100]

1880   Spon Lane Colliery Co closed

1912   Blakeley Hall & Bromford Collieries closed

B. JENSEN BROTHERS & JENSEN MOTORS LTD [REF: 102]

1926 **Alan** (1906-1994) and his younger brother **Richard** (1909-1977) **Jensen** started to design cars and came to the notice of Alfred Wilde of the Standard Motor Company, who persuaded Alan to join an associated company of Standard, the **New Avon Body Co**. For a few years they linked up with **Joe Patrick**, later to be the head of **Patrick Motors** of Bournbrook, Birmingham. They diversified into lorry body-making back in Carters Green, West Bromwich for a few years with a company called W. J. Smith but when the latter died in 1934, the Jensen Brothers changed the company name to **Jensen Motors Ltd.**

The most famous range of vehicles produced by the brothers was in the sports car market with the **Jensen 541R, C-V8** and finally the **Interceptor**. These cars were seen by many rich and street wise as being the ultimate sex symbol during the roaring sixties.

1959　Jensen Motors Ltd was sold to **Norcross Ltd**, an industrial holding company.
1966　 Both Jensen brothers resigned from the company
1967　The company fell short of the American safety regulations
1968　Norcross sold its interest in Jensen and the company was bought by a merchant bank
1970　A Norwegian-American West Coast car distributor **Kjell Qvale** bought majority shares
1973　Sales were disappointing
1976　The company premises were sold

Promotional photo of Jensen Works (date unknown) viewed from the North. The proximity to Spon Lane most northerly lock can be seen. In the foreground is Kelvin Way. In 2020, this site had been cleared again and an industrial site rebuilt.

2.11 OLDBURY RAILWAY CARRIAGE & WAGON WORKS

METROPOLITAN AMALGAMATED RAILWAY CARRIAGE & WAGON CO, METROPOLITAN CARRIAGE, WAGON & FINANCE CO LTD, SIR DUDLEY DOCKER

1873 The **Oldbury Railway Carriage & Wagon Company**, with help of **Merryweather & Sons**, (of Tram Locomotive Works, Greenwich, renowned for its fire-fighting equipment since the Great Fire of London of 1666) [REF: 103] built a tramcar designed by **John Grantham** that ran along an experimental length of track in West Bolton. Grantham was a pioneering engineer fascinated by marine, locomotive and tramway engineering, who after leaving school helped his father survey rail routes before exploring the vehicles that travel along them that he helped design. [REF: 104].

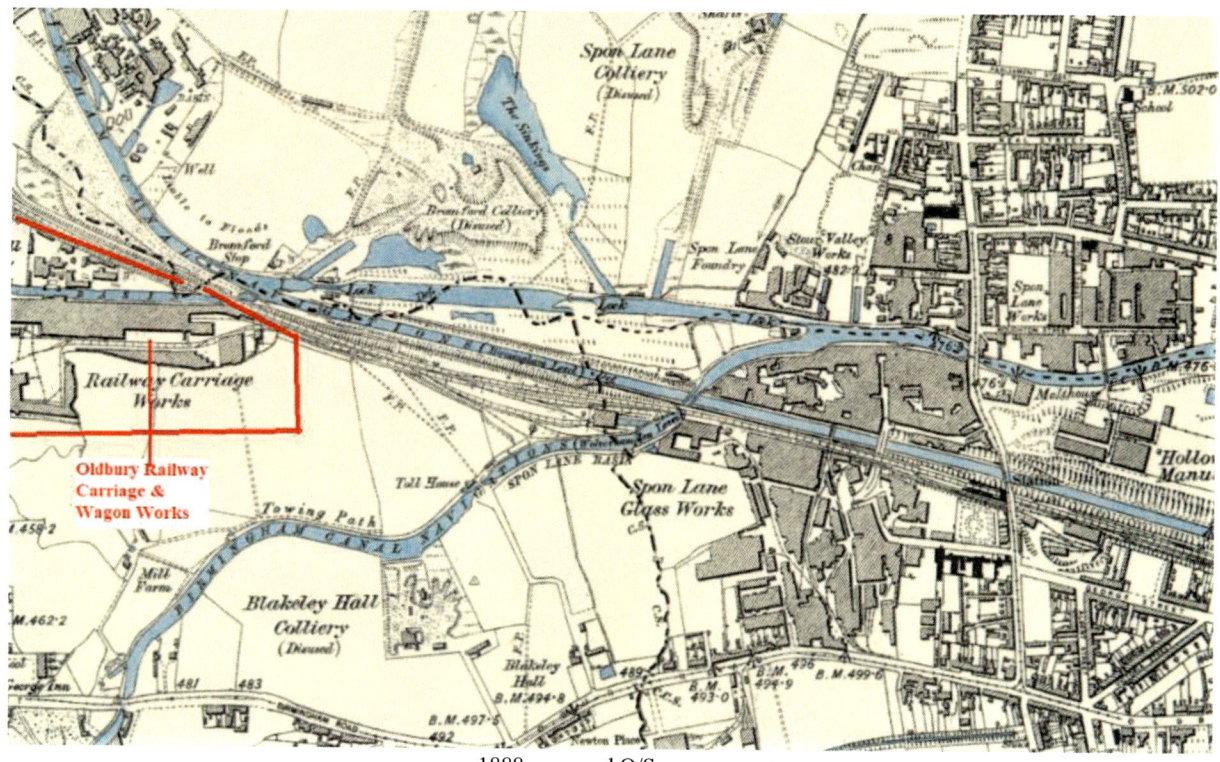

1888 surveyed O/S map

1881 **Percy Wheeler**, (1859-1937) an ex-King Edward VI, Birmingham schoolboy joined the company as works manager [REF: 105]

1886 **Wheeler** became general manager

1897 **Percy Wheeler with his father, Herbert** were elected joint managing director

1902 **Metropolitan Amalgamated Railway Carriage & Wagon Co**, had amalgamated 6 companies including Oldbury Railway Carriage & Wagon Co. Percy Wheeler was appointed director of the Saltley and Oldbury works [REF: 106]. The same year they acquired the Patent Shaft & Axletree Co of Wednesbury, who had built Blackfriars Bridge, London. [REF: 106]

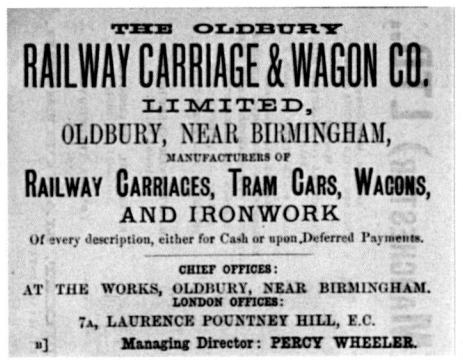

THE OLDBURY **RAILWAY CARRIAGE & WAGON CO. LIMITED,** OLDBURY, NEAR BIRMINGHAM, MANUFACTURERS OF RAILWAY CARRIAGES, TRAM CARS, WAGONS, AND IRONWORK — 1900

1907 **Docker Brothers was acquired**. [*see "Brindley Out Telford Home – A Journey along the Birmingham Canal" Volume 1, p. 41-44*]

1909 Metropolitan manufactured an electrically-powered train for London, Brighton & South Coast Railway.

1912 **Sir Dudley Docker (DD), of Dockers Paint Works, Ladywood** fame, who had acquired a vast number of Directorships and Chairmanships with this being one of them, proposed and carried through a name change to **Metropolitan Carriage, Wagon & Finance Co Ltd**. [*see Brindley Out Telford Home – A Journey along the Birmingham Canal" Volume 1, p. 42*]
[REF: 107]

1921 **Wheeler** age of 62, retired from the Metropolitan Carriage, Wagon & Finance Co Ltd Co.

1928 Wheeler later returned to the board of the company

1934 **Again, Percy Wheeler** retired but died three years later at the age of 78.

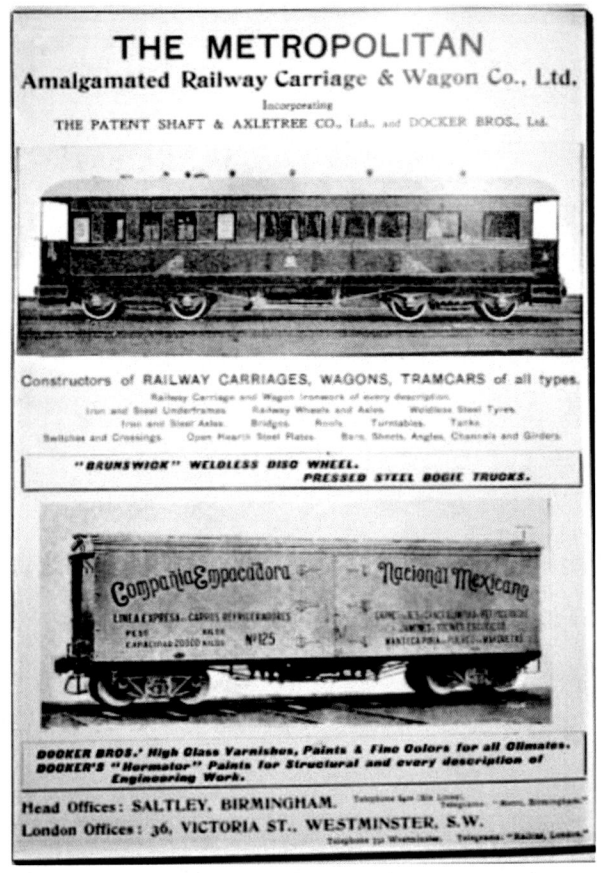

THE METROPOLITAN Amalgamated Railway Carriage & Wagon Co., Ltd., Incorporating THE PATENT SHAFT & AXLETREE CO., Ltd. and DOCKER BROS., Ltd. — 1910

2.12

STEWART AQUEDUCT – GRADE 2 LISTED HISTORIC AQUEDUCT

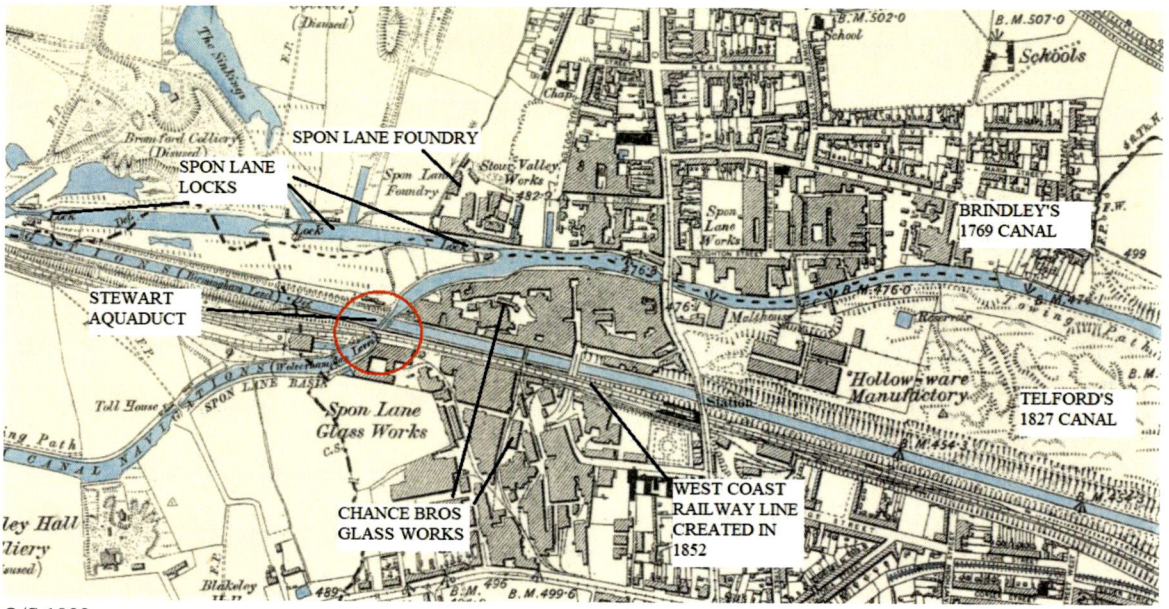

O/S 1888

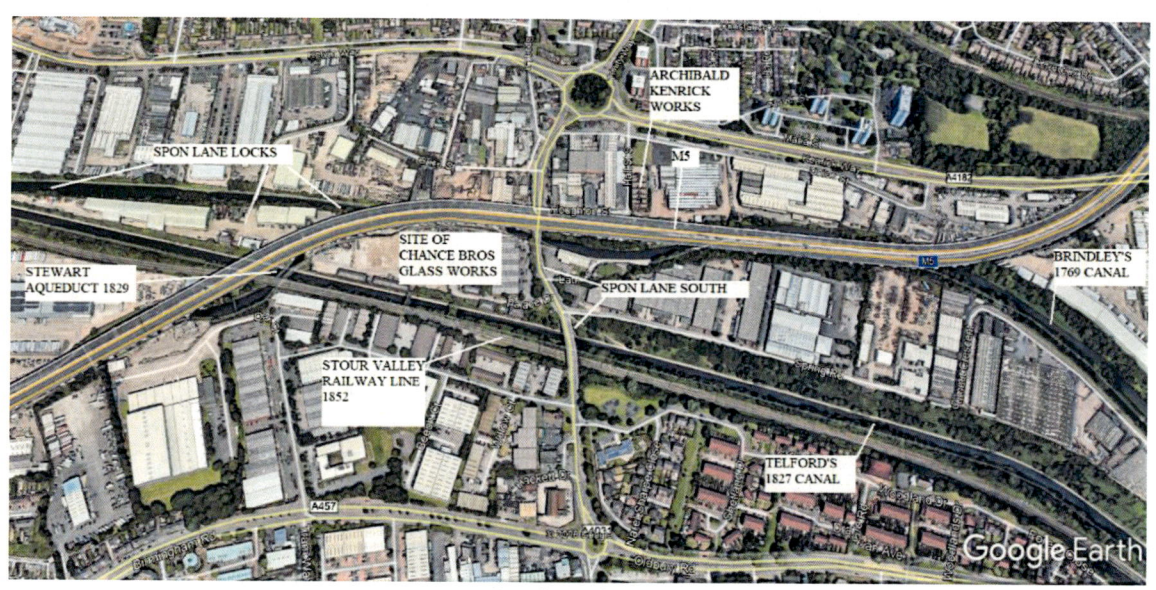

Google Earth 2020.

The **Stewart Aqueduct** in Smethwick dates from 1829 and was constructed under **Telford**'s instruction to take Brindley's earlier canal over his new very straight deep cutting. *[Why was it called Stewart? I have not been able to elicit]* Furthermore, in 1852, like a death knoll to the engineering genius of these two men, the Stour Valley section of the West Coast Main railway line also converged on this juncture, running parallel to Telford's newly constructed canal. Then between 1967 and 1970, the raised section of the M5 ran between junction 4 to the junction with the M6, which capped the lot with its engineering prowess of a motorway on stilts. [REF: 98].

HISTORIC ENGLAND LISTED BUILDING
List Entry No. 1977161 [1987]
STEWARD {STEWART} AQUEDUCT (APPROXIMATELY 400 METRES WEST OF SPON LANE SOUTH) BIRMINGHAM CANAL WOLVERHAMPTON LEVEL
Aqueduct. Built in 1828 by Thomas Telford to carry the Old Main Line (Wolverhampton Level), opened in 1769 and re-aligned in 1790, over his New Main Line, on the Birmingham Level. Brick in English bond with sand- stone dressings. Two elliptical skew arches with chamfered voussoirs. Moulded string course dies into rusticated quoins of abutments. Ashlar capping course carries cast-iron railings with intersecting arched heads. Buttresses added to central cutwaters at uncertain date.

The solid brick Grade 2 Listed Stewart Aqueduct with its elegant cast iron railings taking a limb of Brindley's 1769 canal over Telford's route of 1827. It then passes beneath the Stour Valley railway line of 1852 to the left and the whole scene is then dominated by the raised concrete limbs of the M5. Each generation has attempted to produce an engineering marvel, better than the last. This photo dates from 2010. Behind the camera is the derelict giant site of chance Brothers Glass Works.

--X--

PART 3
STEWART AQUEDUCT BACK TO THE GREEN

Telford's 1825 Engine Arm Bridge carrying the Engine Arm branch over his new Main Line

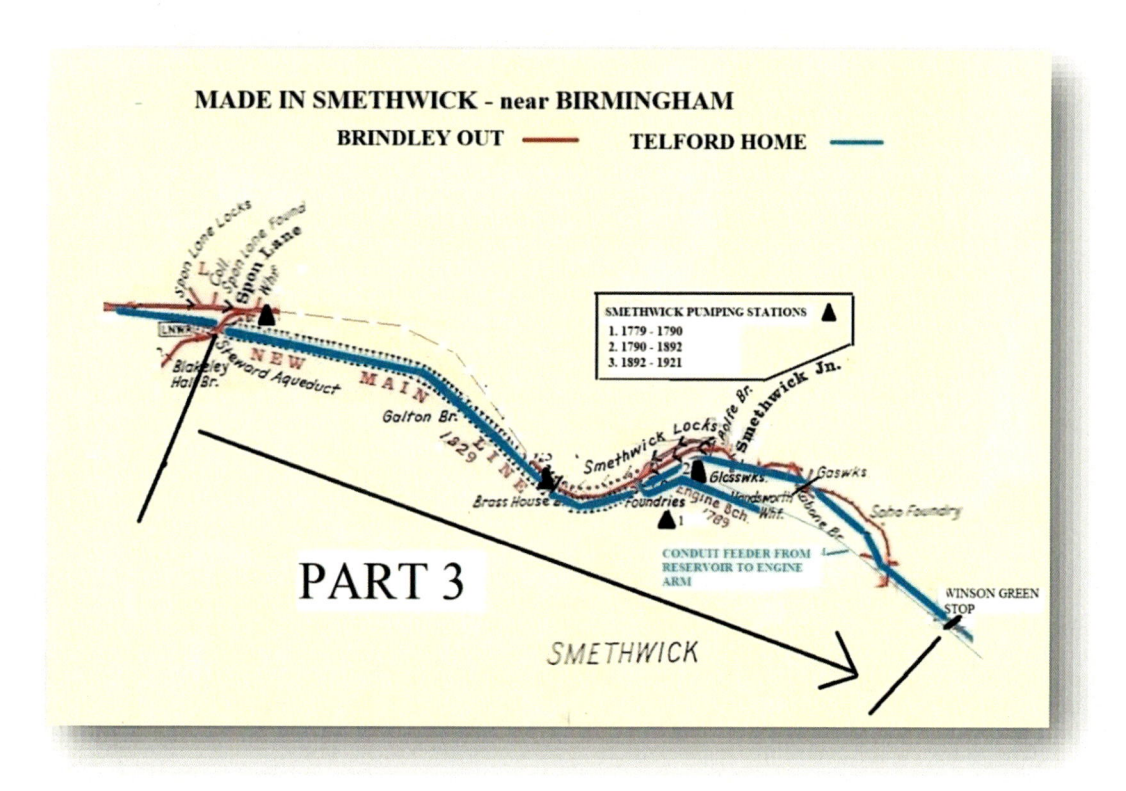

--x—

It is very apparent as one descends from the Brindley Canal heights and turns left to the sharp and straight line of Telford's 1827 canal, that even in 2020, there are high walls of 19th century industrial works all around. Bridges pass across this Smethwick Cutting, ignoring the world below as if another planet. This was the gigantic site of the now defunct Chance Brothers. Part 3 is the return journey to the outskirts of Smethwick's larger neighbour, Birmingham.

--X--

3.1 CHANCE BROTHERS

Much has been recorded in Volume 1 "Brindley Out Telford Home – A Journey along the Birmingham Canal" *[p. 89-93]* about the remarkable Chance Brothers but their national and international importance cannot be stressed enough. Their home was Summerfield Park, just off Dudley Road, Birmingham, now with the house gone, it is a public park by the same name.

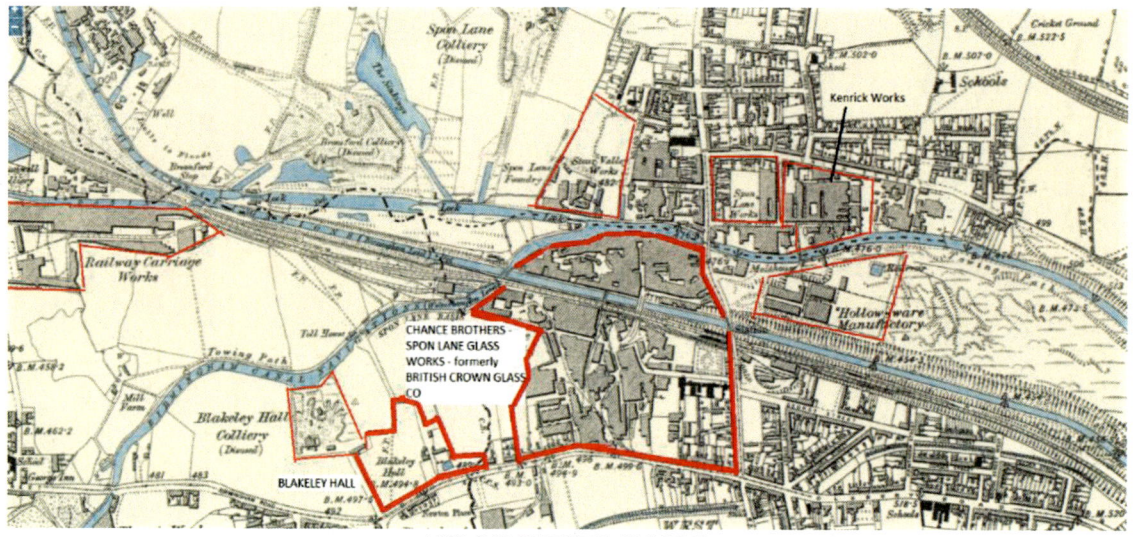

1888 O/S SURVEY 6": MILE

A. BLAKELEY HALL
Blakeley Hall, along with the manors of Smethwick and Harborne had been the family seat of a family called **Cornwallis**, that when it ran out of male heirs, possession passed to families **Grimshaw and Wright**. In 1769, the Birmingham Canal passed through its grounds, when all water in its moat was lost.

B. BRITISH CROWN GLASS CO
1814   Crown window-glass was started in Smethwick by **Thomas Strutt**. He operated from a building on part of the farmland belonging to Blakeley Hall, alongside the Birmingham Canal, north-west of Smethwick.

1816   **British Crown Glass Co. registered**

1822   Thomas Strutt died and the works sold to **Joseph STOCK and Philip PALMER**, partners of **Robert Lucas CHANCE**.

C. CHANCE BROTHERS

1936 Britain from Above. [Historic England]. Chance Brothers site at Spon Lane viewed from the south. Blakeley Hall is just going out of the picture in the bottom left [REF: 1]

After much application, HISTORIC ENGLAND LISTED THIS SITE AS A SCHEDULED MONUMENT IN 2005. LIST NO. 1021387

1824   Chance Brothers was founded in **Spon Lane**, Smethwick by **Robert Lucas CHA**NCE when he bought the **British Crown Glass Company of Spon Lane**.

1832   Company was experiencing financial difficulties and was bailed out by the two brothers, **William CHANCE and George CHANCE**, owners of a thriving iron merchants in Great Charles Street, Birmingham. The company was now changed to **CHANCE BROTHERS & CO.** The same year they achieved success in partnership with a Frenchman, Georges Bontemps from Choisy-Le-Roi, by making the first British cylinder blown sheet glass.

1834   A German process was introduced by Robert Lucas Chance called **cylinder glass sheet**, enabling larger panes and better-quality glass.

1834   The **brothers James & John HARTLEY** became partners in the business forming **CHANCE & HARTLEY.** (One of the numerous bridges that crossed the canal between the different parts of Chance Brothers factory, was named after Hartley).

1835   Chemical manufacture with a method based on the invention of Salt cake by a local man, **Richard PHILLIPS**. This chemical plant was moved to Oldbury, to permit expansion of both sides of the industry.

1836   The partnership with Hartley brothers was short lived as they set up a company in Sunderland. The same year, a nephew of **Robert Lucas Chance, James Timmins**

CHANCE, completed a degree at Cambridge and joined the company. His future with the company was anticipated for whilst a student, he had invented a process for polishing sheet glass to produce a **'patent plate'**

It has been said of J.T. Chance:

*'He is an interesting early example of the graduate entering British industry. Without any previous technical training, he proceeded to add a refinement to the sheet glass process which improved the finished product considerably and made it a much more attractive selling line.' In 1838 he took out an important patent (no. 7618) relating to the polishing of sheet glass. It took some time to develop the idea to practical application. In 1839 one of his earliest customers was **Joseph Paxton**, who used the glass to glaze the conservatory at Chatsworth House. Chance bought the required machinery from Wren and Bennett of Manchester."* [REF: 2]

1837   Chance Brothers provided **Chatsworth House** with 1.2 metre lengths of glass for the Great Conservatory. Until this pioneering event, only 0.9m had been possible.

1838   **Optical Glass** became a product for Chance Bros.

1845   Excise duty on glass was abolished

1850   Dioptric Lenses for light houses started in production.

1889 dioptric lens, Inchkeith Lighthouse. [REF: 71; Grace's Guide]

1851   Grace's Guide states:

"Chance Brothers and Co made the glass for the 1851 Great Exhibition. Other projects included the glazing of the Houses of Parliament, and the white glass for the four faces of the Westminster Clock Tower (being the only firm at the time able to make such glass). The

ornamental windows for the White House in America were also made by Chance Brothers and Co. Other products included stained glass windows, ornamental lamp shades, microscope glass slides, painted glassware, glass tubing and specialist types of glass."

Crystal Palace in its site at Penge Common [REF: 72]

1851   Great Exhibition. The Crystal Palace was designed by Joseph **Paxton** using Chance Brothers glass and originally it was placed in Hyde Park but was subsequently moved to **Penge Common** where it was destroyed by fire in 1936

1851   Abolition of the Window Tax

1852   Dioptric Revolving Lighthouse was first created

1856   The partnership was dissolved after the death of **William Chance** with his son, (also William) starting his own business **William Chance & Co**

1860   **James Timmins Chance** joined **Michael Faraday** in an experiment for Trinity House, improving the process for setting up lighthouses at Whitby Southern Lighthouse, which resulted in great improvements in that industry.

1862   **Chance Brothers & Co** ordered and put into use, 13 of a newly designed **'regenerative furnace,** that **William Siemens** had developed as well as a special one for optical lighthouse lenses. With such equipment, furnaces of this variety became an enormous fuel saver and financial boom. The design won Grand Prix at L'Exposition de Paris 1867.

1873   **John Hopkinson**, a renowned physicist and engineer took over the running of the business from James Timmins Chance and invented **the rotating optics for lighthouses**. The company became a major producer of lighthouse engineering with a vast range of allied materials. **James Timmins Chance placed lamps inside Fresnel lenses** to increase light output. They introduced rotating optics, which enabled identification depending on how many revolutions the light would flash.

1888   Chance Bros introduced **machine rolled patterned glass**. The same year, the **Aluminium Company** constructed a plant next to the Oldbury chemical plant run by Chance Brothers since 1835 and developed a symbiotic exchange of residual sodium carbonate from muriatic acid supplied by Chance Bros.

1890   The Oldbury plant was converted into a private limited company called **Oldbury Alkali Company Ltd.**

1894   The **Oldbury Alkali Co Ltd**, joined ranks with a neighbouring chemical works, **Albright & Wilson** to create **British Cyanide Co. Ltd** under the direction of another member of the family, **Alexander M. Chance**. But with war in South Africa the market collapsed with many companies folding leaving British Cyanide Co as one of the survivors.

1894   Third class award at the Antwerp Exhibition for lighthouse and dioptric lens.

1898   The Oldbury Alkali Co linked up with another established chemical works, **W. Hunt & Sons** of Wednesbury, of which **Alexander M. Chance** was chairman.

1914   Chance Brothers in Spon Lane was the only company making optical glass in the UK and during WW1 and production increased 20-fold. They now had a vast list of products: window glass, optical glass, rolled glass, vitreous tiles, mosaics, lighthouses, searchlights.

1920   Aerial Lighthouses were in production

1937   Lighting equipment for aerodromes and airways was in production.

1945   **Pilkington** acquired a 50% share in Chance Brothers

1913

1946 saw a change in advertising

1946 also saw the advent of the breakup of the Smethwick site. [REF: 74 revolutionaryplayers.org.uk/various-buildings-at-chances- glassworks/]

1952   Pilkington assumed full control of Chance Brothers

1956   Chance Brothers' engineering division was sold to **J. Stone & Co (Holdings) Ltd,** an engineering and marine and railway manufacturer making pumps in Deptford, dating from 1831.

1946 Demolition of House Cone No 10. Originally built in1852/4 for making window glass which was later for rolled Plate [REF: 74 revolutionaryplayers.org.uk/various-buildings-at-chances- glassworks/]

1976   Flat-glass production in Smethwick ceased

1981   Total closure of all Chance works in Smethwick with all operations moving to Malvern as a subsidiary of Pilkington but using the name of **Chance Brothers Ltd.**

1992   The company name changed to **Chance Glass Ltd**

In recent years a Restoration Trust called "CHANCE GLASS WORKS HERITAGE TRUST" has been set up to preserve the country's most important glass producing name. [REF: 73]
https://www.chanceht.org/

Robert Lucas CHANCE (1782-1865)    James Timmins CHANCE (1814-1902) by Joseph Gibbs, 1902
[Wikipedia]

116

--X--

A small virtual detour to the south along Spon Lane South brings the traveller to a road junction with Oldbury Road, a nondescript area. Turn right here and cross to the other side, (south) is a cul de sac of suburban light industrial units called Ruskin Place. A strange name for such a location, on first sight.

--X--

3.2 RUSKIN POTTERY

RUSKIN POTTERY [REF: 92, 93]

Although not immediately on the banks of either canal, it would be inappropriate not to mention this remarkable little gem **Ruskin Pottery** and its creators, **Edward Richard Taylor** (1838-1912) and his son, **William Howson Taylor**, (1876-1935). The partnership called their art ware **Ruskin Pottery** in respect to **John Ruskin**, with whom they had great empathy for his writings and philosophy. The Wikipedia entry for Ruskin Pottery states:

> *"The pottery produced was notable for the innovative glazes used on a range of brightly coloured pots, vases, buttons, bowls, tea services and jewellery. The ceramic glazes devised by William Howson Taylor included misty soufflé glazes, ice crystal effect glazes - 'crystalline', lustre glazes resembling metallic finishes, and the most highly regarded of all, sang-de-boeuf and flambé glazes which produced a blood red effect. The sang-de-boeuf glazes were created using reduction of copper and iron oxides at high temperature. This was a difficult technique, first developed in China in the 13th century and reinvented by several art potters in Europe in the late 19th century. William Howson Taylor was one of the principal exponents of 'high fired' techniques, producing a range of colours and unique 'fissured' glaze effects. "*

1877   Birmingham Council persuaded Edward Richard Taylor, artist and energetic teacher to take over the **Birmingham School of Art** and expand it. The foundation stone of the current Birmingham School of Art building was opened in 1885 and designed by J.H. Chamberlain using sponsored donations from the Tangye Brothers *[see p. 61-3]* and Louisa Ryland, each donating about £10,000 (equivalent to £900,000 in 2020).

1885   The Birmingham School of Art became the first **Municipal School of Art** in the United Kingdom, which went on to be a leading centre of the **Arts & Crafts Movement**.

1898   Edward Richard Taylor with his son, William Howson Taylor started a small pot works, the **Birmingham Tile & Pottery Works** at 173-4 Oldbury Road, Smethwick. Between them the Taylors produced some original and beautiful pottery, which at first was called 'Taylor ware'.

1904   Name of their creations changed to Ruskin Pottery, when Edward retired from teaching. They won the Grand Prize award at the International Exhibition at St. Louis

1906   Further prizes at Milano
1907   Christchurch, New Zealand prize
1908   Exhibited at the London Exhibition
1910   Exposition de Bruxelles Awards

1904 – 2020 [O/S Maps]

- 1911 Turin award
- 1912 Edward Taylor died
- 1913 Ghent prize
- 1914 Became renowned for the manufacture of "Ruskin" artistic pottery, enamels, buttons and hatpins
- 1935 The works closed and in 2020 is the site of an industrial estate, Ruskin Place. William Howson Taylor died after retiring to Devon. Wikipedia entry further states:

  "When the studio closed in 1935 the formulae for the glazes and all the pottery documentation were deliberately destroyed, so that the unique Ruskin products could never be replicated."

Smethwick Public Library carries a small collection, presented by William himself.
The **Wednesbury Museum & Art Gallery** has a display

William Howson Taylor (1876-1935)

Ruskin Pottery

--X--

Return to the canal towpath on the north side, dropping down the slope (National Cycle Route 81), turn around and admire the façade of the Spon Lane Bridge, which has history.

SPON LANE BRIDGE

The original 21ft (6.4m)wide bridge dated from Telford's mammoth cutting of about 1827 but became too narrow for modern day traffic a century later. In 1926, Smethwick Corporation placed an advertisement in the Smethwick Telephone newspaper for tenders to widen it to 46 ft (14m). [REF: 120]. It was to be constructed in the Hennebique system, - using Ferro-Concrete, an invention by a Belgian engineer, Francois Hennebique which was the fore-runner of re-enforced concrete. [REF: 121]. Messr. Mouchell & Partners Ltd, were the appointed engineers to a design by the Borough Engineer & Surveyor, A E Douglas, MICE. It is interesting to not that

Spon Lane bridge looking from the south (2010)

--X—

Continue southwards to a bend to the right which after the impeccably straight Telford route, seems perverse but as one turns this corner between the high banks, once a record depth for a waterway, some engineering features, high up on the banks come into view. The first is the remarkable railway bridge bearing Galton Road Station and then immediately after is the jewel in the crown of this canal; the Galton Bridge

--X—

3.3 GALTON BRIDGE & THE GALTON FAMILY

The **Grade 1, Listed Galton Bridge** [REF:78] is an example of a feat of early 19th century genius which is a combination of Telford engineering perception with exquisite construction by the **Horseley Works**. Like so many understated gems of engineering genius, it is tucked away and not really appreciated by bustling 21st century living. Unlike the iron bridge at Ironbridge, it is difficult to see it from many good angles and contemporary adjustments to accommodate the motor car and train services have seriously overshadowed the site.

HISTORIC ENGLAND LISTED BUILDING
GRADE 1
List entry No. 1214833
GALTON BRIDGE INCLUDING ATTACHED RAILWAY BRIDGE SPAN, ROEBUCK LANE BIRMINGHAM CANAL BIRMINGHAM LEVEL
Road bridge, now footbridge, over New Main Line of Birmingham Canal. 1829 by Telford. Cast iron. Brick abutments have some sandstone dressings. Single segmental arch of 150 foot span carries road across Smethwick cutting. Arch formed by girders pierced in lattice pattern, with lattice bracing in spandrels. "Horsley Iron Works 1829" is said to be cast in four pieces. "Galton Bridge" is cast above the centre on each side. Cast iron railings terminate at stone piers with Gothic blind tracery. Named after Samuel Tertius Galton, one of the BCN committee.

Galton Bridge, early 19th century print by Louis Haghe.

Nigel Crowe of CRT says of Galton Bridge:
"Built with iron cast by Horseley Ironworks in 1829 with diagonal lattice ribs and spandrels, Galton Bridge pre-figures later railway architecture and in some respects makes Telford's Pontcysyllte Aqueduct of 1815 look old-fashioned. Telford wrote that he had designed Galton for 'safety, combined with economy' " [REF: 77]

When first constructed it was the highest and longest single span bridge in the world being 46 metres and was named after **Samuel Tertius Galton** (1783-1844), who was a businessman and scientist from a formidably famous local family. His father was **Samuel John Galton, FRS** (1753-1832) an eminent scientist and member of the **Lunar Society**, a Birmingham Quaker and paradoxically, an arms merchant who lived at **Great Barr Hall**. Apart from the links with Great Barr Hall, the family had a residence called **Galton House** close to the Galton Bridge site between the two canals and another family home was **Warley Woods,** designed and built for another son, **Hubert Galton**. In 1809, Samuel Tertius married **Violetta**, a daughter of **Erasmus Darwin**, a founding member of the Lunar Society and eminent physician, philosopher, inventor and poet. They produced three sons and four daughters. One of the sons, **Francis Galton** (1822-1911) became an eminent scientist.

Thomas Telford's Galton Bridge of 1829 over this deep cutting was constructed by Horseley Works. The bridge in the foreground carries the Galton Bridge railway station and the modern tunnel in the distance, carries Telford Way.

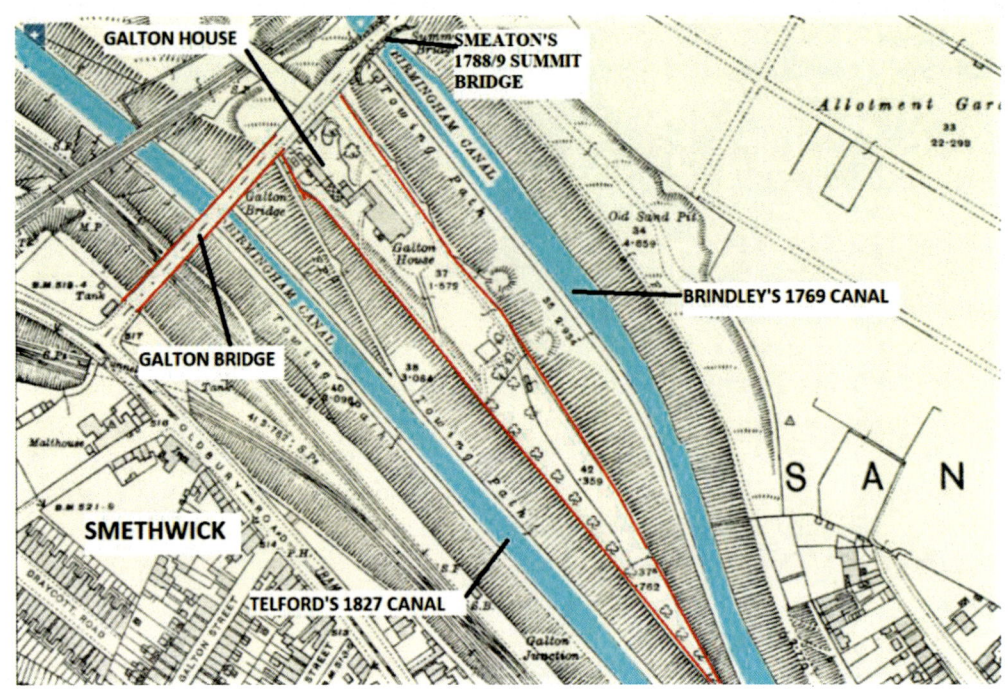

SMETHWICK showing the proximity of Galton House and Galton Bridge [O/S MAPS 1913/14 25"/mile]. Smeaton's later Summit Bridge is shown at the top of the map

—X—

As the journey passes beneath this magnificent hidden homage to early 19th century engineering genius, the canal passes immediately into a tunnel of 20th century construction bearing the Telford Way dual carriageway from urban Smethwick to the M5 at the roundabout engulfing the archway relic of Sandwell Park *[p. 91]*. Emerging from this protracted concrete tube, the Telford straightness continues to Brasshouse Lane, passing the New Pumping Station at the lower level and the gentle bend to the left brings the next amazing early 19th century monument into view; the **Engine Arm Aqueduct.** However, before this is reached, there is another less distinguished Historic England Grade 2 Listed building that requires comment.

--X--

HISTORIC ENGLAND LISTED BUILDING
List Entry No. 1391126 (2004)
RETAINING WALL TO FORMER CORPORATION YARD
GV II Retaining wall. c.1910 for Smethwick Corporation Depot by C. J. Fox Allin, Borough Engineer. Reinforced concrete. Linear stretch of wall approx. 50m long running parallel to the south side of the Birmingham Canal. To the south face, only the parapet is visible. To the north face, there is a band below the parapet then the rest of the approx. 10m high wall. In profile, the wall is canted towards the Canal side, with triangular buttresses positioned along the south land side, both parts supported by concrete footings.

Listed for its technological interest as an early reinforced concrete wall, as well as for its strong group value with the Grade I Engine Arm Aqueduct; there is an interesting juxtaposition between these two works of engineering that each took full advantage of the innovative structural and design of their respective periods.

--X--

3.4 ENGINE ARM & AQUEDUCT

HISTORIC ENGLAND LISTED BUILDING
GRADE 2*
List Entry No. 1391874
ENGINE ARM AQUEDUCT, BIRMINGHAM CANAL WOLVERHAMPTON LEVEL
An iron trough aqueduct with tow path roving bridge. Built circa 1828 by Thomas Telford to carry the Engine Arm of the Wolverhampton level canal over the deep cutting of Telford's new Birmingham mainline navigation and thus ensure the continued supply of water from the Rotton Park Reservoir.
PLAN: The aqueduct is orientated north west to south east and has a tow path on both east and west side. The towpath roving bridge lies on the north west end of the aqueduct, is orientated north east to south west, and has blue engineering brick with stone copings and rusticated stone arch details. It was conceived as an integral part of the aqueduct scheme to allow the towpath to cross the entrance to the aqueduct.
MATERIALS: The aqueduct is an iron trough supported on a single span, cross braced to counter the outward thrust of the weight of water carried, springing from stone and brick abutments. ELEVATION: Both the east and west face of the aqueduct are of the same design with decorative ironwork tracery of three orders; the grid-work of the cross bracing rises from a single span arch with fluted gothic columns supporting pointed arches and pierced quartrefoil spandrels above; plain square section railings, rising to trefoil arches

immediately below the simple rolled hand rail. The handrail terminates in short octagonal stone end piers, seven faces of which have recessed oblong panels with decorative blind tracery, echoing the trefoil arches of the railings. Sloping octagonal stone copings, cap the piers. The abutments are constructed in engineering brick in English bond with deep rusticated stone coins and copings. The towpath has a brick surface with raised footholds [hoofholds]. The humpbacked towpath roving bridge is constructed of blue engineering brick, in English bond with a flattened elliptical arch, and vermiculated rustication to the stone quoins. Sloping abutments set at 90° to bridge, or its south side, carry the tow path from the level of the aqueduct over the bridge, and have plain curved stone copings.

The Engine Arm Aqueduct from the Engine Arm canal towpath looking north across the 1825 iron construction that passes over Telford's route (finished in 1827) to join the Brindley 1769 original route firstly passing beneath a towpath bridge. A modern housing estate on the north side of Brindley's Smethwick locks now occupies the site of the Sandwell Iron & Axle Works.

The **Engine Arm** was opened in 1825 as Telford's answer to bringing water to the highest point of his new main line. Brindley's winding route of 1769 always had problems of inadequate water supply and despite **John Smeaton's** attempt in 1780 to rectify this difficulty by removing three of the six locks and drilling through the hillside at the **Summit Tunnel**, it only partially solved the problem and other remedies were essential to permit the passage of working boats through this part of the BCN. Grace's Guide states about the Smethwick Engine [REF: 83]

"The Smethwick Engine is a steam engine made by Boulton and Watt and brought into service in May 1779. [PUMPING STATION 1.] Originally, it was one of two engines used to pump water back up to the 491 ft summit level of the BCN Old Main Line (Birmingham Canal) canal at Smethwick, not far from the Soho Foundry where it was made. The other engine, also built by Boulton and Watt, was at the other end of the summit level at Spon Lane. In 1804 a second Boulton and Watt engine was added alongside the 1779 engine." [PUMPING STATION 2]

In the 1820s, Telford designed a canal system at a much lower level than Brindley's and constructed a brick-lined miniature canal conduit from **Rotton Park Reservoir** (now Edgbaston Reservoir) - for the most part being parallel with his main one but high on the west bank to the **Engine Arm**, where water could then be pumped into the canals at the high point.

LEFT: Sadly, in 2019 the ravages of 21st century neglect and abuse has left the channel in an extremely poor state negating the recognition deserved to the genius who had it constructed
RIGHT: The Engine Arm (2010) looking east before it turns south under Bridge St and where Boulton & Watt's beam engine was housed and brought into service in 1790. It is now in the Think Tank Museum, Birmingham.

There had been three pumping stations in total to the south east of the summit tunnel which functioned during different eras. The first, built nearby at the **Soho Foundry** by **Boulton & Watt** opened in 1779 with another being on the north west side of the hill at Spon Lane, (also built by Boulton & Watt). This first Smethwick Pumping Station functioned until 1790 but was then replaced by a more powerful pump that carried in service until 1892, when it too wore out. These two early pumps were situated on Bridge Street. The third was constructed at Brasshouse Lane and has been totally rebuilt, listed as Grade 2 and sitting juxtaposed between Brindley's high route to the north and Telford's low one to the south.

For the Engine Arm Canal pumps to function properly, solid fuel was needed and therefore water had to be passed across Telford's new canal resulting in the construction of the Aqueduct in 1829/30, which is itself a work of art. It is constructed of an iron trough supported on a cast iron latticed arch with brick and stone abutments. Coal boats brought coal to the Smethwick Pumping Stations on this limb of water as an 1830 improvement. It was restored in 1985.

Very soon, the Engine Arm became another useful waterway for factories and industry to find a vector of their goods away from their site of construction and this canal limb was hemmed in on every side; e.g. Birmingham Plate Glass Works, Anchor Iron Works, Credenda Steel Tube Works, Patent Rivet Company, Smethwick Iron Foundry, Corporation Depot, Etna Iron Works, Eagle Iron Works, Soap works, to name but a few!

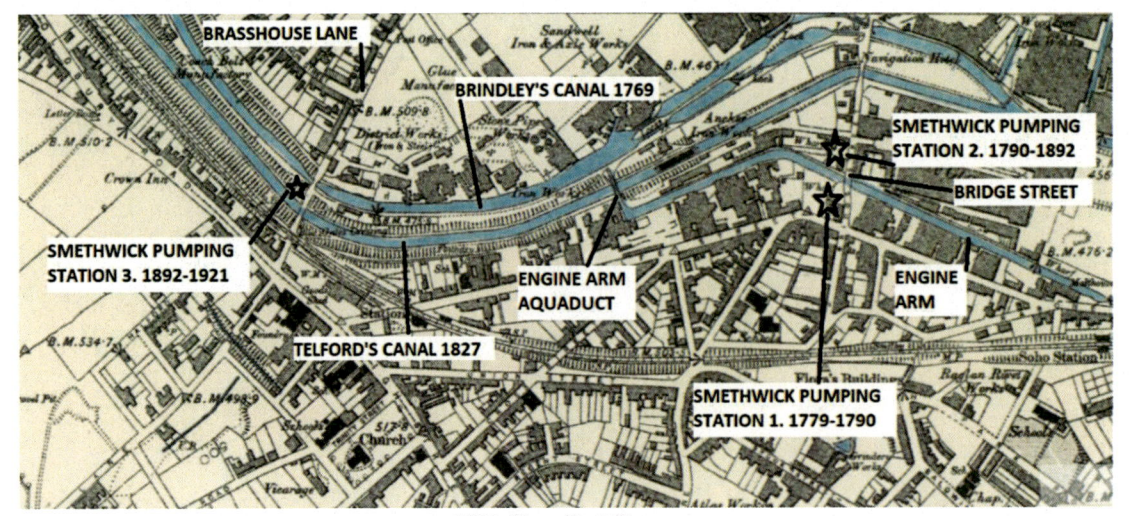

1888 6" : mile O/S map

An old sepia photograph of 1897 during the time of the demolition of the pumping station 1, clearly shows the hammer beam format of the engine, which is now housed in the Thinktank Museum in Birmingham and is the **'oldest working steam engine in the world'**. It must be added that the 32" bore cylinder was replaced in 1803 by one of 33" diameter with a new valve operating mechanism.

LEFT: The demolition of Pumping Station 1 [Courtesy of Ray Shill]
RIGHT: Smethwick Engine. Thinktank Museum, Birmingham [REF: 103]

The Engine Arm Aqueduct of 1829/30 – On the left is the leading edge of the Smethwick Stop

—X—

Throughout Smethwick, and, close to the canal banks there were many iron works that sprang up whose proximity to the water's edge enabled the raw materials, as well as the finished goods, to be distributed throughout the kingdom and further afield to the Empire. They came and went; often gobbled up by bigger and more successful competitors, or as market needs changed and their flexibility was not sufficient to maintain commercial viability. Some merely closed their doors when the proprietor died or retired with there being no one to continue with the production. A handful of these iron works lay alongside the Engine Arm. Not a great deal seems to have been written about them but a few of their advertisements remain.

--X--

3.5 IRON WORKS OF SMETHWICK
ANCHOR, EAGLE, ETNA & SANDWELL IRON & AXLE, SMETHWICK IRON FOUNDRY

Smethwick became a major centre for iron works. The term 'Iron Works' seemed ubiquitous for anything made from iron: the wide range of advertisements promoted virtually anything. E.g. The street call of "any old iron, any old iron, ..." supported the revolution that was occurring in the use of iron. There were a handful of these works along both sides of the Birmingham Canal in Smethwick. At Smethwick Locks stood **Smethwick Iron & Axle Works** and on the edge of the Feeder Arm was the **Anchor and Smethwick Iron Foundry** close to the locks and then further to the east, three further iron works, including **Eagle** and **Etna** (sometimes spelt Aetna Works).

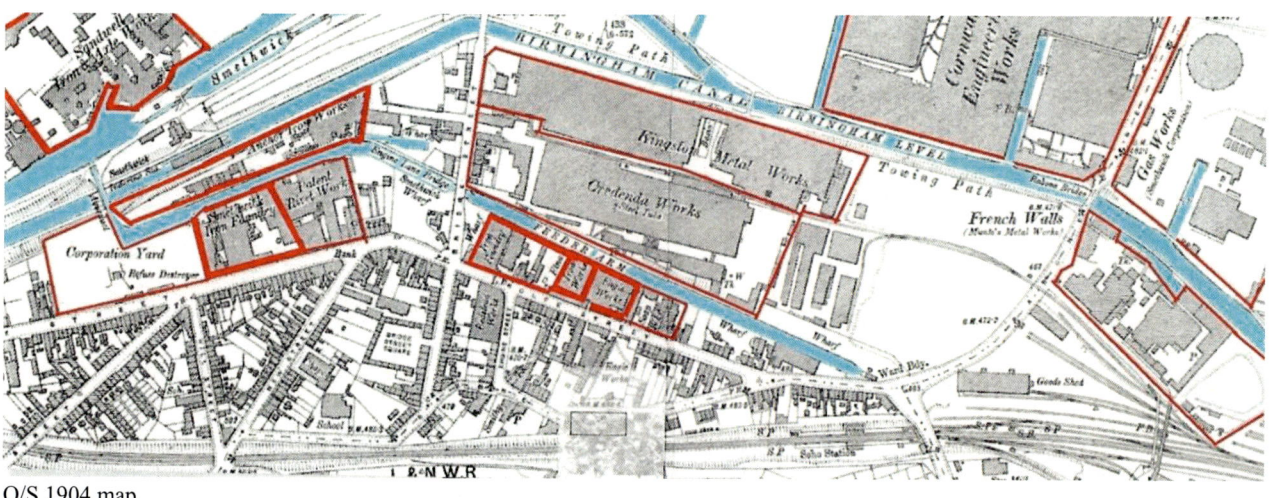

O/S 1904 map

127

PARKES' CUT NAILS
[ONLY AWARDS MELBOURNE, 1880; PARIS, 1867. HIGHEST AWARD SYDNEY, 1879.]
SHOE TIPS.
HIGHEST AWARD SYDNEY, 1879.
Eagle Works, Smethwick.

JOHN I. PARKES LTD.
EAGLE WORKS
SMETHWICK

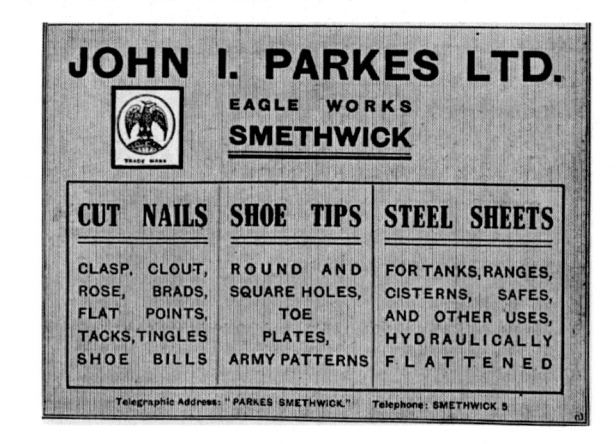

CUT NAILS	SHOE TIPS	STEEL SHEETS
CLASP, CLOUT, ROSE, BRADS, FLAT POINTS, TACKS, TINGLES SHOE BILLS	ROUND AND SQUARE HOLES, TOE PLATES, ARMY PATTERNS	FOR TANKS, RANGES, CISTERNS, SAFES, AND OTHER USES, HYDRAULICALLY FLATTENED

Telegraphic Address: "PARKES SMETHWICK." Telephone: SMETHWICK 5

1849 Joshua & William HORTON - "Makers of boilers, land and marine steam engines, gasometers, tanks, boats, punts"

ADVERTISEMENTS.   17

NEAL AND TONKS,
JEWELLERS, LAPIDARIES,
BLACK ORNAMENT & BUTTON MANUFACTURERS.

BROOCHES, GLASS BUTTONS, COAT LOOPS, SHIRT STUDS,
NECKLACE AND OTHER SNAPS, CLOAK CLASPS,
AND VARIOUS ORNAMENTS IN GLASS, PEARL, AND IVORY.
Glass Benders, Quickers, Stainers, &c.
PEARL, TORTOISE SHELL, & IVORY WORKERS,
WRITING FOLIOS, WORK BOXES,
TEA CHESTS & CADDIES, INK STANDS, CIGAR CASES,
Ladies' Companions, Card Cases, &c.
NO. 13, GREAT CHARLES ST., BIRMINGHAM.

JOSHUA & WILLIAM HORTON,
ÆTNA BOILER MANUFACTORY,
SMETHWICK, NEAR BIRMINGHAM.
MANUFACTURERS OF
WROUGHT IRON BOILERS,
OF EVERY DESCRIPTION, FOR
LAND & MARINE STEAM ENGINES,
GASOMETERS, SHIP'S TANKS, SALT PANS, SUGAR PANS,
CLARIFIERS, BOATS, PUNTS, &c.
N.B.—BOILERS REPAIRED ON THE SHORTEST NOTICE.

EDWARD HOLDEN,
GLASS, LUSTRE, AND
CHANDELIER MANUFACTURER,
DEALER IN
TOILETS, CRUETS, & SMELLING BOTTLES,
GIBSON MILL,
CAMBRIDGE STREET, BIRMINGHAM.

—X—

Returning to Telford's main canal and initially proceeding eastwards on the northside, several big sites come into play that over the years, have seen many changes of ownership and function. Two such works, Credenda and Kingston Works were crammed in between the Engine Arm to the south and the Main line to the north. As one re-joins Smethwick Junction, cross over to the south side and follow the grassier footpath. It is here that two other major players were present on the right side of the canal; Muntz's Metal and London Works. In Brindley's day, the route of the canal wound into the sites in a more tortuous way and signs of these old relics can still be seen by the discerning eye. Just east of the junction there is evidence of a deviation into what was the Kingston Works. Further along, just past Rabone Lane Bridge, the towpath climbs sharply over the infilled bridge of French Walls.

—X—

3.6 CREDENDA WORKS

CREDENDA WORKS [Credenda means 'matters of faith'] [REF: 2]

1880   **William Micklewight** was appointed works manager at **Credenda**. He was born at Harborne, Birmingham in 1850 and having been educated locally then served an apprenticeship with **James Watt & Co at the Soho Foundry** where he remained for a decade.

1887   There was a dissolution of the Credenda partnership of three; William C. Stiff of Hagley Road, Birmingham, Herbert B.S. Bennett and Thomas W. Piggott who had been working from premises at Ledsam St, Ladywood, Birmingham called **Credenda Cold-drawn Seamless Steel Tube Company**. Bennett and Piggott retired leaving **William C. Stiff** to continue.

1888   A new company called **Seamless Steel Tube Company Ltd** was created with a capital of £100,000 (in money of 2020 = £8.5 million) in £10 shares. This company had been created originally by **Sir Joseph Whitworth & Co** of Manchester.

1889   The company, Credenda Seamless Tube Ltd bought the Bridge Street factory **Birmingham Plate Glass Co,** alongside the Feeder Arm and converted the factory into a tube mill.

1893   The company lasted four years and then was placed in receivership

1894   Micklewight moved to John Russell, Alma Tube Works in Walsall.

1896   the company was sold to the **New Credenda Tube Company Ltd** and bought by **Birmingham Star Tube Co.** The former was subsequently wound up a year later.

1897   Star Tube Co was absorbed into **Weldless Tubes Ltd**.

1901   **William Micklewight** went to Russia on government business, returned to become the **Chief Engineer for John Russell**

1906 **Allen Everitt & Sons**, [see p. 133] a company specialising in the manufacture of condenser tubes moved from Birmingham to the adjacent **Kingston Works** as **Tubes Ltd** until 1929 when it was acquired by **I.C.I.** and trade continued until 1958.

1907/8 A Birmingham bicycle manufacturing firm (making brakes and pedals), **J.A. Phillips & Co** of Bath Row, Birmingham bought the Credenda Works, giving up its Birmingham premises. J.A Phillips had two partners; John Alfred Phillips and Ernest William Bohle. The latter was born in Cologne, came to Birmingham, married a local lady and lived in Moseley, Birmingham.

1909 Patent was opened. **and J. A. Phillips and Co.** produced improvements in means of attaching brakes and other parts and fittings to cycles and like machines.

1910 The partnership of J.A. Phillips was dissolved, with John Alfred retiring being replaced by Henry Charles Church.

1914 It was reported:

> 'The Smethwick magistrates were occupied for nearly six hours yesterday in hearing evidence in a case in which Messrs. J. A. Phillips and Co. (Limited), of the Credenda Works, Bridge Street, Smethwick, were summoned charges under the Trading With the Enemy Act. Sixteen summonses were issued in all - six against the firm, four each against **Ernest William Bohle**, (naturalised subject and resident of the UK for 20 plus years) the Credenda Works, and Otto Hesmer, of the same address,(naturized for 2 years) and summonses were also issued against Henry Charles Church, of the Credenda Works.'

Later that years, the works employing 1000 were destroyed by fire!!! *[REF: 2]*

A report of 1910 by Bohle, himself sheds some light upon the dissolution of the partnership [REF: 16]

"CAPTAINS OF INDUSTRY"
MR E. H. BOHLE

Mr E. H. Bohle, partner with Mr H. C. Church in the successful concern of J. A. Phillips and Co., Ltd., Birmingham, is a forceful personality, and a master of detail, and a strong believer in the economic benefits of thorough standardisation. Some years ago he met Mr J. A. Phillips, and discovered that their mutual interest lay in forming a partnership. They concentrated their energies on the sole manufacture of brakes and pedals for the trade, and the business has steadily grown to its present large proportions. Mr Bohle holds himself responsible for the entire works department, while also supervising the commercial side, Mr Church being the travelling partner"

1916 William Micklewight died

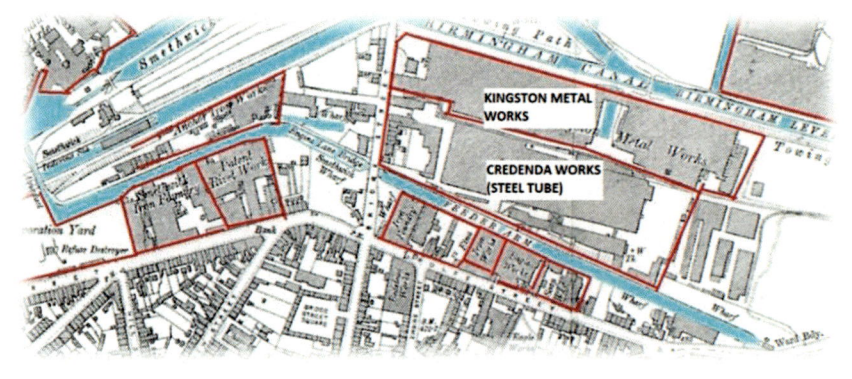

1904 O/S map of part of Smethwick.

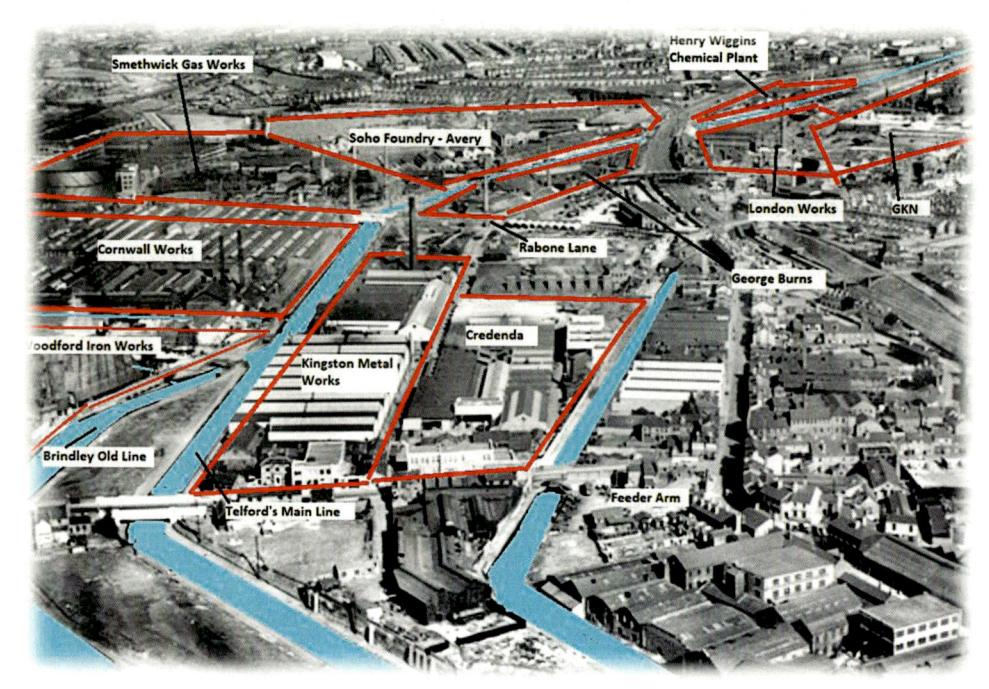

1934 Britain from Above. From the North

1916 **J.A. Phillips & Co** consolidated by amalgamating with **Rolfe Manufacturing Co**. The latter produced motorcycles between 1911 and 1913 but had been previously successful in 1905 with the production of a 2,75 h.p. Rolfe-Goode motorcycle.

1920/1 The **Smethwick Tube Co** set up in Rolfe St, becoming part of **George Burn Ltd. [see p. 138-9]**. Meanwhile **Tube Investments** acquired Phillips, manufacturer of bicycle parts.

1920s & 30s Many of the Rolfe Street premises were acquired by George Burn, including the **soap works of William Cliff & Sons**, which he replaced with tube mills.

1937 the company became **George Burn City Tube & Conduit Mills** and operated from Rabone Lane on the site of Muntz's **'Old Side Works'**. Burns sold the Birmingham works.

1971 The works closed in Rabone Lane and moved to Shirley, Warwickshire.

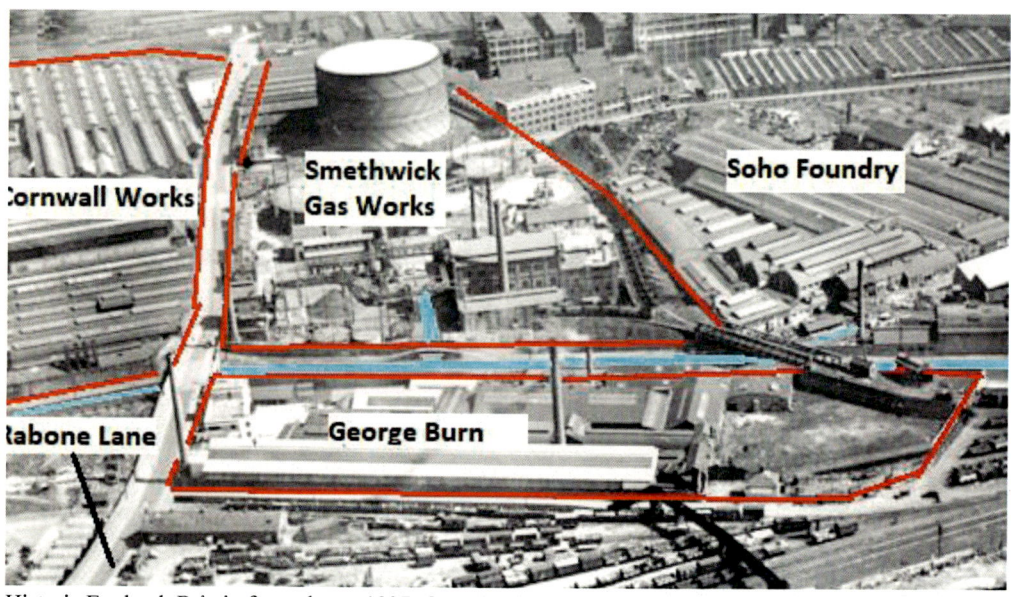

Historic England: Britain from above. 1937. George Burn Ltd on the old site of Muntz Metals 'Old Side Works' [REF: 15]

131

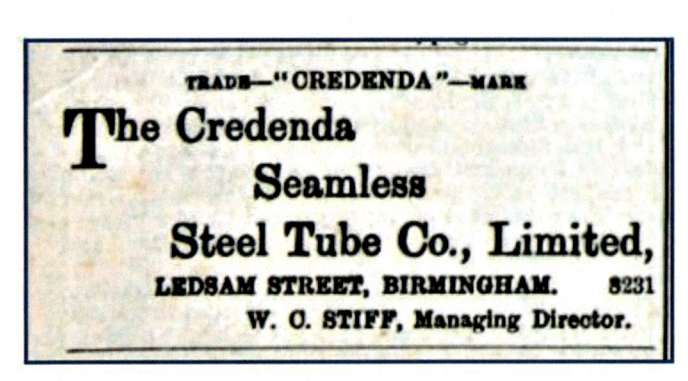

1889

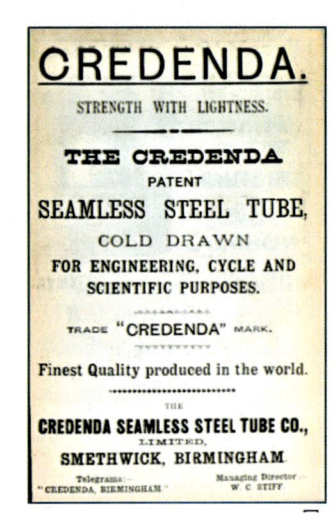

1891

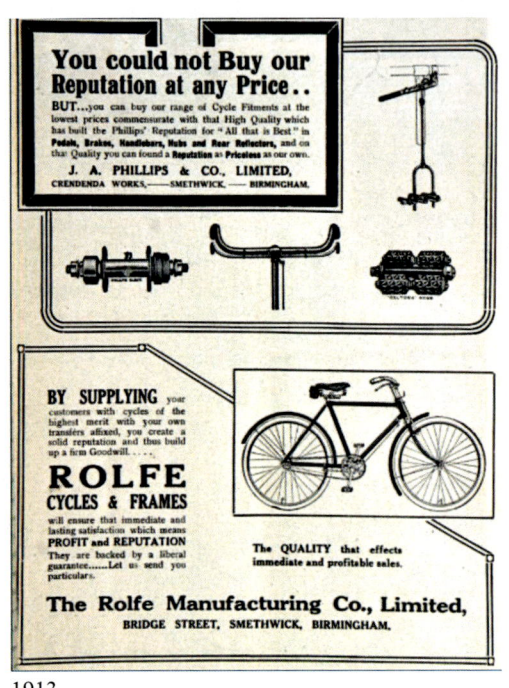

1913

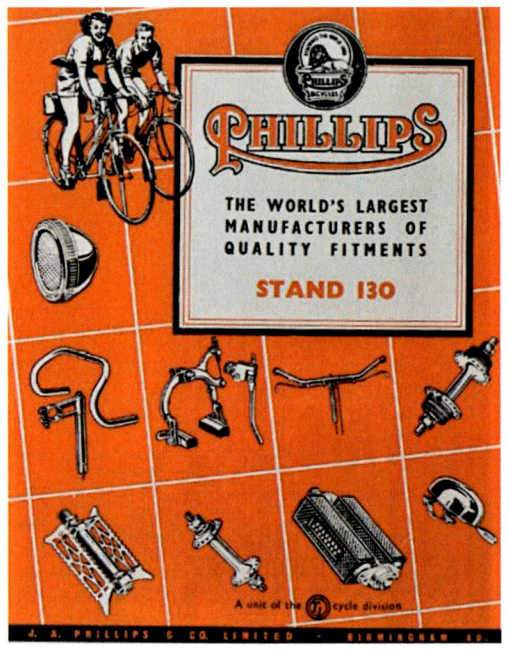

1955

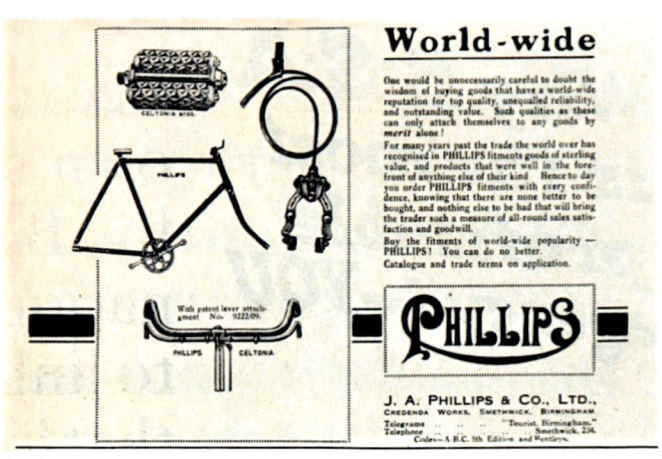

1927

3.7 - KINGSTON METAL WORKS
Allen Everitt & Sons

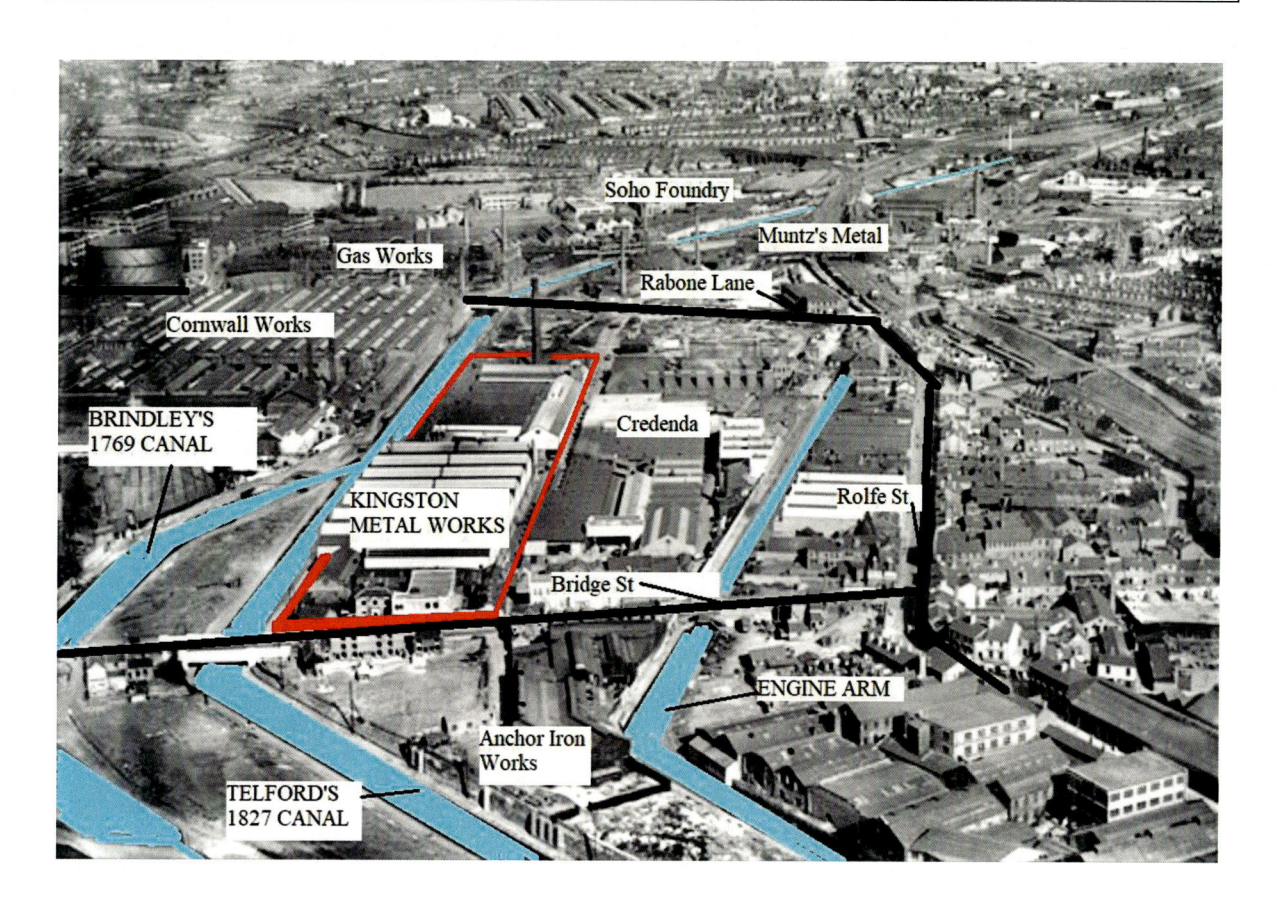

1769   **Allen Everitt & Sons** first mentioned in Birmingham [REF: 61, 62, 63, 64]

1800   Business working from three Birmingham sites; Adderley St, Liverpool St, Glover St.

1823   **George Allen Everitt** was born in Birmingham

1851   C/R George Allen Everitt was described as a wire and tube manufacturer who employed 120 men and lived in Deritend with his family.

1864   George & Maria had made a great deal of money from this industry for their son, **Neville Henry Everitt,** born in 1864 in Edgbaston, who was educated at Harrow and Oxford University and after serving a 5-year apprenticeship with **Patent Shaft & Axle Co.** (manufacturers of steel pipes of large diameter), in Wednesbury became a director of the renowned **'Messrs Thomas Piggott & Co,'** manufacturers of bridges, girders, gasholders and engines. [See Hiscock: "Brindley Out Telford Home – A Journey along the Birmingham Canal", page 48].

1868   A wide range of products were being made by Allen Everitt & Sons' on both sides of the canal'. They were smelting iron ore and dealing with every aspect associated with the manufacture of their product including 'the refining of pig copper, casting of ingots to the final scouring and annealing They also manufactured sheet and foil copper and brass.'

1890   Allen Everitt & Sons Ltd acquired the **Kingston Works** site and started moving from Birmingham to Kingston Works over a period of years until 1902. They specialised in the manufacture of copper / nickel condensing tubes 'from a state-of-the-art factory.'

1929   **I.C.I.** acquired the company

1958   **Yorkshire Imperial Metals Ltd** was created and acquired the interests of I.C.I.

1971   **Yorkshire Imperial Metals Ltd**. were making non-ferrous tubes, fittings and plates at the Kingston Works.

> **HUNDREDS of TONS of**
> **ÆCOPPER PIPES**
> have been used all over the country for
> **HEATING & WATER INSTALLATIONS,**
> which is only one of many tributes to
> **Æ SERVICE.**
> SOLE MAKERS
> **ALLEN EVERITT & SONS, Ltd.** SMETHWICK, BIRMINGHAM.
> KINGSTON METAL WORKS,
> Established 1769

One little curiosity associated with Allen Everitt, appears in Grace's Guide: [REF: 91]

1921 Obituary

Engineer-Captain WALTER GEORGE KENT, C.B.E., R.N., died on September 15, 1921. Engineer-Captain Kent entered the Royal Naval Engineering College at Devonport in 1880, leaving it in 1886 to proceed to the Royal Naval College at Greenwich.

In 1887 he left Greenwich and joined H.M.S. Bellerophon in the West Indies, later serving on the Pacific Station on board H.M.S. Champion, a corvette, during a commission of 31 years. In 1896 he was appointed to a destroyer building by Messrs. Laird Brothers, Birkenhead, and went to sea in 1897 in H.M.S. Thrasher. Later he served in H.M.S. Orwell, leader of the Mediterranean destroyer flotilla.

In 1902 he left the Orwell and destroyers after an experience of seven years and was again sent to the Mediterranean in H.M.S. Venus. He became Admiralty Overseer for the Midland district at Birmingham in 1906, and in 1909 was appointed Engineer-Commander of H.M.S. Bulwark, flagship at Sheerness, where he managed the machinery department with conspicuous success, and was selected in 1911 to carry out the mechanical training of stoker ratings at Chatham. Here he was highly successful, making the training a thorough one and obtaining excellent results.

*At the outbreak of war, he was appointed to H.M.S. Diligence at Portsmouth, and early in 1915 returned to Birmingham as Overseer, accomplishing the necessarily enormous amount of work with characteristic energy and acumen. In addition to the regular duties attaching to the post of Admiralty Overseer of the Midland district, his work in Birmingham included the organization of the supply of non-ferrous materials for the Admiralty and Ministry of Munitions until the Director of Materials and Priority was appointed. He was promoted to Acting Engineer-Captain in 1916, and received the C.B.E. after the war terminated, in recognition of his services, retiring in 1919, when he joined the firm of **Messrs. Allen Everitt & Sons, Ltd., Kingston Metal Works,** Smethwick, as assistant managing director, which position he held at the time of his death.*

His strict integrity and unfailing kindness of heart, together with his scrupulous devotion to duty, and his thorough knowledge of naval machinery and its manufacture, have earned for Captain Kent the highest respect and esteem of his many friends in naval and engineering circles, who will lament his loss.

Engineer-Captain Kent was elected member of the Institute of Metals on June 10, 1920.

3.8 FRENCH WALLS
George Muntz, Muntz's Metal, George Burn Ltd

A. FRENCH WALLS, George Muntz & Muntz's Metal

1660   First mention of **French Walls**

1771   Sir John Peshale sold the estate to a Birmingham merchant, John Turner, with a lease being granted to John Jennens.

1790   A gun foundry and manufactory was operating on this site by a John Whately.

1791   Whately ordered a 20 h.p. engine to power the forge, gun barrel grinding and boring mill.

1795   John Whately's brother Henry was now running the works, when the 20 h.p. engine finally arrived, at which time it only powered the grinding and boring mill; another 9 h.p. engine was purchased to operate the forge.

1798   The works were passed **to Henry Piddock Whately**, when a lease was granted to Edward Croxall of Shustock and a Birmingham button maker, Joseph Gibbs for the operation of a farm.

1807   **George Muntz** joined the family business that his father **Philip Frederick Muntz** was involved in; **Muntz & Purden**. Phillip F. Muntz had taken advice from Matthew Boulton and invested in this company.

1811   Phillip Muntz died and George managed the works in Water Street, Birmingham.

1812   French Walls was mortgaged to Isaac Spooner and Mathias Attwood, when the property included a mill and a steam engine.

1815   Grace's Guide:
"All those substantial and excellent buildings known as the **French Walls Flour Mill**" were auctioned. They were described as three miles from Birmingham on the banks of the Birmingham Canal. There were twenty dwelling houses in the lots of sale, and among these were three houses, described as having been the outbuildings that used to belong to the homestead of French Walls Farm."

1816   **James Watt Jnr**. [p. 37-42] bought the French Walls Mill including 2 engines.

1820   James Watt leased the French Walls to **Henry Downing** and lent him money to develop an ironworks.

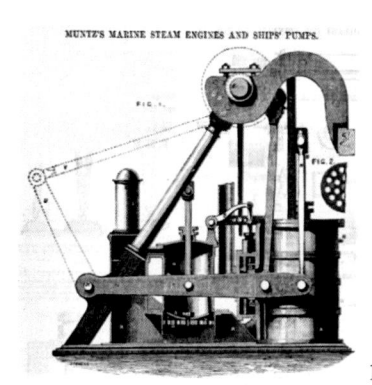

1861

1829   Downing went bankrupt and Watt leased the site to Bordesley Steel Co but some years later, Watt took over the ironworks, calling it **French Walls Works** and ran it alongside the **Soho Foundry** on the other side of the canal. It was a symbiotic relationship where French Walls Works provided the Soho Foundry with boiler plates and turned-out merchant iron and steel with scrap from the Foundry being returned to French Walls for recycling. [REF: 5]

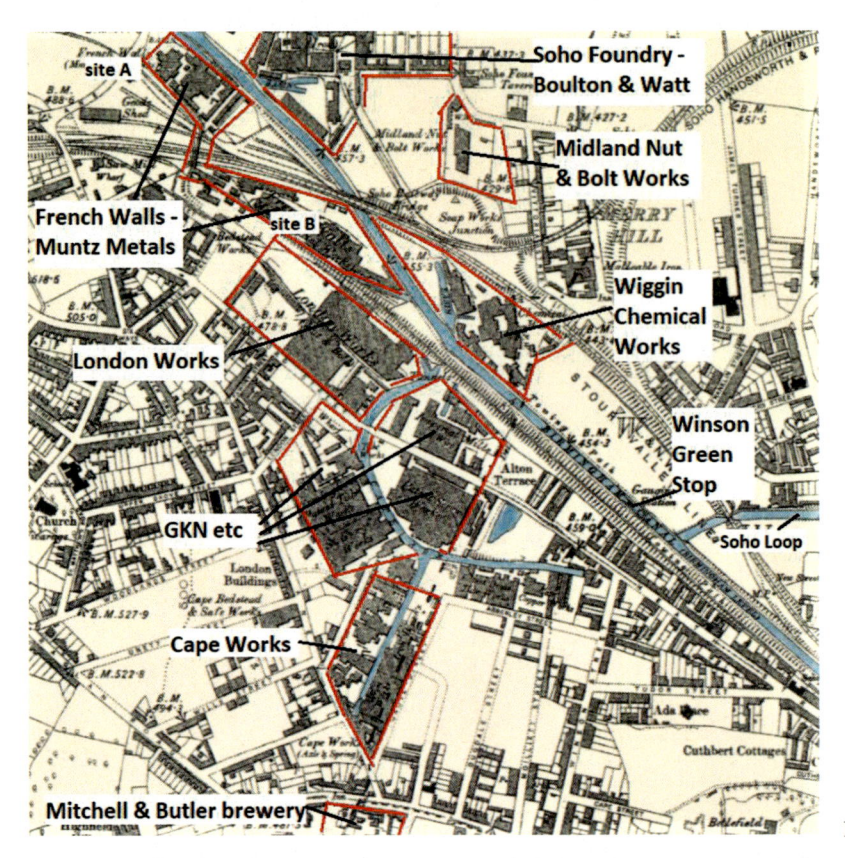

1888 6"/mile O/S map annotated

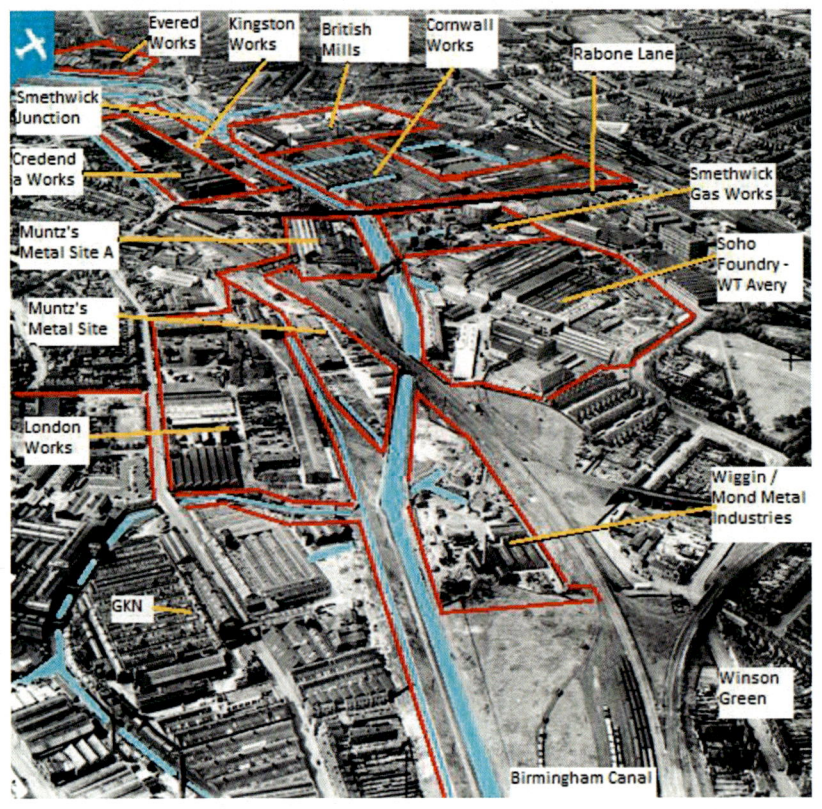

1946

1832   George Muntz gained patents for **Muntz's Metal** [REF: 27] and for ships' bolts made of the metal

1837   **Patent Metal Co** (not to be confused with the Patent Nut & Bolt Co, at the London Works, next door that was to go bust in 1865), was formed and Muntz 's metal was transferred to Swansea

1842   James Watt, now elderly, gave up on French Walls Works which were bought by **G.F. Muntz**, already an established engineer and famed for inventing an alloy of copper and zinc, ultimately being called 'Muntz's Metal'. Muntz needed a larger site and initially, the 4.5-acre **site A 'Old Site Works'** he had bought to the north of the Wolverhampton & Stour Valley Railway was sufficient.

1843   **P.H. Muntz** was **deputy chairman of Birmingham Chamber of Commerce**

1850   Muntz had outgrown his current site and a further 6.5 acres were bought to the West on the other side of the railway line, just north of **The London Works, site B, 'New Side Works'**.

1852   The new site was completed which was linked to site A by a private bridge over the railway.

1857   G.F Muntz died and the business continued under his son's direction, also G.F. Muntz

1864   **G. F. Muntz Jnr**, sold the company to a newly formed **Muntz's Metal Ltd** but another member of the family continued to run the company for making his yellow metal sheathing and rods

1890   The company restructured but continued to have Muntz family members at the helm.

1912   Muntz's Metals were leading exhibitor at the Non-Ferrous Metals Exhibition at the Royal Agricultural Halls

1921   As well as the now world-famous **patent yellow metal sheathing and rods**, Muntz's Metal Co made a range of non-ferrous articles

1925   Muntz's Metal Co amalgamated with **Elliotts Metal Co,** Selly Oak Works, Birmingham, which had been established since 1853

1932   **ICI Metals Division** incorporated Muntz's Metal Co

More recently, the company name became Muntz & Barwell, when Douglas Barwell bought the semi-derelict Lower Avon Navigation and was integral in its renovation. [Graham Wigley]

Brass Boiler Tubes.—Muntz's METAL COMPANY, LIMITED, French Walls, near Birmingham.—Manufacturers of Solid Drawn Brass Boiler Tubes, Condenser Plates and Tubes, Pump Rods, Screw Bolts, &c.

B. GEORGE BURN LTD

1889   A newly formed company **Credenda Seamless Tube Co** [see p. 129-132] bought the Bridge Street factory of the former **Birmingham Plate Glass Co** and converted it to a tube mill; **Credenda Works**

1896   **Star Tube Co** bought the company

1897   Star Tube Co was absorbed into **Weldless Tubes** (Later to be called **Tubes Ltd**)

1906   The Credenda Works closed

1908   A Birmingham bicycle manufacturer, **J.A. Phillips & Co** bought the Credenda Works and moved to the site [see p. 130-132]

1920   **Smethwick Tube Co** set up in nearby Rolfe Street, and became part of **George Burn Ltd**

1920S & 30S George Burn bought up several premises in Rolfe Street, including the soap works of **William Cliff & Sons** and replaced these sites with tube mills.

1937   George Burn opened the **City Tube & Conduit Mills** in Rabone Lane on the site of Muntz's 'Old Side Works' and made this the HQ.

1971   George Burn moved to Shirley [REF; 84]

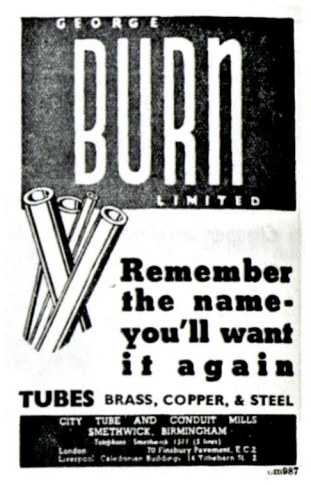

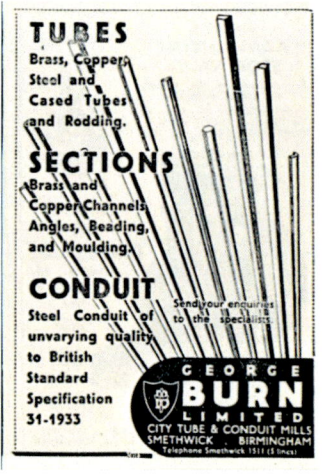

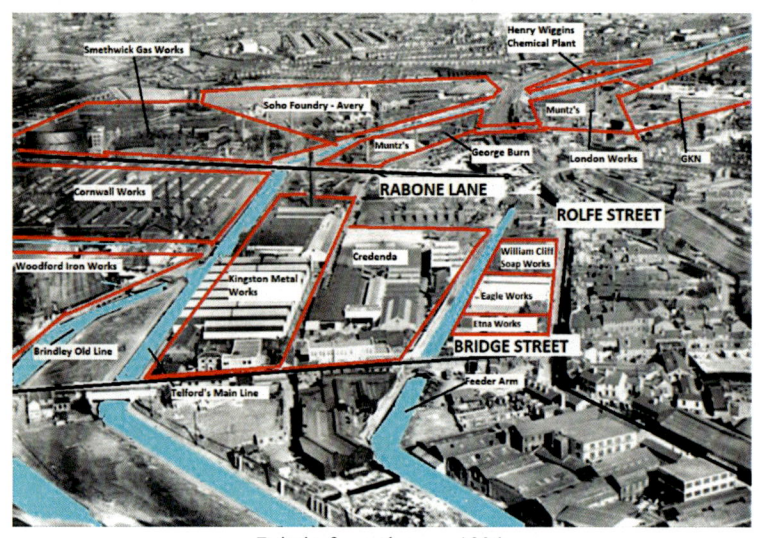

1925   1938

Britain from above – 1934

3.9 LONDON WORKS

SMETHWICK GROVE, FOX HENDERSON & CO, THOMAS ASTBURY & SONS, PATENT NUT & BOLT CO, WATKINS & KEEN

This area known as London Works portrays a complex picture of how many companies worked from here but it must be remembered that a few small companies would share a power source and work under the same roofs. From time to time, one would go out of business another would expand, or simply amalgamate or take over. Times were very fluid, businesses were changing at a phenomenal speed and there was great interplay and reliance on the neighbours, both big and small; this site was a perfect example of this behaviour. Initially, the London Works was an independent and prosperous centre but as emphasis and inventions changed, take-overs occurred with the London Works being no exception. This section of the journey is devoted to the major manufacturers and how they evolved alongside each other.

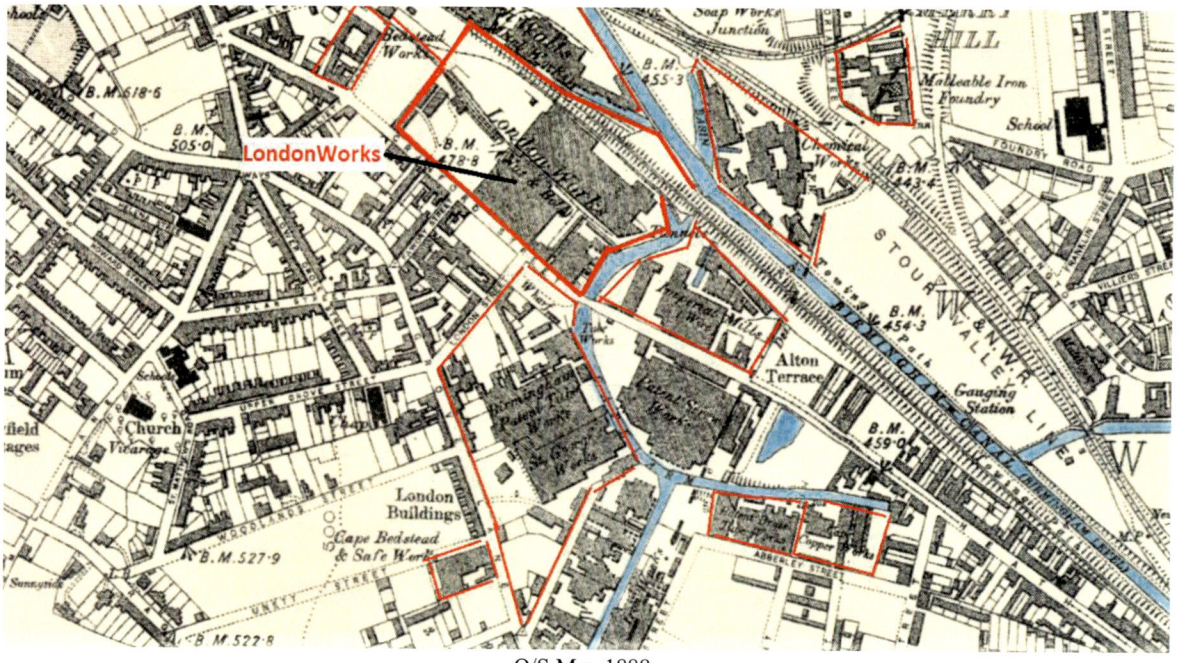

O/S Map 1888.

A. Smethwick Grove, Jean-Louis Moilliet and James Keir [REF: 14]

1790s   A house called **Smethwick Grove** stood on the site south-west of the main railway line and to the west of the Birmingham Canal for years and was recorded as being present in the late 1790s.

1797   it was the home of **James Keir**, a Scotsman of whom James Watt said Keir; was "a mighty chemist and an agreeable man." He was also regarded as a man of letters, an inventor and man of science and he became a member of the **Lunar Society.**

1790s   was a period when a young Swiss engineer called **Jean-Louis Moilliet** from Geneva arrived at **Soho Foundry** with £10,000 (equivalent in 2020 = £1,212,000) and a letter of introduction to meet Matthew Boulton. The latter, being an hospitable man and recognising his capabilities (as well as the £10,000), introduced Moilliet to colleagues and other like-minded engineers, including James Keir and his daughter, Amelia.

139

1801 Jean-Louis and Amelia married; he naturalised and changed his name to **John Lewis Moilliet** and moved in with the Keir family.

1813 Moilliet bought Smethwick Grove and the 16-acre estate bordering the eastern edge of Birmingham Canal. There are both a street and a pub named after him in the vicinity of the historic site of Smethwick Grove.

Smethwick Grove and site of the London Works some years later

1819 A celebrated novelist, **Maria Edgeworth**, a friend of Amelia's visited her a couple of times at Smethwick Grove and commented in a letter that "Amelia was most affectionate in her whole manner and conduct to us, …..herself is fatter even than when you saw her – quite a heavy mass in person – much older in appearance than her age. …. The young Moilliets, (of whom there were five) were fine, fat, chubby slow creatures." Maria Edgeworth's father was a celebrated writer and inventor from Ireland called **Richard Lovell Edgeworth**, *[see p. 152]* who was born in Bath but moved to Ireland. He was another member of the **Lunar Society**. [REF: 15]

1824-27 **Telford** altered the route of Brindley's 1769 route which cut through the Smethwick Grove estate. Moilliet took advantage of the changes and took over the loop of truncated canal making it into an ornamental lake.

1828 Moilliet had increased the estate to 59 acres. Ultimately, Moilliet moved to **Hampstead Hall** and let the Grove to **George Bacchus**, a partner in a Birmingham firm of flint-makers

1830 George Bacchus left Smethwick Grove, when, being close friends of the Quaker family of **Samuel Tertius Galton**, (son of Samuel John and Lucy of Great Barr Hall and Warley Woods), John Lewis Moilliet's son, **James married Lucy Harriot Galton**. The Galton family was full of strong social connections, eminent scientists, arms dealers and philosophers and local landowners at Galton Hall. After their marriage, James & Lucy moved back to Smethwick Grove.

James Moilliet sold the mansion to **Thomas Adkins** [see p.29-31]of Handsworth; a soap manufacturer and the house became known simply as The Grove. There is a street name The Grove in 2020.

1846 Smethwick Grove was bought by **George Selby** of **Birmingham Patent Iron & Brass Tube Co**. [See GKN: Patent Iron & Brass Tube Co]

B. Fox, Henderson & Co

1784 **Joseph Bramah** [see p.98] established a lock making, hydraulic press, and other items in Denmark Street, London. They developed the 2Challenge Lock" which remained unbreakable for 60 years

1787 Bramah's catalogue included water closets

1790 Grace's Guide records:

"the company famously had a "Challenge Lock" which was displayed in the window of their London shop from 1790 mounted on a board containing the inscription: *The artist who can make an instrument that will pick or open this lock shall receive 200 guineas the moment it is produced.* The "Challenge" withstood attempts to open it for over 60 years."

1793 A water closet was supplied by Bramah to Lord Anson of Shugborough Hall.

1814 Joseph Bramah died.

1818 **Francis and Edward Bramah** joined the family business in Pimlico where they made famous locks and condensing engines.

1830 The brothers fell out with John Joseph Bramah leaving the partnership

1839 Grace's Guide:
"John Joseph Bramah is reported to have taken over his deceased uncle's business. He was said to possess his uncle's business skills and love of mechanisms if not his inventiveness. He gathered together a huge business in railway plant at Pimlico, with the help of George and Robert Stephenson, and subsequently transferred it to Smethwick as the **London Works**, joining himself with **Charles Fox and John Henderson as partners**".

Charles Fox, had been a protegee and principal assistant of **Robert Stephenson** during the construction of the London Euston to Birmingham railway, who when he teamed up with **John Joseph Bramah** a son of this notable family of engineers and iron-founders, between them they bought 5 acres of land that had previously been part of **Moilliet's** large estate and started **Bramah, Fox & Co** on the purchased site now referred to as **the London Works**

1840 Francis Bramah died The same year a site started being erected at Smethwick

1841 The works were operational and although Charles Fox was the junior partner, he was apparently the brains in the team, having designed and supervised the construction of the factory. Bramah retired from the business in the early 1840s.

1843 Birkenhead Commissioners approved plans for a market designed by Fox Henderson & Co

1844 **Fox Henderson constructed the Birkenhead market** but it went way over budget. In the same year, they were in court due to the death during the construction of a glass roof at the Bricklayer's Arms Station, London. And finally, a wall blew down during construction at Birkenhead market!

1845 Fox was now joined by **John Henderson**, a Scottish engineer and the company became **Fox, Henderson & Co**. Fox drew on his railway experience with Stephenson and he invented various improvements to railway routes as well as a complete railway plant and stock.

1846 John Joseph Bramah died

1848 Fox, Henderson & Co teamed up with **William Siemens**, inventor of the regenerative furnace, to produce a **regenerative steam-engine and condenser**. It was not a great success.

1848 Bramah & Co took over Horseley Iron Works

1850   Fox, Henderson & Co were producing "wrought-iron pipes, steam engines, boilers, gasometers and ships' tanks" [REF: 5] . The London Works, at this time was described as *"the finest and most compact range of buildings in South Staffordshire"*. By this time expansion had been extensive with a vast boiler house containing two 75 h.p. engines, surrounded by workshops and a smithy containing 70 forges, and probably the largest in the world at that time. They were producing 300 tons of castings per week and had a workforce of between 800 and 1200 men.

Grace's Guide states:

> "Fox and Henderson's expertise with structural ironwork led **Joseph Paxton** to invite them to build his iron and glass scheme for The Crystal Palace for The 1851 Great Exhibition. They built all the ironwork for the building, starting work before the formal contract had been agreed. Due to its innovative modular design and construction techniques, it was ready in nine months. Some of the work was carried out at the Renfrew works.
>
> 1851 Award at the 1851 Great Exhibition. See details at 1851 Great Exhibition: Reports of the Juries: Class V."

1851   **Charles Fox was knighted** for ingenious design and supervision of Joseph Paxton's Crystal Palace, making most of the iron work. The company were also responsible for many large iron framework railway station constructions: Liverpool Tithebarn Street, Bradford Exchange, Paddington, Birmingham New Street. Fox was the designer and Henderson dealt with the construction.

Crystal Palace c. 1901 (courtesy of cpfc.co.uk)

1852   Fox, Henderson & Co were employed by **Crystal Palace Co.** to move the structure of the exhibition hall to Sydenham, where they re-erected and enlarged it on Sydenham Hill, (now Crystal Palace).

1852   The relationship of Fox, Henderson with Siemens came to an end with endless financial losses.

1856   The company, **Fox Henderson failed** due to massive financial losses and vacated the premises. However, a partnership between Francis Watkins and Arthur Keen started as **Watkins & Keen**, (initially at Victoria Works, Rolfe Street, but latterly from London Works, Smethwick). [*See p. 23-25. GKN: Arthur Keen*]

1857   Charles Fox started a practice of a civil and engineering consultancy with two of his sons; **Sir Charles Fox & Sons.** The London Works closed putting 2000 employees out of work which caused great hardship for the people of Smethwick.

C. Thomas Astbury & Sons, Patent Nut & Bolt Co, Watkins & Keen

1849   There is an entry in the 1849 History & Directory of Birmingham under the heading 'Iron Founders' of **Thompson, Astbury & Co**, Smethwick but no other information. It is possible that Thomas Astbury was in partnership with a Mr. Thompson before he moved to London Works. The cast iron roving bridge on the Birmingham Canal called 'Lee Bridge' is likely to date from when Telford pushed his straight line through in 1827.

1858   Thomas Astbury & Sons occupied part of the London Works. An interesting family connection occurred when **Thomas Astbury's daughter, Hannah** married **Arthur Keen** of Guest, Keen & Nettlefold. Thomas Astbury recognised the potential of the patent for the Nut-making machine that Francis Watkins was trying to sell in 1856.

1860   The **Patent Nut & Bolt Co Ltd.** moved to London Works, Smethwick. "Near Birmingham"

1862   It is recorded by Grace's Guide:

"All fastenings for the "immense structure" of the International Exhibition were supplied by the Patent Nut and Bolt Co, the premises of the late firm Fox, Henderson and Co, London Works, now in the possession of Messrs Watkins and Keen; Watkins had arrived in England about 1856 from America; the works had become one of the largest of its kind in the world, covering more than 4 acres and employing 500 people. The contract for the Exhibition had been granted largely on the basis of the uniformity of the product arising from machine production."

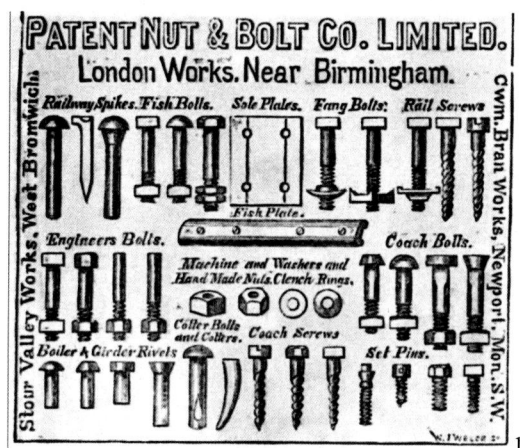

1868 [REF: 2]

1864   Rapid expansion by Watkins and Keen, displaced Thomas Astbury from London Works while simultaneously, the Patent Nut & Bolt Co set about levelling their yard and was launched as a joint-stock company

1865   **Patent Nut & Bolt Co, Watkins & Keen and Thomas Astbury** all three occupied the London Works for a period.

1865   The partnership of **Patent Nut & Bolt Co** being Francis Watkins and Arthur Keen, dissolved.

1865   A **William Weaver Vaughan** was recorded as occupying the works trading as the **London Works Iron Co**

1867   London Works was advertising the sale of sections of iron; Ts, angles, etc. and coach axles, wrought iron boxes and military gun barrels

1873   A partnership between William Weaver Vaughan, William Beasley & William Brown, Iron Manufacturers of the **London Works Iron Co**, at The London Works was dissolved with Brown and Vaughan continuing to trade at the site.

Meanwhile the partnership of Thomas Astbury and James Astbury was dissolved but continued to trade as **Thomas Astbury & Sons**

1876   A new Patent 690 was registered for the manufacture of 'unwelded or open jointed steel and iron tubes' by William and David Brown & William Weaver Vaughan.

1881   Again there was a dissolution of partnership of **London Works Iron Co** with William Brown retiring. At this time their business was recorded as being at London Works and at the Cape Works, Smethwick

1887   Thomas Astbury & Sons was supplying shells to the British Government. [REF: 2]

1894   Grace's Guide reports that the Patent Nut & Bolt Co:
"Exhibited at The Antwerp Exhibition. 'Every description of bolts and nuts, black and polished and galvanised, of iron, steel, brass, gun-metal and copper, from the smallest size up to 3.5 inch and 4-inch diameter'. Awarded Gold medal for metallurgy and for Railway Plant."

1900   Proposal from Arthur Keen, the chairman for the reconstruction of the company by amalgamation with the Dowlais Iron Co and Guest and Co would give the company its own coal and iron supplies and a diversified range of products; the company would be called **Guest, Keen and Co.**

A **Thompson, Astbury & Co. Smethwick** roving bridge close to the junction of Soho Loop, Icknield Port Loop and the Birmingham Canal

—X—

After passing beneath the railway bridge on the right bank, the high wall on that side once was the perimeter of the London Works, which precedes the double bridge construction to the Cape Loop and a final few hundred metres of straight grassy track takes one back to the Winson Green Stop.

—X—

4. THREE TITANIC CANAL ENGINEERS
BRINDLEY, SMEATON & TELFORD

A. James BRINDLEY

James Brindley was born into a comfortably wealthy family from Tunstead in Derbyshire but spent many years living in Leek, Staffordshire. As a teenager, he received a sound education from his mother and then served an apprenticeship in a millwright's shop, after which he set himself up as a wheelwright, becoming a good friend of the **Wedgwood family**. His reputation as a skilled engineer spread; it seemed no engineering problem was beyond him. In 1752 he designed a successful engine for draining coalmines.

This success reached the ears of the **3rd Duke of Bridgewater** who hired him to assist with difficult parts of the construction of a canal designed to move coal from his mine at Worsley to Manchester. It was Brindley's job to design the Barton Aqueduct, an important link carrying water 12 metres above the river Irwell.

This put Brindley in a very prominent position for when plans were afoot to build a canal from Birmingham to Wolverhampton in the late 1760s.

James BRINDLEY (1716 -1772)
painted by Francis PARSONS 1770 [REF 108]

In 1880, Robert Dent published a local tome of history *"Old & New Birmingham: A history of the town and its people"* in which he quoted from a report of 1766 by a lawyer of that time, John Meredith:

> We read further, in the *Gazette* of July 15th, that—
>
> Birmingham Navigation, July 10th, 1766.—Whereas several numerous public Meetings have been held at the Swan Inn, to consider of a Plan for making a navigable Canal through the principal Coal Fields in this Neighbourhood by Smethwick, Oldbury, Tipton Green, and Bilston, in the Counties of Salop and Stafford, to join the Canal now making between the Trent and Severn, at Adderaly, near Wolverhampton, Mr. James Brindley having made a Survey of it, estimated that the Expence would not exceed the Sum of £50,000 and on the Friday the 12th Day of June last, in Pursuance of an Advertisement for that Purpose, a Subscription was opened to apply to Parliament for Powers to make such Canal, and for compleating the same. There is already £35,000 subscribed; the Subscription Deeds will continue open at Mr. Meredith's, Attorney at Law, Birmingham, until the 28th of July Inst. unless the whole sum of £50,000 be sooner subscribed. At the same Place the proceedings of the Committee appointed for the Conduct of the application may be referred to. By Order of the Committee.
>
> JOHN MEREDITH, Solicitor.

The report continued:

> By this time upwards of £35,000 was already subscribed towards carrying out this project. A bill "for making a Navigable Canal from Birmingham to Wolverhampton" was introduced in Parliament during the next session, (1768,) and received the royal assent on the 26th of July in that year. On the "agreeable news" reaching Birmingham, "the bells were set to ringing, which were continued the whole day."
>
> The length of the canal was about twenty-two miles, and the expense of making it about £70,000, divided into shares of £140 each, of which no one was allowed to purchase more than ten. From "A List of the Proprietors of the Birmingham Canal Navigation," (issued March 30, 1770,) we find that these shares were five hundred in number, and that the full number of ten were held by the following gentlemen: Thos. Anson, Esq., of Shuckbro'; Ann Colmore; Jer. Clarke, Esq., of Westbromwich; Peter Capper, Redland; Henry Carver, Esq.; the Earl of Dartmouth; James Farquharson; John Francis; Samuel Galton; John Galton, Bristol; the Earl of Hertford; Sir Lister Holte, Bart., of Aston Hall; John Kettle; John Lane, jun.; Thomas Lee; Henry Venour; Joseph Wilkinson; and William Welsh. John Ash, M.D., (founder of the General Hospital,) held five shares, as also did Richard Rabone, John and Edward Sneyd, (respectively,) Dr. Wm. Small, Thomas Westley, and others whose names are well known and (in many cases,) honourably represented by their descendants in Birmingham to-day. Strange to say, the Father of Soho held only three shares. Among other shareholders may be mentioned, Poet Freeth, (who held one share,) Joseph Guest, Samuel Aris, James Brindley, (the engineer,) Joseph Carles, John Grew, Michael Lakin, Samuel Pemberton, jun., Daniel and Josiah Ruston, etc.
>
> "This grand work," says Hutton, "like other productions of Birmingham birth, was rather hasty; the managers, not being able to find patience to worm round the hill at Smethwick, or cut through it, wisely travelled over it, by the help of twelve locks,—with six they mount the summit, and with six more descend to the former level; forgetting the great waste of water, and the small supply from the rivulets, in climbing this curious ladder, consisting of twelve liquid steps."
>
> The summit of this watery ladder is said to have been 460 feet above the level of the sea; but the inconvenience of the numerous locks being a source of continued complaint, the company eventually called in the aid of Telford to remove them; hills were cut through to a perpendicular depth of more than seventy feet, and other improvements effected, so that "the aspect of this canal," says Mr. Bates, writing in 1849, "is not surpassed in stupendous magnificence by any similar work in the world."
>
> The first boat-load of coals was brought to Birmingham by this canal Nov. 7th, 1769, the year of the Stratford Jubilee;

Pages from Dent's record of the raising of money to build the canal in the 1960s [REF 17]

With these distinguished names bringing their pots of cash to the table, the finances of the Birmingham Canal were secure. The expression "the Father of Soho held only three shares" could have referred to either James Watt or Matthew Boulton but one presumes the latter. By contrast, the impressive ownership of a share by James Brindley, must have indicated he was well on his way to being financially secure and that he truly believed in the job to have bought shares.

--X--

B. **John SMEATON**

James Smeaton was born in Austhorpe, Leeds in 1724 and 8 years younger than Brindley, attended Leeds Grammar School, then joining his father's law firm but he preferred a career in mathematical instrument construction and joined the York watch making firm of Henry Hindley, where he designed a **pyrometer to study material expansion.**

John SMEATON (1724-1792) by George ROMNEY [Courtesy of National Portrait Gallery]

1753   at the age of 29, he was **elected to the Royal Society**.

1755/9 Smeaton designed the third **Eddystone Lighthouse**, 12 miles south of Plymouth Sound, the first two having been destroyed by storm and fire respectively. It was subsequently removed to make way for a fourth one designed by James Douglass and is re-erected on **Plymouth Hoe** as a monument called Smeaton's Tower. [REF: 88]. It was during the construction of the lighthouse that Smeaton **discovered the properties of modern cement**, (leading ultimately to the invention of Portland Cement and concrete), that enabled him to build his Eddystone Lighthouse of considerable strength to withstand the elements that previous constructions had not survived.

1759   was awarded the Royal Society's prestigious **Copley Medal** for his research into the mechanics of waterwheels and windmills, in which he constructed small-scale models and tested various configurations over seven years of experiments. [REF: 87]. This was a vital link in the development of the Industrial Revolution as it enabled understanding of the power of water. During this era, he established a concept, known as **Smeaton's Coefficient**.

Then followed a catalogue of successes:

1761   designed a water engine for Royal Botanic Garden, Kew
1763/6 Coldstream Bridge over the River Tweed
1765/70 River Lea Navigation (London) improvements
1766/71 Perth Bridge over the River Tay, Scotland
1766/73 Ripon Canal
1767/70 Smeaton's Pier at St. Ives, Cornwall
1768/70 Smeaton's Viaduct over the River Trent, Nottinghamshire
1768/77 Forth & Clyde Canal from Grangemouth to Glasgow
1771   Smeaton founded the Society of Engineers, which continues into modern day
1775/80 Aberdeen Bridge
1775/81 Peterhead Harbour, Scotland
1789   Summit Bridge, Smethwick [REF: 90] *[See p. 87-89]*
1782/89 Birmingham & Fazeley Canal, Birmingham construction

Wikipedia: *The canal was completed in August 1789. The benefits of the co-operation with the other canal companies were that when all the links were completed in 1790, it immediately generated a great deal of freight traffic. This created problems, as the flights of locks at Aston and Farmer's Bridge became congested, and this became worse when the Warwick Canal built a junction onto the Digbeth Branch. The problem was not solved until 1844, when the Birmingham and Warwick Junction Canal to the south east and the Tame Valley Canal to the north west were opened. The name of the Birmingham & Birmingham & Fazeley Canal Company was changed to Birmingham Canal Navigations in 1794.* [REF: 89]

1792   St. Austell's Charlestown Harbour, Cornwall
1792   John Smeaton died

1860/94 The reverse side of the English coin, the penny, displayed Smeaton's Lighthouse on the reverse side behind Britannia.

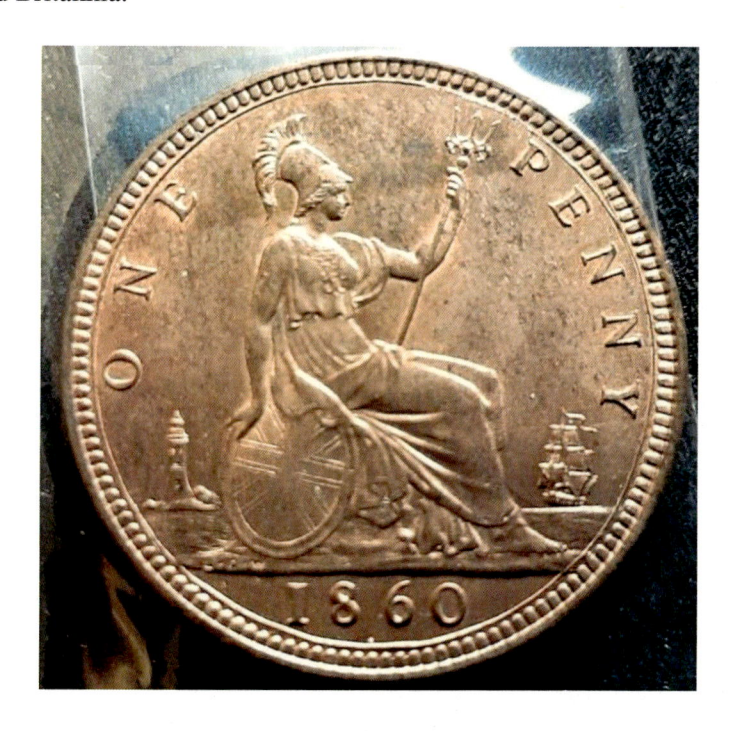

--X--

C. Thomas TELFORD

Thomas Telford was a Scottish civil engineer and architect and 40 years Brindley's junior. He was a trained stonemason and a noted builder of roads, bridges and canals. He came from an extremely poor family and went on to become the **godfather of civil engineering**. His vision and creativity were the prime factors behind the architecture of bridges, roads and canals of the 18th century.

Thomas TELFORD (1757 – 1834)
by George PATTEN. [Courtesy of the Resource Centre, Glasgow Museums].

1782   Telford moved to London, met two Scottish architects, (one of whom was **Sir William Chambers)**, who were involved in the building of Somerset House: they accepted him to join the team. The following year, he met up with a childhood friend and future very wealthy benefactor, **Sir William Pulteney**, one of Britain's richest men, architectural sponsor, (notably in Bath) and who rapidly became his patron. By 1784, Telford was working in Portsmouth docks learning the great variety of skills of construction and civil engineering necessary for boat building.

1786 -1792 Telford turned his competent hands to many different areas of engineering; the stone Montford Bridge over the River Severn, conversion of a Norman motte and bailey at Shrewsbury Castle, and overall, Pulteney put a great number of projects his way with each successful project earning him a reputation as the 'man for all engineering projects'. One of his greatest projects was pioneering the building of bridges in iron and not stone. The following year, he was charged with the construction of the **Ellesmere Canal**, involving the construction of the **Pontcysyllte Aqueduct**, which took the water course 36m (121 ft) above the River Dee with a span of 305m (1007 ft).

1803 Telford returned to Scotland to construct the **Caledonian Canal**, which although a very prestigious project giving employment to local Scots, was a failure in commercial terms; overshooting its budget and taking ten years to finish, being 3 years late. By this time ship design had enlarged and the canal was a catastrophic failure being too narrow to take the bigger craft.

1820s His reputation as a canal engineer continued and he returned to England with a highly ambitious project of joining **Birmingham to Ellesmere Port**. He was the first to ignore contours and cut his waterways directly using locks to raise and lower levels and it was during the middle years of the 1820s that he set about the Midlands end of his scheme with the new canal being opened in 1827, which also included the enlargement of the Rotton Park Pool into the Reservoir, we know today.

Professional jealously on the part of Telford hindered the building of the **Avon Gorge Bridge by Brunel.** Telford, being the first President of the Institution of Civil Engineering was asked to be chairman of the committee to appoint a designer and engineer, but he consistently blocked Brunel's appointment many times until a public outcry forced him to submit.

1826 However, his greatest personal bridge success was the construction of the iron **Menai Suspension Bridge**, essentially being done at the same time as the **Birmingham Canal Main Line**.

He developed a reputation for ingenious design and strong, long-lasting road building in his lifetime creating over 1000 miles throughout the country, for which he received the nickname from a poet friend, Robert Southey, of 'Colossus of Roads'. It was Telford who proposed that road surfaces should have a camber to assist drainage.

1834 Thomas Telford returned to London to live during the escalation of failing health. He died in 1834, failing to see the completion of his vast canal project, **the Shropshire Union** and is buried in Westminster Abbey. [*REF: 136*]

His designing supremacy was unchallenged and he created some of Britain's finest roads and bridges. He introduced the concept of suspension bridges and experimented with cast iron as a bridge material. His constructions established connections among different people and their cultures. People were able to migrate from one place to another through roads and bridges to earn a living and lead a better life. He was a visionary who managed to look ahead of his time. He will always be remembered for his magnificent expertise and significant contribution towards the progress of mankind. [*REF: 42, 43*]

--X--

5. OTHER MEN OF THE BIRMINGHAM LUNAR SOCIETY

A. LUNAR SOCIETY OF BIRMINGHAM

1765   The LUNAR SOCIETY OF BIRMINGHAM, firstly being called the **Lunar Circle**, starting in 1765 and was an informal dinner club of 18th century intellectuals, many being scientists, philosophers and industrialists, who were at the forefront of the Industrial Revolution and who had been colleagues, great friends and joined by family marriages since the 1750s.

1775   It was not until 1775, that the formal name of the **Lunar Society** was given to this formidable group who met on the night of a full moon, which offered them clearer light for their journey home after the dinner. They used to meet at a variety of venues but predominantly the homes of **Erasmus Darwin** in Lichfield, **Matthew Boulton**'s home of Soho House and **Samuel John Galton**'s home at **Great Barr Hall**. This small tribute to these great men is only a tug of a forelock to them and relates to those who had a connection with the canal system of the Birmingham Canal Network, the BCN.

The Lunar Society was not free from the problems of clubs today in as much support waned amongst the members in their attendances. It seemed to befall a hard nucleus of regular attenders that kept it alive. Fourteen individuals are known to have attended the meetings regularly:

Matthew BOULTON – **Erasmus DARWIN** – Thomas DAY – Richard Lovell EDGEWORTH [see p.140] – **Samuel John GALTON** – Robert Augustus JOHNSON – **James KEIR** – **Joseph PRIESTLEY** – **William SMALL** – Jonathan STOKES – **James WATT** – Josiah WEDGWOOD – John WHITEHURST – William WITHERING

Other notable members from the industrialists were:
Richard KIRWAN – **John SMEATON** – **John BASKERVILLE** – John WYATT – John ASH – **James BRINDLEY** – Alexander BLAIR – Joseph WRIGHT – Benjamin FRANKLIN

Although these monthly meetings were important, many of the members, particularly those local to Birmingham, met regularly and discussed matters together and it is thought by some that the monthly meeting were used for representatives of larger groups to meet and take matters forward to the celebrated inner circle of Boulton, Watt *[see p.36]* and Small *(below)*.

1776   Matthew Boulton had become pivotal in the reliability of holding meetings and is recorded to have stated before a meeting:
"to make many Motions to the Members respecting new Laws, and regulations, such as will tend to prevent the decline of a society which I hope will be lasting."

However, this pivotal importance was matched by his need to attend his own business as it coincided with the pinnacle of his steam engine development and thus he was frequently absent from his own meetings.

1791   Members came and went but certain incidents influenced the decline. One of these was that Joseph **Priestley** had come to Birmingham, become a member but was victim of 1791 riots called the **Priestley Riots**, when he was forced to flee the city with his home of **Moseley Hall** being set on fire by an angry mob; the aetiology of such dissent seems to be complex but the proximity of the French Revolution of 1789 was more than a coincidence.

1813   Eventually, the society fizzled out.

Wikipedia records: *Historian Jenny Uglow wrote of the lasting impact of the Society:*

The Lunar Society['s] ... members have been called the fathers of the Industrial Revolution ... [T]he importance of this particular Society stems from its pioneering work in experimental chemistry, physics, engineering, and medicine, combined with leadership in manufacturing and commerce, and with political and social ideals. Its members were brilliant representatives of the informal scientific web which cut across class, blending the inherited skills of craftsmen with the theoretical advances of scholars, a key factor in Britain's leap ahead of the rest of Europe.

Soho House.

MOONSTONES: [REF: 80] [grid reference SP062949] Carved in 1998, placed and unveiled the following year in the carpark of supermarket ASDA in Queslett Road, Birmingham are 9 sandstone memorial stones dedicated to nine members of the Lunar Society:

> Josiah WEDGEWOOD (1769-1843)
> Eramus DARWIN (1731-1802)
> Samuel John GALTON (1753-1832)
> William MURDOCK (1754-1839)
> Matthew BOULTON (1728-1809)
> James WATT (1736-1819)
> Joseph PRIESTLEY (1733-1804)
> James KEIR (1735-1820)
> William WITHERING (1741-1799)

B. MEMBERS OF THE LUNAR SOCIETY

The members explored here were essentially associated in some way, either directly or loosely with the Birmingham Canal. The total membership was far too complex to comment in this context.

a. Erasmus DARWIN (1731-1802) [REF: 112]

Erasmus Darwin (1770) by Joseph Wright of Derby [kind permission of Birmingham Museum & Art Gallery]

Erasmus Darwin was not directly associated with the Birmingham Canal (apart from a generic design he made for a canal boat hoist). However, he was an over branching umbrella figure whose involvement with the Birmingham Lunar Society was integral with its function and whose affinity acted as a catalyst for original thought by all participants. He was primarily an English physician, physiologist, naturalist, philosopher, poet, inventor and staunch anti-slave abolitionist – *[that is all!]*. His family connections spread through the Lunar group by marriage and kin, being connected to the Samuel Tertius Galton, Josiah Wedgewood and Thomas Day, (a writer and man of considerable eccentricity). Furthermore, he was grandfather to the famous Charles Darwin. He married twice produced at least 14 children and possibly more by different women if rumours were to be believed. He was a great friend of **Benjamin Franklin**, an American statesman, with whom he showed support for the latter's quest for the American Independence. Through Franklin, **William Small** (see below) returned to Britain and settled in Birmingham as a physician and was introduced to the Lunar Society.

----

b. Matthew BOULTON (1728-1809) [REF: 115]

Matthew Boulton. (1728-1809) (Courtesy of Birmingham Museum & Art Gallery)

1728   **Matthew Boulton** unlike most of his circle, was born in Birmingham to a small-metal 'toy' manufacturer, also Matthew.

1743   At the age of 15, he left school

1745   Boulton had invented a technique of inlaying enamel into buckles, which through their popularity, he started exporting to France, after which, they were returned to Britain as the latest chic French style.

1749   Matthew Boulton married a distant cousin from Lichfield, **Mary Robinson**, daughter of a wealthy mercer (fabric merchant) and later that year after his father made him a partner in the family business, he and Mary moved to the Snow Hill area of Birmingham.

1757   **Matthew Boulton Snr.** retired leaving his son in total control of the business at the age of 29.

1759   Matthew Snr died in the same year that Mary Boulton died having lost three babies during the decade. During that year Matthew Jnr took control of his father's not inconsiderable wealth and toy making business

1760   Matthew Boulton married his wife's sister, **Anne Robinson**. Needless to say, this union was opposed by the brother Luke, "who feared Boulton would control much of the Robinson family fortune." [REF: 115]

1761   Boulton leased 5.3 hectares (13 acres) of an old mill on the Hockley Brook in **Soho**, just north of the centre of Birmingham and rapidly converted the site into his **Manufactory**. He then converted a cottage on the site into a residence called **Soho House**, firstly giving it over to some family members.

1762   Boulton put his first major business partner **John Fothergill** into Soho House. Fothergill was a very experienced trader who had travelled widely in France and Germany but as a partnership. They were not extraordinarily successful, despite having built one of Birmingham's major factories. [REF: 116]

1764 **Luke Robinson died** with the family estate passing to Anne with the obvious consequence Boulton ultimately did control the Robinson fortunes. It is fair to say that this vast fortune was put to immensely useful purpose and without it, the inventions of James Watt and others may never have come to fruition.

1766 Matthew Boulton evicted Fothergill from Soho House and went there himself to live. The same year he was a founding member of the **Birmingham Lunar Society**

1768 Boulton, like his contemporaries, was a great philanthropist and lover of Handel's music and he decided he would start a fund to raise money to build a hospital for Birmingham and his close physician friend, **Dr John Nash** (a fellow Lunar Society member). Putting these two facts together, Boulton ran a Birmingham Music Festival, which lasted over three days and raised large funds.

1769 The initial part of **Brindley's** new **Birmingham Canal** opened and passed close to Soho House and Manufactory. [It was finally all opened in 1771]. Boulton ironically was not in favour at first as he anticipated that the canal would abstract from the vital brook that fed his lake and Manufactory Mill. However, he did hedge his bets and bought three shares investment in the scheme when money was being raised. He later stated that : *"Our navigation goes on prosperously; the junction with the Wolverhampton Canal is complete, and we already sail to Bristol and to Hull."*

1770 **Matthew Robinson Boulton** was born to Matthew & Anne Boulton.

1770 Boulton visited the Royal Family and sold some ormolu to the **Queen Charlotte (wife of George III)**

1771 Wikipedia records words by Boulton: *"I am very desirous of becoming a great silversmith, yet I am determined not to take up that branch in the large way I intended, unless powers can be obtained to have a marking hall [assay office] at Birmingham."* He petitioned Parliament to request and justify the opening of an Assay office in Birmingham. There was considerable objection from London goldsmiths but he was successful and achieved the passing of an Act that enabled the setting up of offices in Sheffield and Birmingham. It is often stated that the reason Sheffield silver was marked by a crown and Birmingham an anchor is that the decision for these two silver hallmarks was derived from the venue of the deciding discussion having been a pub called the Crown and Anchor.

1775 Boulton bought the patents of James Watt's partner, **Dr John Roebuck**, *[see p. 38]* who had gone bust and settled on taking on 2/3 share in James Watt's business as settlement of a debt by Roebuck. Boulton was during this period very prolific from his Manufactory in Soho, producing very ornate works of art, some of it being purchased from Wedgewood's factory in Stoke on Trent.

1776 **Boulton & Watt** erected two new engines with favourable publicity.

1778 Adequate funds had been raised to build the Birmingham General Hospital

1779 Boulton & Watt took on **William Murdoch** *[see p. 38-40, 160]* who went to Cornwall to manage their interests there as the popularity of the pumping engines was growing.

1779 Birmingham General Hospital opened

1782 **John Fothergill** died. In the same year, the firm modified Watt's pumping engine to work in a rotary motion thus adapting it for use in mills and factories. This was a massive and important diversification for the team, who had saturated the Cornwall tin mine industry. Orders poured in from around the world. Between 1775 and 1800, Boulton & Watt had produced 450 engines. This development of an efficient steam engine opened the world to develop large-scale industry with the large British industrial cities expanding exponentially.

Soho Manufactory Ormolu. (Grace's Guide)

1784   The Birmingham Triennial Festival started on the back of Boulton's initial three-day concert of 1768, initially being held in St. Philip's Cathedral and Theatre Royal in New Street but the venues rapidly became inadequate, which became a lever to the city having a proper concert hall in 1834 in the form of the Town Hall. [REF: 118]

1785   Both Boulton and Watt were elected to the Royal Society as Fellows

1789   **Samuel Wyatt** was commissioned to expand and upgrade Soho House and grounds. Today, a Grade 2* Listed building. [REF: 117]

1794   **Boulton was elected High Sheriff of Staffordshire**. He had for a long time concerned himself with the crime of the city and had put up finances to support the local militia. [REF: 115]

1797   Boulton was awarded the license to produce coins of the realm and turned out one and two penny pieces made of copper.

1800   Both **Boulton and Watt** retired from their business as the patents ran out in that year and they handed the control of the Foundry and Manufactory over to their sons, Matthew Robinson Boulton and James Watt Jnr.

1806   Boulton's copper coinage came to an end.

1808   The Soho Mint made 90,000,000-coin pieces for the East India Company. He said:

> *"Of all the mechanical subjects I ever entered upon, there is none in which I ever engaged with so much ardour as that of bringing to perfection the art of coining."*

1809   **Boulton's health deteriorated rapidly and he died**, being buried in the church yard of St Mary's Church, Handsworth, Birmingham.

--X--

c. **James WATT. (1736-1819) [REF: 113]**

James Watt (1736-1819). By Carl Frederik von Breda

James Watt was reputedly one of the country's greatest engineers and thinkers.

1736   He was born at Greenock, Scotland, the eldest son of five children to a Presbyterian shipwright and ship-owner father and an influential and forceful mother of some standing. After his schooling, James worked with his father in the design workshop, where he showed considerable originality in engine modelling.

1754   Watt's mother died when he was 18 and with his father's health declining, he travelled to London and trained as an instrument maker.

1755   He returned to Glasgow with the intention of setting up his own business designing and making instruments. Over a short period of time, he was able to use some astronomical instruments bequeathed to Glasgow University by a Jamaican astrologist, **Alexander Macfarlane.**

1759   Watt went into partnership with an architect, **John Craig**, with whom he made musical instruments and toys, employing 16 workers.

1764   James Watt married his cousin **Margaret Miller**; they had 5 children, two of them made it to adulthood. James Jnr. ultimately was to take over his father's partnership in Boulton & Watt and the great man's esteemed workshop at the beginning of the 19th century.

1765   Partner, John Craig died

1772   Wife, **Margaret died in childbirth**.

1777   James Watt married again; to **Ann MacGregor**, with whom he had a further two children. They moved to Birmingham. Watt became dependent on a fellow associate inventor Dr Roebuck, who went bankrupt but the company was rescued by one **Matthew Boulton** of the Soho Manufactory, who bought all the patent rights and restored financial equilibrium.

The story of the Soho Foundry is already recorded [p.32 to 49] and shall not be repeated here. James Watt built up a long friendship with many contemporary inventors and was a great speaker but a man of modesty with poor business acumen. It was said of James Watt, by **Humphry Davy,** (of Davy Lamp fame) that:

"Those who consider James Watt only as a great practical mechanic form a very erroneous idea of his character; he was equally distinguished as a natural philosopher and a chemist, and his inventions demonstrate his profound knowledge of those sciences, and that peculiar characteristic of genius, the union of them for practical application"

1796   **The Soho Foundry opened.**

1800   James Watt retired in 1800 at the time his patents were coming to an end and the company's success was booming with the production of 41 large engines. He lived at **Heathfield Hall,** in Handsworth, Birmingham, where he created a garret workshop to work on many different inventions.

1819   James Watt died at the age of 83 and was buried in Handsworth Parish Church graveyard.

Soho Foundry after the name change of 1849 from Boulton & Watt to James Watt & Co. (Courtesy of Avery-Berkel)

---

   d.   **William MURDOCH (1754-1839) [REF: 114]**

William Murdoch (1754-1839)

1754 **William Murdoch** was born in Ayrshire, Scotland, being the third of seven children of a millwright, John Murdoch, whom he assisted in the mill. He had an excellent schooling and possessed a natural comprehension of mathematics and mechanics.

1763 At the age of 9, he and his father built a wooden horse on wheels, which was a hand-cranked propelled tricycle . Although no documentation survives, it is said that as a young man, he experimented with heating coal gas in a copper kettle.

1773 At the age of 23, **Murdoch travelled to Birmingham** to ask for a job working with the famous James Watt. Apparently, Boulton was extremely impressed by the wooden hat Murdoch had designed and wore, which he had turned on a lathe. He started to work in the Pattern Shop of Boulton & Watt.

1779 Boulton, on writing to Watt spoke of Murdoch,
"I think William Murdoch a valuable man and deserves every civility and encouragement." [REF: 60].

During that year, Boulton & Watt sent him to Cornwall to manage the installation and maintenance of their many new engines that were being bought by the Cornish Tin Mines. Watt described the company policy as :

> *"Our profits arise not from making the engine, but from a certain proportion of the savings in fuel which we make over any common engine, that raises the same quantity of water to the same height."*

1781   There is written evidence that Murdoch invented a **'Sun & Planet Gear'** which permitted the power of steam to achieve a 'rotative or circular motion around an axis or centre'. This meant that 'motion was given to the wheels of mills' by converting the vertical motion of a steam driven beam into circular motion using a planet (cogwheel) fixed at one end of a rod connected to the beam of the engine'. The credit went to James Watt, who patented it that year.

1782   Boulton said:
> *"We want more Murdocks, for of all others he is the most active man and best engineer erector I ever saw."* [When Murdoch arrived in England from Scotland, he changed the spelling of his name to Murdock in an attempt to be accepted locally.]

1782   Murdock and Watt collaborated on several inventions and improvements concerning engines

1784   His best hidden design in Britain, was the **first working model of a steam carriage**, which his employers tried to discourage but hedged their bets with patenting the same. Murdoch's working model of his steam carriage still survives in **the Birmingham Thinktank Museum**. This is the model that caused so much alarm when he first piloted it one dark night around the streets of Redruth. [see p. 38]

1784   Murdoch experimented with **gases and chemistry**. He made **'iron cement'** from ammonium chloride and iron filings. The final product was used on boilers and joints to form a durable seal

1791   He filed a patent on the production of aniline dyes (first industrial purple) & coatings

1792   Murdoch will be remembered for his application of **gas lighting in replacing tallow and oil** to produce artificial light.

1794   **He was producing coal gas from a small retort** containing heated coals. His house in Redruth was the first domestic building to be lit by gas.

1798   Murdoch returned from Cornwall to work again at the **Soho Foundry, where he lit the factory with gas light,** making it the first one in the world to operate in this new invention

1799   He invented a **steam wheel**, a precursor of the steam turbine.

1808   The Royal Society had a presentation by Murdoch entitled **"Account of the Application of Gas from Coal to Economical Purposes"**

1810   He became a partner in the Boulton & Watt business, joining the two sons of the original firm

1815   He designed and installed the **first gravity-fed piped hot water system** since Roman times at Leamington Spa Baths

1817   Murdoch moved into his large new house **'Fair House'**, Sycamore Hill, Queens Head Road, Handsworth, Birmingham.

1830   The partnership with Boulton & Watt company was dissolved due to his diminishing health and economic failures in the company.

1839   **William Murdoch died** at the age of 85 and is buried in St Mary's Church, Handsworth

----

e.   **William SMALL. (1734-1775) [REF: 82]**

William Small, [1765 c.] by Tilly Kettle

William Small is not a name much known in the West Midlands but he was another eminent Scotsman who went to the United States to become confident and advisor to **Thomas Jefferson**, Third President of the United States. Jefferson said of William Small:

> *"a man profound in most of the useful branches of science, with a happy talent of communication, correct and gentlemanly manners, and a large and liberal mind... from his conversation I got my first views of the expansion of science and of the system of things in which we are placed."*

Small returned to Britain in 1764 with a letter of introduction to Matthew Boulton from **Benjamin Franklin**, when he set up a medical practice in Birmingham, became a great friend of Boulton as well as being his physician. He became a close friend of **Erasmus Darwin** and **Thomas Day**. He was integral with his colleague, **John Ash** in setting up the Birmingham General Hospital. [REF: 82]

----

f. James KEIR (1735-1820). [REF: 89]

James Keir (1735-1820)

1735 Born in Sterling, an 18th child! He studied medicine at the University of Edinburgh where he met his lifetime friend, Erasmus Darwin.

1757 At age of 22, he took a commission in the army but after 10 years resigned feeling a lack of sympathy by his colleagues for his scientific bent. Ultimately, he came to West Bromwich to study chemistry and geology.

1768 Keir resigned his commission but kept one sympathetic friend from the forces, **Captain Alexander Blair**.

1772 He took a long lease on an established glassworks at Amblecote, Stourbridge, with some colleagues, two being Samuel Skey, (a vitriol manufacturer in Bewdley) and John Taylor, (a Birmingham manufacturer).

1776 He wrote a renowned paper, entitled "On the Crystallisations observed on Glass", which was read to the Royal Society and published in its Philosophical Transactions (1776).

1768 Having been good friends with **Matthew Boulton** he met **James Watt** at the former's home of **Soho House**.

1778 Keir resigned from his glass undertakings and took over control of **Soho Manufactory**, refusing a partnership based on 'poor financial risk'.

1780 **Keir and Alexander Blair** (now retired from the army) started a **chemical works at Tipton** manufacturing alkali from Potassium sulphate and Sodium Sulphate, and subsequently they commenced a soap factory based on their discovery.

1780 **Joseph Priestley** visited Birmingham and **worked with Keir** on gases and in particular carbon dioxide with its different properties from atmospheric air.

1785 Keir was elected to be a **Member of the Royal Society of London**

1787 He sent some new findings from "Experiments on the Congelation of the Vitriolic Acid" to the Royal Society.

1788 His paper of 1787 was followed up with "Remarks on the Principle of Acidity, Decomposition of Water and Phlogiston". The same year another paper by him appeared in the Transactions of the Society of Arts entitled "Fossil Alkali".

1789 Keir published Part 1 of his "**Dictionary of Chemistry".**

1790 He communicated to the Royal Society "Experiments & Observations on the Dissolution of Metals in Acids and their Precipitations".

1794 Keir and Blair established the Tividale Colliery on the border of Dudley and Tipton.

1798 Keir wrote an article in Stebing Shaw's important History of Staffordshire on the **"Mineralogy of Staffordshire"**

1800 Whilst visiting the Watt family in Birmingham, Sir Humphry DAVY, (of Davy Lamp fame and 1st Baronet and President of the Royal Society) met James Keir.

1807 There was a house fire at Keir's home, Finchpath Hall, Charlemont, West Bromwich whilst he was away

1820 **James Keir died** and is buried in West Bromwich

Sculptor William Bloye's gilt sculpture of the three titans Boulton, Watt and Murdoch set outside the old Registrar's Office, Broad Street, Birmingham. Currently shrouded during massive building works of 2020

APPENDIX

Soho Railway Bridge, Merry Hill railway viaduct and environs, Soho 1946

PART A   The Statutory Legislation for declaring a scheduled Monument

PART B   1888 Surveyed Ordnance Survey 6" : Mile Maps (annotated)

PART C   Paintings & Sketches by the author

PART D.   References

PART A – THE STATUTORY LEGISLATION FOR DECLARING A SCHEDULED MONUMENT

Why should a building be defined as being A Scheduled Monument? This need is clearly outlined in a series of Historic England and Department for Culture, Media & Sport (DCMS documents) and dates from 1913. Aspects relevant to Soho Foundry are excerpted here before demonstrating the failure of application on page 169.

Historic England: - Scheduled Monuments [REF: 1]
- *"Scheduling is our oldest form of heritage protection. It began in 1913, although its roots go as far back as the 1882 Ancient Monuments Protection Act, when a 'Schedule' (hence the term 'scheduling') of almost exclusively prehistoric monuments deserving of state protection was first compiled."*
- ***Scheduling is the selection of nationally important archaeological sites.*** *Although archaeology is all around us, Scheduled sites form a carefully chosen sample of them,* ***which are closely managed.***

Historic England: Industrial Sites [REF: 2]
1. HISTORICAL SUMMARY: 1.5 1700-1800
- p11. By the closing years of the eighteenth-century specialist foundries producing steam engines and other machinery were being established. **Notable** amongst these were Boulton and Watt's Soho Foundry at Smethwick in the West Midlands. Despite wholesale clearance of most of these sites, *the archaeological investigation of surviving buildings and surrounding of Boulton and Watt's Soho Foundry, is demonstrating their archaeological potential. [REF:2; p 11]*
- p12. Demand was further compounded by the development of the steam engine. … but it was not **until James Watt's 1769** patent and other subsequent improvements that the steam engine was widely adopted away from the coalfields. [REF: 2; p12]

2. OVERARCHING CONSIDERATIONS
2.1 Scheduling & Protection.
- p19. Scheduling, *through triggering careful control and the involvement of Historic England,* ***ensures that the long-term interests of a site are placed first.*** It is warranted for sites with real claims to national importance which are the most significant remains in terms of their key place in telling our national story, **and the need for close management of their archaeological potential. Scheduled monuments possess a high order of significance: they derive this from their archaeological and historic interest.**
- The Schedule aims to capture a representative sample of nationally important sites, rather than be an inclusive compendium of all such assets.
- Given that archaeological sensitivity is all around us, **it is important that all means of protecting archaeological remains are recognised.**

2.2 Heritage Assets & National Importance
- p20. Paragraph 194 and footnote 63 of the National Planning Policy Framework (July 2018) states **that any harm to, or loss of, the significance of a designated heritage asset should require clear and convincing justification and for assets of the highest significance should be wholly exceptional;**
- These assets are defined as having National Importance (NI). This is the latest articulation of a principle first raised in PPG16 (1990-2010) and later in PPS5 (2010-2012).

2.3 Selection Criteria

p20. The particular considerations used by the Secretary of State when determining whether sites of all types are suitable for statutory designation through scheduling are set out in their Scheduled Monuments Policy Statement. [ref: 5]

3. SPECIFIC CONSIDERATIONS
3.8 Historic Importance p.23 Where a site is associated with a famous and especially an innovative industrialist, engineer, or company, or saw new processes pioneered, this may add to its significance. That will be especially so where innovation has impacted on, and can be read in, the form of the asset.

3.9 Group Value
p.23 Another form of group value occurs where there are a number of different industrial concerns clustered together, especially where there were historical linkages.

3.10 Survival & Condition
 p23. ... **given that the aim of scheduling is to secure the long-term preservation of a monument for the benefit of future generations, ...**

Historic England; Heritage at Risk; Soho Foundry [REF: 9]
SOHO FOUNDRY HERITAGE AT RISK
"Foundry built in 1795: the world's first integrated steam engine manufactory, established by Boulton & Watt. Historic England and the Local Authority grant **aided a temporary roof to stabilise the structure in 2009.** That roof is still protecting the core historic building."

Dept. for Culture, Media & Sport: - Scheduled Monuments [REF: 3, 10]
- 15. The preservation of Scheduled Monuments often requires little or no direct intervention, but on occasion this is necessary and / or desirable. To help protect them from uncontrolled change or unauthorised geophysical surveys, the 1979 Act introduced two dedicated consent regimes: Scheduled Monument Consent and Section 42 licences
- 16. *It is a criminal offence to demolish, destroy, damage, remove, repair, alter or add to a Scheduled Monument,* or to undertake flooding or tipping operations on land in, on or under which there is a Scheduled Monument, unless prior consent has been obtained from the Secretary of State in the form of Scheduled Monument Consent (SMC). *It is also an offence to fail to comply with the terms of such consents.*
- 24. In certain circumstances English Heritage can offer 'funding of last resort' to help ensure the recording of unexpected discoveries of national importance that are threatened by imminent damage or destruction – including those identified during the implementation of SMC.
-

ANNEX 1 – Principles of Selection for Scheduled Monuments.
p10 Their importance can be gauged by the level of heritage interest they hold for current and future generations. This is defined in terms of their archaeological, architectural, artistic, historic or traditional interest, particularly their:

> • Archaeological Interest in carrying out expert investigations at some point into the evidence places hold, or potentially may hold, of past human activity. Monuments with archaeological interest form a primary source of evidence relating to the substance and evolution of places, plus the people and cultures that made them.

• Historic Interest in how the present can be connected through a place to past people, events and aspects of life. Monuments with historic interest provide a material record of our nation's prehistory and history, whether by association or through illustration.

P11. *Fragility / vulnerability. The significance of some monuments can be destroyed by a single ploughing or unsympathetic treatment, while there are standing structures of particular form or complexity whose significance can be severely reduced by neglect or careless treatment; vulnerable monuments of this nature could particularly benefit from the legal protection that scheduling confers.*

ANNEX 4 Q&A
P15. Is the condition of nationally important monuments regularly monitored?
- **The condition of Scheduled Monuments is monitored as part of English Heritage's Heritage at Risk programme.** Local government archaeological services, plus independent national & local heritage organisations and community groups, can also play important roles in their curation, plus that of non-scheduled but nationally important monuments.
- **The Secretary of State has powers to repair Scheduled Monuments and to compulsorily acquire ancient monuments deemed to be at risk.**

MAP SEARCH – SOHO FOUNDRY
Closer examination of the Historic England Scheduled Monument area of Soho Foundry shows there to be two separate listed items within the Scheduled Monument site:
- The Foundry Pattern Stores & Erecting Shops [Grade II*]
- Towpath Bridge at Soho Foundry [Grade II]

(Grade II* buildings are particularly important buildings of more than special interest; 5.8% of listed buildings are Grade II*)

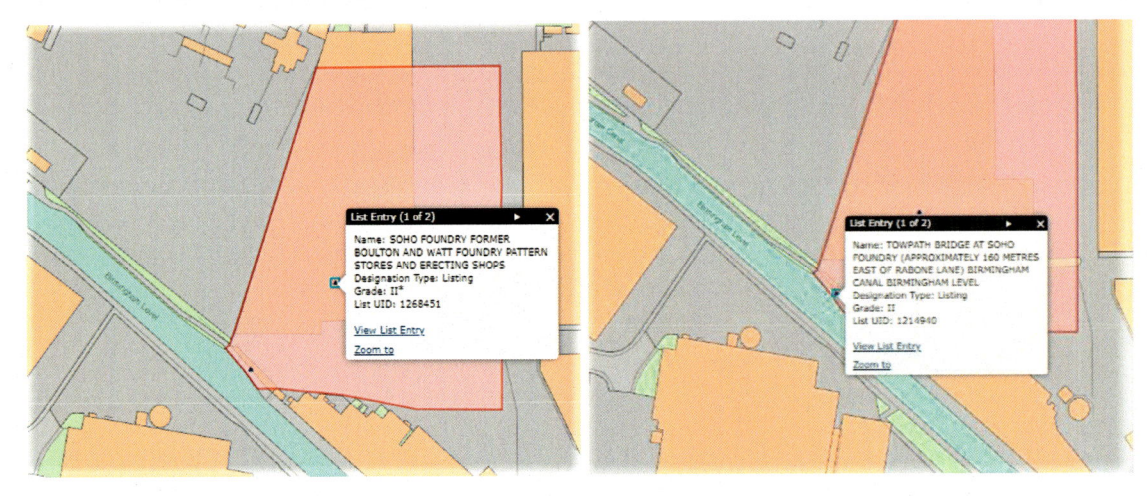

RESUMEE OF LEGISLATIVE CRITERIA FOR A SCHEDULED MONUMENT WITHIN THE CONTEXT OF SOHO FOUNDRY

"Scheduling is our oldest form of heritage protection.

Scheduling is the selection of nationally important archaeological sites. ..... which are closely managed.

By the closing years of the eighteenth-century specialist foundries producing steam engines and other machinery were being established. <u>*Notable*</u> *amongst these were Boulton and Watt's Soho Foundry at Smethwick*

it was not until James Watt's 1769 patent and other subsequent improvements that the steam engine was widely adopted away from the coalfields.

Scheduling, through triggering careful control and the involvement of Historic England, ensures that the long-term interests of a site are placed first

the need for close management of their archaeological potential. Scheduled monuments possess a high order of significance: they derive this from their archaeological and historic interest.

it is important that all means of protecting archaeological remains are recognised.

Where a site is associated with a famous and especially an innovative industrialist, engineer or company, or saw new processes pioneered, this may add to its significance.

Another form of group value occurs where there are a number of different industrial concerns clustered together, especially where there were historical linkages.

given that the aim of scheduling is to secure the long-term preservation of a monument for the benefit of future generations, ...

Historic England and the Local Authority grant aided a temporary roof to stabilise the structure in 2009. That roof is still protecting the core historic building.

It is a criminal offence to demolish, destroy, damage, remove, repair, alter or add to a Scheduled Monument. It is also an offence to fail to comply with the terms of such consents.

Fragility / vulnerability. The significance of some monuments can be destroyed by a single ploughing or unsympathetic treatment, while there are standing structures of particular form or complexity whose significance can be severely reduced by neglect or careless treatment; vulnerable monuments of this nature could particularly benefit from the legal protection that scheduling confers.

The condition of Scheduled Monuments is monitored as part of English Heritage's Heritage at Risk programme.

Local government archaeological services, plus independent national & local heritage organisations and community groups, can also play important roles in their curation, plus that of non-scheduled but nationally important monuments.

The Secretary of State has powers to repair Scheduled Monuments and to compulsorily acquire ancient monuments deemed to be at risk.

The remains of the Boulton and Watt Soho foundry and mint survive well!
[HE   Listing Summary]

HE - REMAINS OF BOULTON & WATT SOHO FOUNDRY [REF: 12]

Remains of the Boulton and Watt Soho foundry and mint, Birmingham Canal, Smethwick

Overview

Heritage Category: Scheduled Monument
List Entry Number: 1021388
Date first listed: 17-Apr-2008
Map

District: Sandwell (Metropolitan Authority)
National Grid Reference: SP 03421 88863

Reasons for Designation   The remains of the Soho foundry **provide a unique example of an early industrial Foundry. Soho was one of the first purpose-built steam engine manufactories in the world**, founded by the pioneering firm of Boulton and Watt and associated with other renowned engineers and new techniques. William Murdoch, John Southern and Peter Ewart all worked for Boulton and Watt.

In establishing this ground-breaking manufactory Boulton and Watt established a format which was copied and developed by many later steam engine firms and general engineering concerns. At the date of its inception in 1795, the engineering industry had barely developed and the steam engine manufactory represented a pioneering venture of fundamental importance to the origins of an industry for which Britain became renowned.

- The site may be considered as one of the founders of the great industrial lineage in which Britain was pre-eminent in the world for much of the C19.
- In addition to steam engines, Boulton and Watt had important associations with the development of steamships from 1804 and the Boulton and Watt marine engine business was one of the most important in the country during the C19.
- Its most celebrated contract was the provision of the screw engines for Brunel's Great Eastern, which successfully laid the first transatlantic cables.
- In 1788 Boulton and Watt manufacturing was also the first to introduce steam powered mint machinery, which was then exported worldwide, for example to Mexico, Russia and India.
- The works were also the first gas-lit factory building in the world and responsible for pioneering the production of gas lighting equipment on a commercial basis. **The remains of the Boulton and Watt Soho foundry and mint survive well.**
- They will help to illuminate this pioneering phase of industrial development in the West Midlands.
- The significance of the site is enhanced by the exceptional archive associated with it which includes the papers of the Boulton and Watt company as well as the separate collections of the personal papers of James Watt and Matthew Boulton which are housed in the Birmingham City Reference Library.

PART B. HISTORIC ENGLAND GRADED LISTING ALONG THE BIRMINGHAM CANAL

Along this journey of the Birmingham Canal limbs as they pass through the often-forgotten gem of historical heritage called Smethwick there are:

   1 GRADE 1 Listed
   3 GRADE 2*
   23 GRADE 2
   2 SCHEDULED MONUMENTS

PAGE 28:   LIST ENTRY NUMBER 1977155 DATE FIRST LISTED 1987 **GRADE 2** "TOWPATH BRIDGE AT SP 036 884 (APPROXIMATELY 640 METRES SOUTH EAST OF RABONE LANE). BIRMINGHAM CANAL BIRMINGHAM LEVEL

PAGE 34:   LIST ENTRY 1268451 DATE FIRST LISTED 1996 **GRADE 2*** "**SCHEDULED MONUMENT** SOHO FOUNDRY FORMER BOULTON AND WATT FOUNDRY PATTERN STORES AND ERECTING SHOPS, FOUNDRY LANE"

PAGE 34:   LIST ENTRY 1214940 DATE FIRST LISTED 1987 **GRADE 2** "TOWPATH BRIDGE AT SOHO FOUNDRY (APPROXIMATELY 160 METRES EAST OF RABONE LANE) BIRMINGHAM CANAL BIRMINGHAM LEVEL

PAGE 67:   LIST ENTRY NUMBER 1214908 DATE FIRST LISTED 1987 **GRADE 2** "FOOTBRIDGE AT JUNCTION WITH WOLVERHAMPTON LEVEL (APPROXIMATELY 230 METRES EAST OF BRIDGE STREET) BIRMINGHAM CANAL BIRMINGHAM LEVEL"

PAGE 68:   LIST ENTRY NUMBER 1342672 DATE FIRST LISTED 1987 **GRADE 2** "FOOTBRIDGE AT JUNCTION WITH BIRMINGHAM CANAL,SMETHWICK JUNTION (APROXIMATELY 190 METRES EAST OF BRIDGE STREET) BIRMINGHAM LEVEL WOLVERHAMPTON LEVEL"

PAGE 74:   LIST ENTRIES 1077129, 1215330, 1077162 DATE FIRST LISTED 1987 **GRADE 2** "THREE SETS OF SMETHWICK LOCKS"

PAGE 85:   LIST ENTRY NUMBER 1077154 DATE FIRST LISTED 1978 **GRADE 2** "SMETHWICK NEW PUMPING HOUSE APPROXIMATELY 50 METRES NORTH OF BRASSHOUSE LANE BIRMINGHAM CANAL BIRMINGHAM LEVEL"

PAGE 88:   LIST ENTRY NUMBER 1391875 DATE FIRST LISTED 2007 **GRADE 2*** "SANDWELL SUMMIT BRIDGE"

PAGE 88:   LIST ENTRY NUMBER 1215275 DATE FIRST LISTED 1987 **GRADE 2** "RAILWAY BRIDGE 15 METRES NORTH OF SUMMIT BRIDGE/ROEBUCK LANE BIRMINGHAM CANAL WOLVERHAMPTON LEVEL

PAGE 95:   LIST ENTRY NUMBERS 1215249, 1342651, 1288230, 1077160, 13342645, DATE FIRST LISTED 1987 **GRADE 2** "THREE LOCKS & TWO FOOTBRIDGES , SPON LANE

LOCKS, WITH ATTACHED FOOTBRIDGE BIRMINGHAM CANAL WOLVERHAMPTON LEVEL"

PAGE 108:   LIST ENTRY NUMBER 1977161 DATE FIRST LISTED 1987 **GRADE 2** "STEWARD {STEWART} AQUEDUCT (APPROXIMATELY 400 METRES WEST OF SPON LANE SOUTH) BIRMINGHAM CANAL WOLVERHAMPTON LEVEL"

PAGE 111:   LIST ENTRY NUMBERS 1021387, 1077127, 1077153, 1214811, 1279456, 1287117, 1342646, 1977128. DATE FIRST LISTED 2005 GRADE 2, "HISTORIC ENGLAND LISTED THE CHANCE BROTHERS SITE WITH ITS BRIDGES AND RUINED BUILDINGS, DESPITE BEING IN A STATE OF POOR REPAIR" & ENTERED AS A **SCHEDULED MONUMENT IN 2005**".

PAGE 120:   LIST ENTRY NUMBER 1214833 DATE FIRST LISTED 1972 **GRADE 1** "GALTON BRIDGE INCLUDING ATTACHED RAILWAY BRIDGE SPAN, ROEBUCK LANE BIRMINGHAM CANAL BIRMINGHAM LEVEL"

PAGE 122:   LIST ENTRY NUMBER 1391126 DATE FIRST LISTED 2004 **GRADE 2** "RETAINING WALL TO FORMER CORPORATION YARD"

PAGE 123:   LIST ENTRY NUMBER 1391874 DATE FIRST LISTED 2007 **GRADE 2*** "ENGINE ARM AQUEDUCT, BIRMINGHAM CANAL WOLVERHAMPTON LEVEL"

PART C. 1888 SURVEY ORDNANCE SURVEY MAPS 6" : MILE
annotated to show industries along the Birmingham Canal

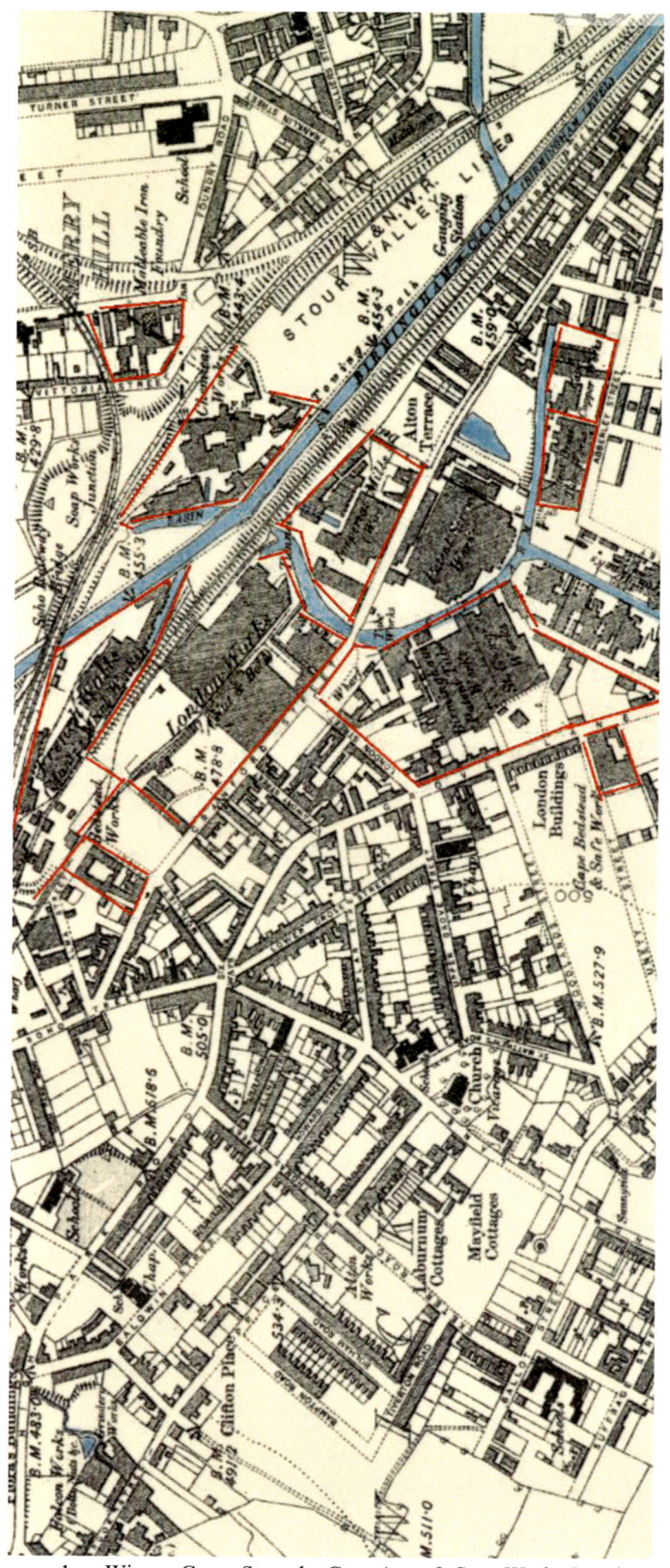

1. Winson Green Stop, the Cape Arm & Soap Works Junction

173

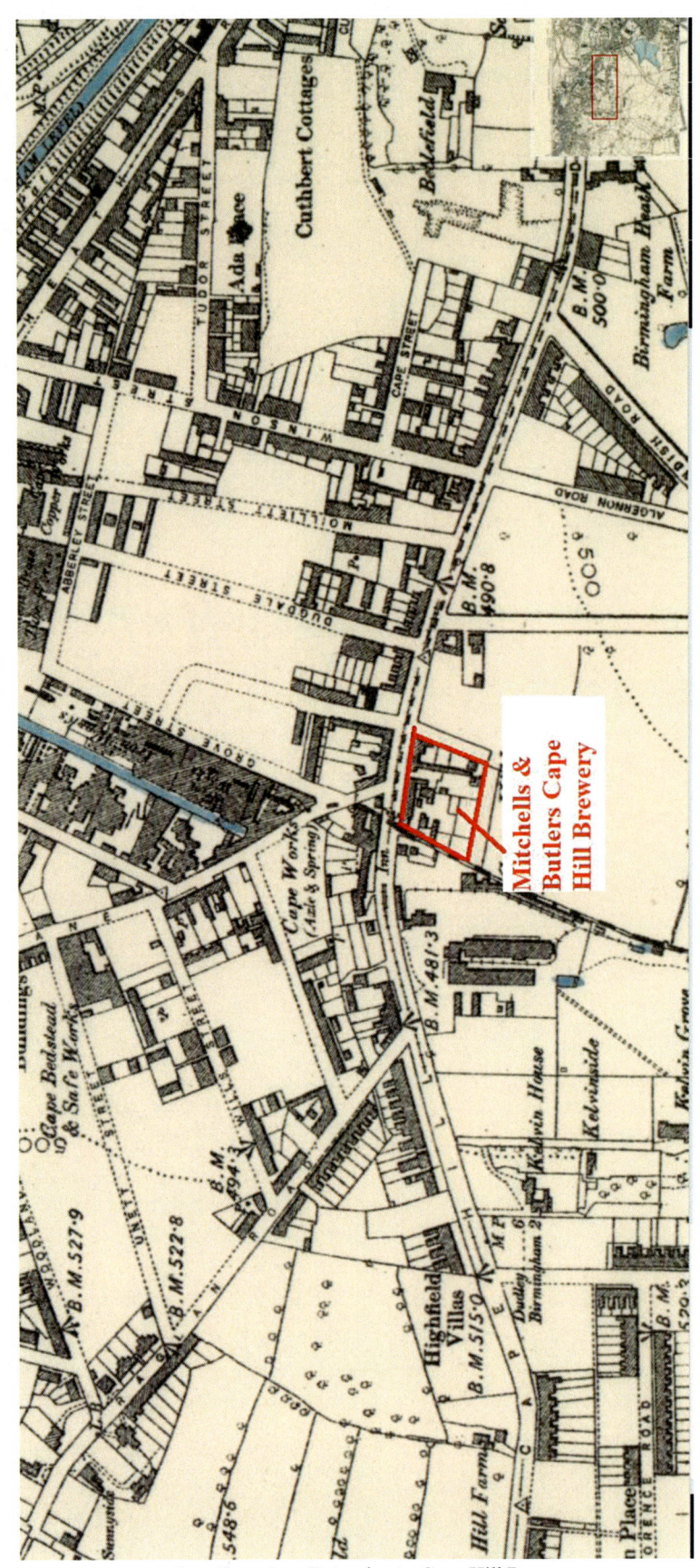

2. Cape Arm Extension to Cape Hill Brewery

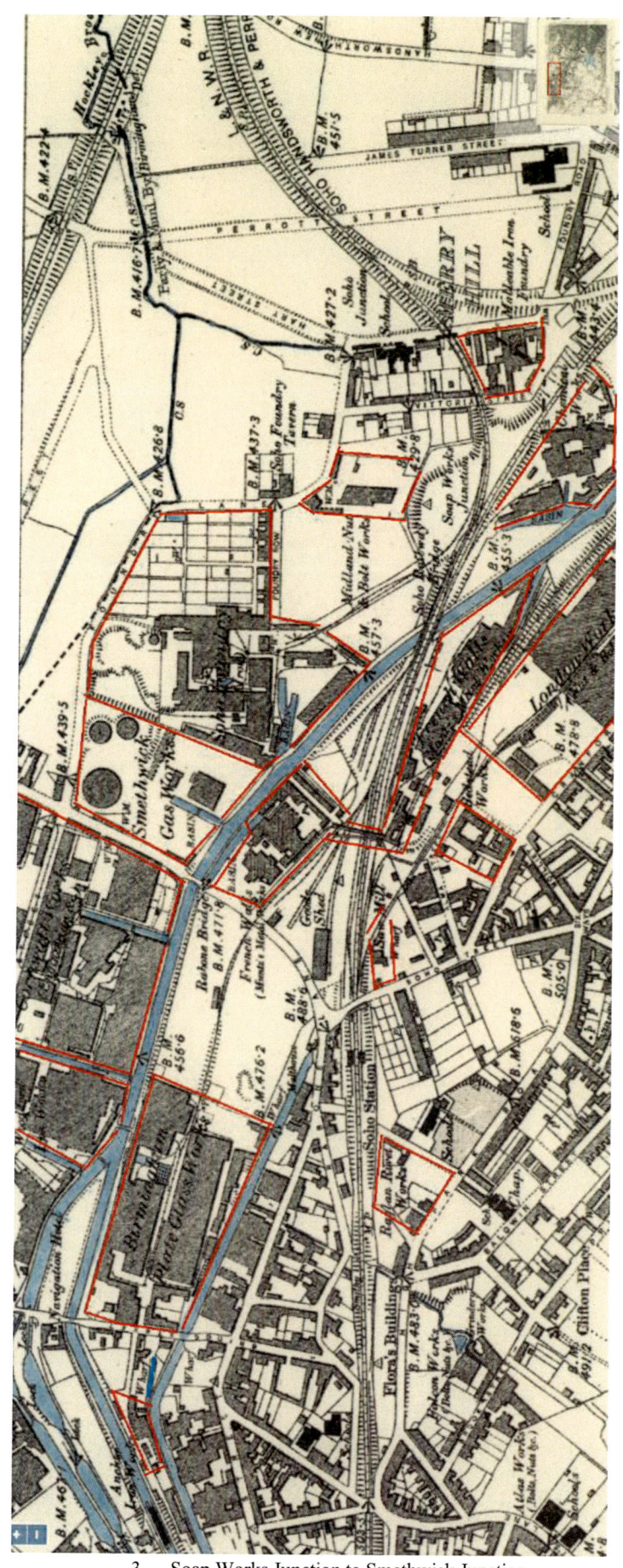

3. Soap Works Junction to Smethwick Junction

4. Smethwick Junction, Engine Aqueduct & Engine Arm

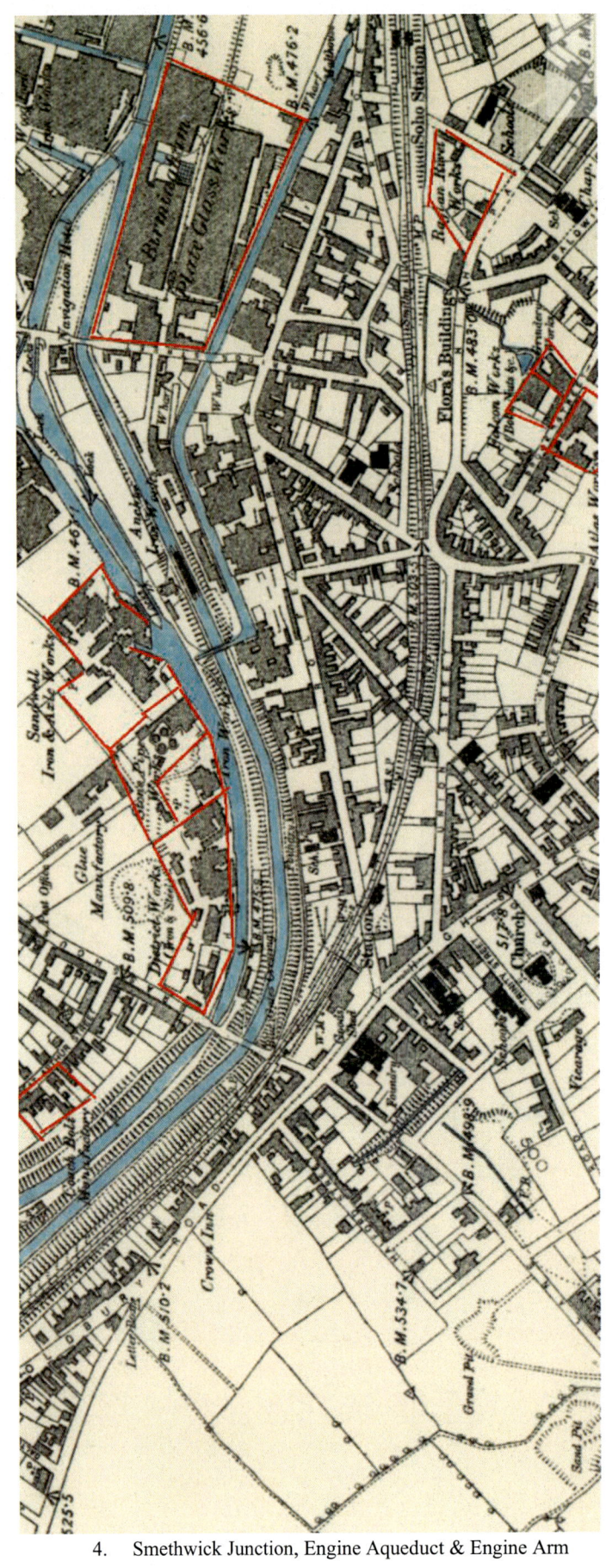

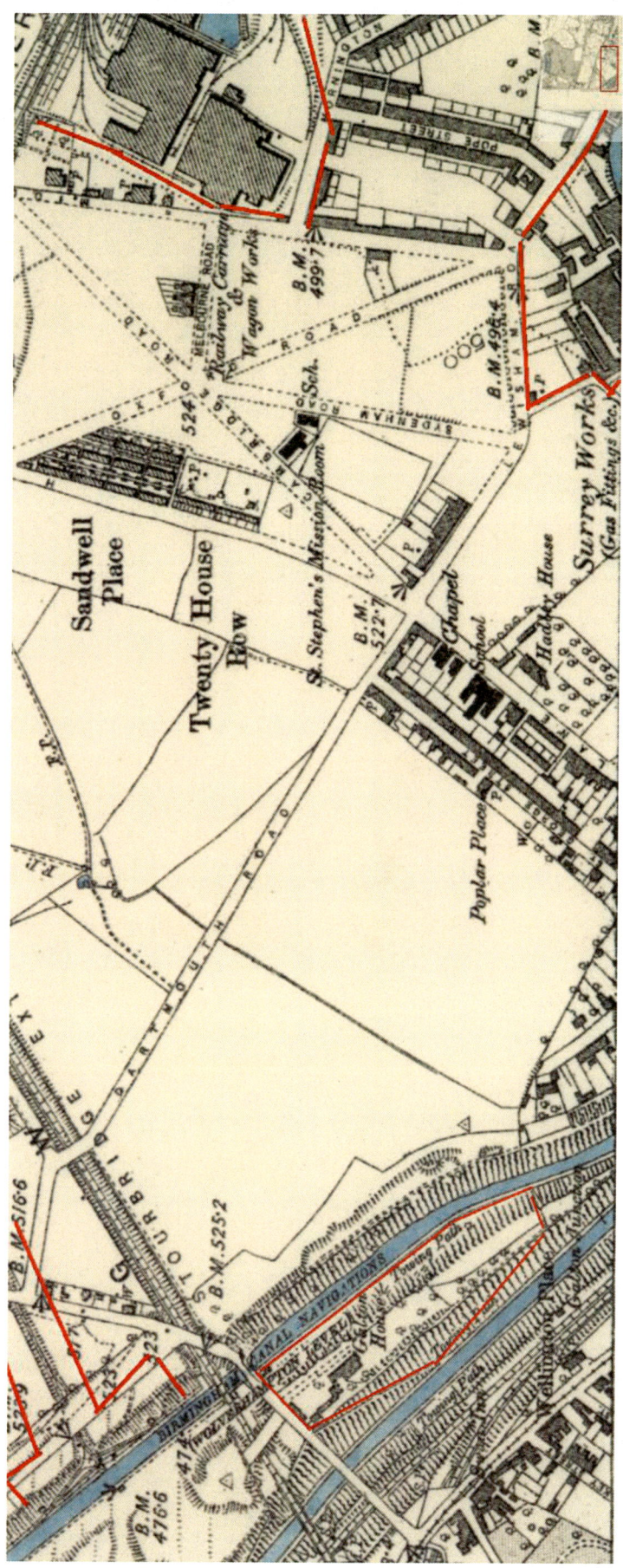

5. Birmingham Carriage & Wagon Works, Summit Tunnel, Sandwell Park Colliery Wharf, Galton House & Bridge

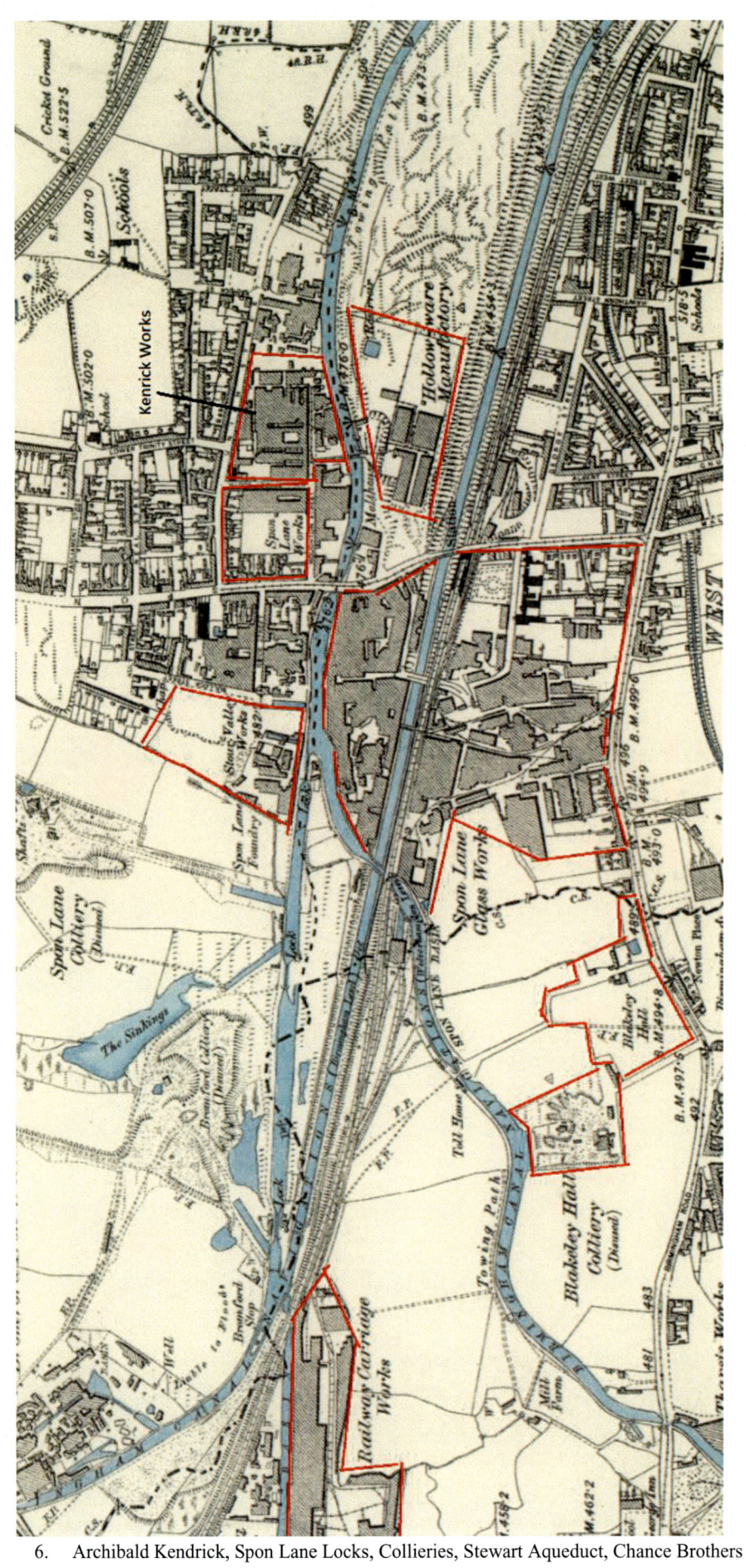

6. Archibald Kendrick, Spon Lane Locks, Collieries, Stewart Aqueduct, Chance Brothers

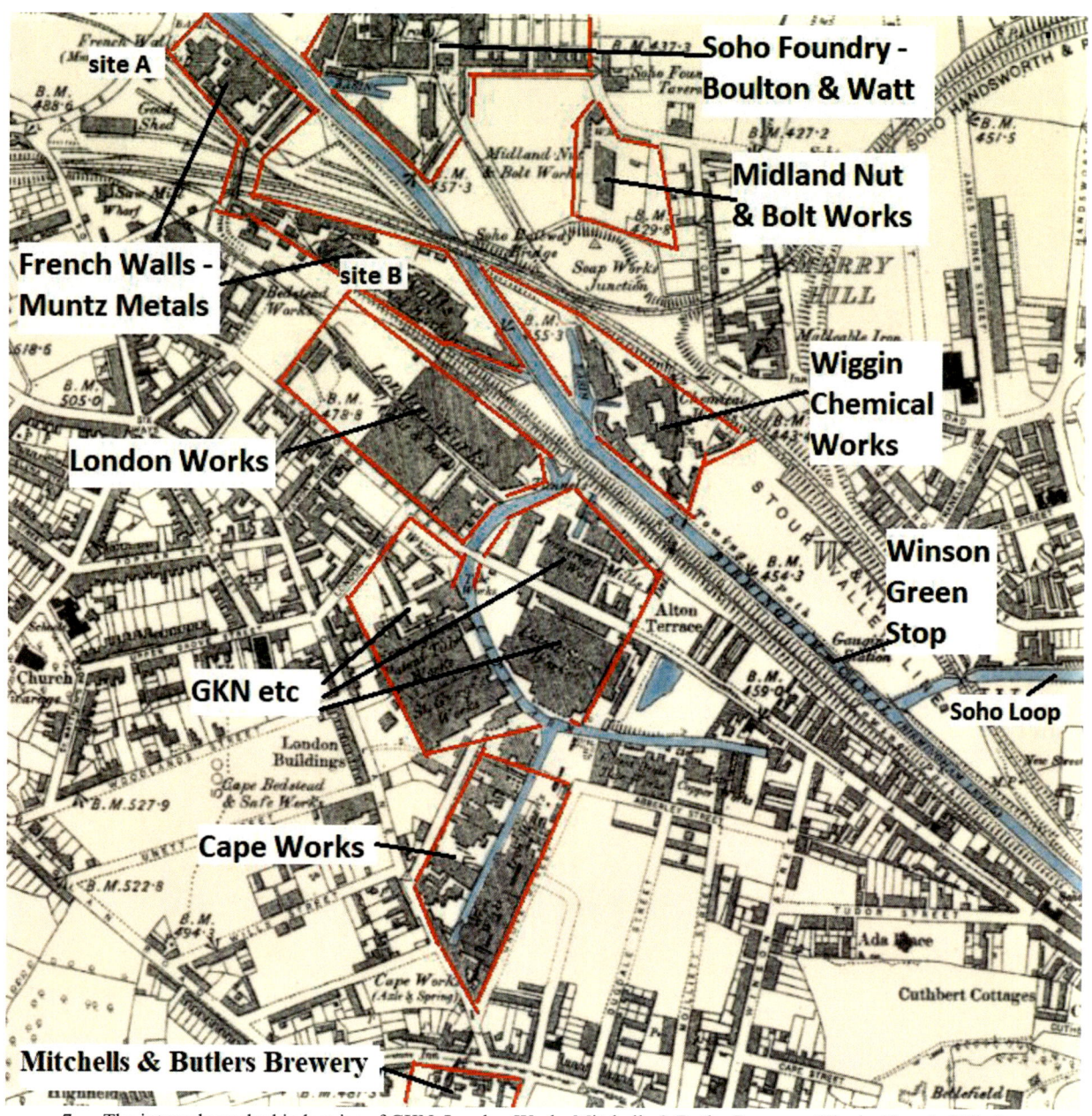

7. The intensely packed industries of GKN, London Works Mitchells & Butler Brewery, Wiggin Chemical Works

PART D.   PAINTINGS & SKETCHES BY THE AUTHOR

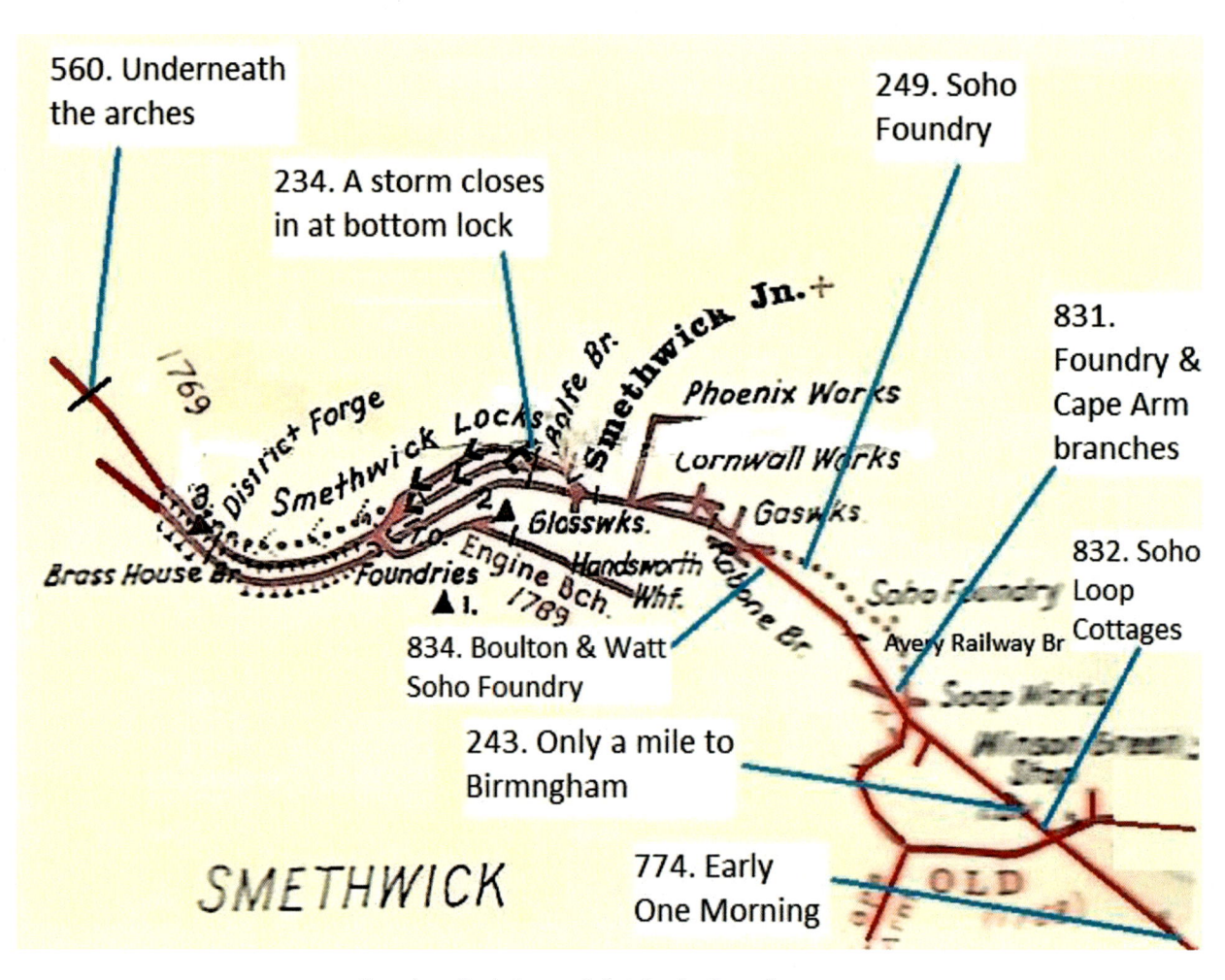

Title of painting		page
"234. A storm closes on bottom lock (2006)"	Oil on Canvas	72
"243. Only a mile to go to Birmingham" (2006)	Oil on Canvas	11
"249. Soho Foundry from the towpath" (2006)	Oil on Canvas	10
"268.1 Soho Loop Junction" [2016].	Ink on Paper	12
"560. Underneath the Arches. (2012)"	Oil on Canvas	89
"800.73 New Smethwick Pumping Station" (2020)	Ink on Paper	84
"800.74 1938c.Smethwick Junction, looking North-west." (2020)	Ink on paper	67
"800.78 The Engine Arm Aqueduct of 1829/30" (2020)	Ink on paper	126
"831. Foundry & Cape Arm branches (2020)"	Oil on Canvas	28
"834. Boulton & Watt Soho Foundry (2020)"	Oil on Canvas	35

Location of paintings and sketches by the author

PART E. TIMELINE

DATE	SPECIFIC JOURNEY REFERENCE	EVENT	CHAPTER REF.
1531	SANDWELL PARK COLLIERY	SANDWELL PRIORY TAKEN BY DAME LUCY CLIFFORD AFTER THE DISSOLUTION OF THE MONASTERIES	2.7
1611	SANDWELL PARK COLLIERY	THE PRIORY WAS THEN CALLED SANDWELL HALL	2.7
1660	FRENCH WALLS	FRENCH WALLS FIRST MENTIONED	3.8
1701	SANDWELL PARK COLLIERY	SANDWELL HALL WAS PURCHASED BY 1ST EARL DARTMOUTH	2.7
1711	SANDWELL PARK COLLIERY	SANDWELL HALL COMPLETELY REBUILT	2.7
1736	BOULTON & WATT	JAMES WATT BORN	1.5
1753	SANDWELL PARK COLLIERY	THE EARLS OF DARTMOUTH MOVE TO PATSHULL HALL	2.7
1759	GKN	DOWLAIS IRONWORKS, S. WALES	1.3
1761	MATTHEW BOULTON & JOHN FOTHERGILL	START A TOY MANUFACTORY AT SOHO MILL	1.5
1766	MATTHEW BOULTON	SOHO MANUFACTORY & GROUNDS DESIGNED BY JAMES WYATT	1.5
1769	**JAMES BRINDLEY**	**1st part BIRMINGHAM CANAL OPENED**	1.1
1769	ALLEN EVERITT & SONS	FIRST MENTIONED AS A COMPANY	3.7
1772	BRINDLEY CANAL	OPENED FOR TRAFFIC	2.6
1777	WILLIAM MURDOCH	MURDOCH IS EMPLOYED AT SOHO FOUNDRY	1.5
1779	BOULTON & WATT	BUILT 2 STEAM ENGINES FOR CANAL ALSO STARTED JAMES WATT & CO WITH NEW PARTNER JAMES KEIR	1.5
1780	ARCHIBALD KENRICK WORKS	KENRICK MOVED INTO BIRMINGHAM MAKING BUCKLES	2.8
1781	WILLIAM MURDOCH	DESIGNED SUN & PLANET GEAR	1.5
1782	JAMES WATT	FIRST WORLD STEAM-POWERED MINT	1.5
1782	JAMES WATT	NOTION OF HORSEPOWER DEFINED	1.5
1784	WATT & BOULTON	PATENT OF PARALLEL MOTION ENGINE	1.5
1784	MURDOCH	DESIGNED STEAM CARRIAGE	1.5
1784	LONDON WORKS	JOSEPH BRAMAH STARTED IN BUSINESS	3.9
1785	JAMES WATT	WHITBREAD ENGINE INVENTED	1.5
1788	SUMMIT BRIDGE	JOHN SMEATON OPENS THE SUMMIT BRIDGE 1788/9	2.6
1788	JAMES WATT	INVENTED STEAM-POWERED COINING PRESS	1.5
1789	SUMMIT BRIDGE	OPENED THE SUMMIT REVISION OF TUNNEL & REMOVAL OF 6 LOCKS	2.6
1790	LONDON WORKS	SMETHWICK GROVE MENTIONED	3.9
1791	ARCHIBALD KENRICK WORKS	SET UP AN IRON FOUNDRY IN WEST BROMWICH	2.8
1792	THOMAS ADKINS, HENRY WIGGIN	THOMAS ADKINS JNR BORN	1.4
1792	WILLIAM MURDOCH	INVENTED GAS LIGHTING	1.5
1795	GKN	THOMAS GUEST INTRODUCED STEAM POWER	1.3
1797	WATT & BOULTON	CARTWHEEL PENNIES MINTED	1.5
1797	LONDON WORKS	JAMES KEIR LIVED AT SMETHWICK GROVE	3.9
1798	WILLIAM MURDOCH	RETURNS TO SOHO FOR FIRST GAS LIGHTING IN A FACTORY	1.5
1800	WATT & BOULTON	BOTH RETIRE	1.5
1807	FRENCH WALLS	GEORGE MUNTZ FOINED HIS FATHER'S FAMLY BUSINESS	3.8
1809	SURREY WORKS	RICHARD EVERED ESTABLISHED A METAL TUBE WORKS	2.1
1810	MITCHELLS & BUTLER	HENRY MITCHELL BORN	1.2
1812	ARCHIBALD KENRICK WORKS	A NEPHEW SAMUEL KENRICK JOINS THE FIRM WITH SITE EXPANSION	2.8
1813	SPON LANE FOUNDRY & HORSELEY IRON WORKS	AARON MANBY TOOK OVER HORSELEY IRON CO	2.9

Year	Company/Location	Event	Ref
1813	LONDON WORKS	JEAN-LOUIS MOILLIET BOUGHT SMETHWICK GROVE	3.9
1814	WILLIAM AVERY	INHERITED SCALE-BEAM BUSINESS FROM HIS COUSIN JOSEPH BALDEN	1.5
1814	CHANCE BROTHERS	BRITISH CROWN GLASS CO STARTED IN FARMLAND OF BLAKELEY HALL	3.1
1814	LONDON WORKS	JOSEPH BRAMAH DIED BUT COMPANY NAME CONTINUED	3.9
1816	FRENCH WALLS	JAMES WATT BOUGHT FRENCH WALLS	3.8
1818	THOMAS ADKINS, HENRY WIGGIN	THOMAS ADKINS BOUGHT SMETHWICK GROVE RESIDENCE	1.4
1818	THOMAS ADKINS, HENRY WIGGIN	THOMAS ADKINS JNR & JOHN NOCK START A SOAP WORKS	1.4
1818	LONDON WORKS	FRANCIS & EDWARD BRAMAH JOIN JOSEPH BRAMAH	3.9
1819	GKN	JOHN SUTTON NETTLEFOLD & MARTHA CHAMBERLAIN MARRY	1.3
1819	BOULTON & WATT	JAMES WATT DIED	1.5
1820	FRENCH WALLS	JAMES WATT LEASES THE SITE TO HENRY DOWNING FOR AN IRON WORKS	3.8
1821	SPON LANE FOUNDRY & HORSELEY IRON WORKS	FIRST IRON STEAMER BUILT "PS AARON MANBY"	2.9
1823	ALLEN EVERITT & SONS	GEORGE ALLEN EVERITT BORN	3.7
1825	ENGINE ARM AQUEDUCT	ENGINE ARM CANAL OPENED BY TELFORD	3.4
1827	**TELFORD'S MAIN LINE**	**TELFORD'S AMENDED ROUTE OPENED**	**1**
1828	ENGINE ARM AQUEDUCT	THIS IRON AQUEDUCT BUILT BY TELFORD	3.4
1829	GALTON BRIDGE	OPENED & NAMED AFTER A BENEFACTOR, SAMUEL TERTIUS GALTON & LOCAL RESIDENT AT GALTON HALL	3.3
1829	STEWART AQUEDUCT	AQUEDUCT CONSTRUCTED	2.11
1829	SPON LANE FOUNDRY & HORSELEY IRON WORKS	GALTON BRIDGE BUILT BY HORSELEY WORKS	2.9
1829	FRENCH WALLS	DOWNING WENT BANKRUPT, WATT LEASED IT TO BORDESLEY STEE CO THEN TOOK IT OVER HIMSELF CALLING IT FRENCH WALLS WORKS	3.8
1830	LONDON WORKS	MOILLIET SOLD SMETHWICK GROVE TO THOMAS ADKINS	3.9
1832	FRENCH WALLS	GEORGE MUNTZ PATENTS MUNTZ'S METAL	3.8
1833	CORNWALL WORKS	SIR RICHARD TANGYE BORN	1.7
1834	CHANCE BROTHERS	BROTHERS HARTLEY BECAME PARTNERS WITH CHANCE BROS.	3.1
1834	CHANCE BROTHERS	CHANCE BROS. BOUGHT BRITISH CROWN GLASS	3.1
1835	BLAKELEY HALL, BROMFORD & SPON LANE COLLIERIES, JENSEN MOTOR LTD	WILLIAM H. DAWES WORKED 2 SHAFT BROMFORD COLLIERY	2.1
1835	GKN	ARTHUR KEEN BORN	1.3
1835	ARCHIBALD KENRICK WORKS	ARCHIBALD KENRICK DIED	2.8
1836	CHANCE BROTHERS	HARTLEY BROS LEAVE. A NEPHEW JAMES TIMMINS CHANCE JOINS THE COMPANY FROM CAMBRIDGE UNIVERSITY	3.1
1837	CHANCE BROTHERS	GLASS FOR THE GREAT CONSERVATORY OF CHATSWORTH HOUSE IS MADE	3.1
1838	CHANCE BROTHERS	DIOPTIC LENSES ARE MADE FOR LIGHTHOUSES	3.1
1839	LONDON WORKS	JOSEPH BRAMAH APPOINTS CHARLES FOX AS PARTNER	3.9
1841	THOMAS ADKINS, HENRY WIGGIN	HENRY ADKINS DIED	1.4
1842	FRENCH WALLS	JAMES WATT SELLS FRENCH WALLS TO GEORGE F MUNTZ.	3.8
1843	MITCHELLS & BUTLER	WILLIAM BUTLER IS BORN	1.2
1843	W & T AVERY	THOMAS & WILLIAM AVERY IN COMPANY	1.5
1844	DISTRICT IRON WORKS	JOHN BROCKHOUSE MADE VEHICLE AXLES	2.4
1845	LONDON WORKS	CHARLES FOX JOINED BY JOHN HENDERSON TO MAKE COMPANY NAME FOX HENDERSON & CO	3.9

Year	Company	Event	Ref
1846	GKN	GEORGE SELBY OF PATENT IRON & BRASS TUBE CO, BUYS SMETHWICK GROVE	1.3
1846	LONDON WORKS	SMETHWICK GROVE BOUGHT BY GEORGE SELBY OF BIRMINGHAM PATENT IRON & BRASS TUBE CO (GKN)	3.9
1848	LONDON WORKS	FOX HENDERSON TEAMED UP WITH WILLIAM SIEMENS	3.9
1849	BOULTON & WATT	NAME CHANGED TO JAMES WATT & CO	1.5
1849	LONDON WORKS	THOMAS ASTBURY WAS AN IRON FOUNDER	3.9
1850	FRENCH WALLS	MUNTZ METALS EXPANDS TO HAVING 2 SITES ON EITHER SIDE OF RAILWAY	3.8
1851	CHANCE BROTHERS	GLASS MADE FOR CRYSTAL PALACE, GREAT EXHIBITION, HOUSES OF PARLIAMENT, WHITE HOUSE, WASHINGTON	3.1
1851	LONDON WORKS	CHARLES FOX WS KNIGHTED	3.9
1852	FRENCH WALLS	MUNTZ FINISHES SITE EXPANSION WITH A PRIVATE BRIDGE OVER THE RAILWAY	3.8
1852	LONDON WORKS	FOX HENDERSON CHARGED WITH MOVING THE CRYSTAL PALACE TO SYDENHAM	3.9
1853	SPON LANE FOUNDRY & HORSELEY IRON WORKS	SPON LANE WORKS STARTED	2.9
1854	BIRMINGHAM CARRIAGE & WAGON CO.	COMPANY LAUNCHED AT SALTLEY, BIRMINGHAM	2.2
1854	GKN	NETTLEFOLD & CHAMBERLAIN START IN HEATH ST, SMETHWICK	1.3
1856	GKN / LONDON WORKS	WATKINS & KEEN STARTED AT VICTORIA WORKS, SMETHWICK. FOX HENDERSON CLOSED LONDON WORKS SITE	1.3 / 3.9
1857	FRENCH WALLS	GEORGE MUNTZ DIED	3.8
1858	JAMES WATT & CO	BUILT SCREW ENGINE FOR GREAT EASTERN	1.5
1858	LONDON WORKS	THOMAS ASTBURY OCCUPIED PART OF LONDON WORKS	3.9
1859	CORNWALL WORKS	MOVE PREMISES TO CLEMENT ST, BIRMINGHAM	1.7
1860	CHANCE BROTHERS	JAMES T CHANCE JOINS FARADAY IN EXPERIMENT FOR TRINITY HOUSE	3.1
1860	GKN	WATKINS & KEEN MOVE INTO LONDON WORKS	1.3
1860	LONDON WORKS	PATENT NUT & BOLT CO MOVED TO LONDON WORKS	3.9
1862	CORNWALL WORKS	MOVE FROM CLEMENT ST TO RABONE LANE, SMETHWICK	1.7
1864	BIRMINGHAM CARRIAGE & WAGON CO.	COMPANY MOVED FROM SALTLEY TO MIDDLEMORE ROAD, SMETHWICK	2.2
1865	THOMAS ADKINS, HENRY WIGGIN	GEORGE ADKINS BOUGHT LIGHTWOODS PARK & HOUSE	1.4
1865	W & T AVERY	WILLIAM AVERY TAKES SOLE CHARGE OF COMPANY	1.5
1865	LONDON WORKS	PATENT NUT & BOLD CO, WATKINS & KEEN, THOMAS ASTBURY ALLOCCUPIED LONDON WORKS	3.9
1866	CORNWALL WORKS	AN AMERICAN CALLS BY WANTING DIRECT-ACTING STEAM PUMPS MADE	1.7
1867	DISTRICT IRON WORKS	COMPANY ESTABLISHED	2.4
1868	W & T AVERY	THOMAS MADE MAYOR OF BIRMINGHAM	1.5
1870	SANDWELL PARK COLLIERY CO	COLLIERY FORMED BY A CONSORTIUM & A COAL SHAFT DRILLED OUT	2.7
1870	SANDWELL IRON & AXLE WORKS	COMPANY STARTED AS LONES, RAYBOULD & VERNON	2.3
1873	BLAKELEY HALL, BROMFORD & SPON LANE COLLIERIES, JENSEN MOTOR LTD	BROMFORD COLLIERY CO FLOATED	2.10
1873	CHANCE BROTHERS	JOHN HOPKINSON RUNS THE BUSINESS & INVENTS ROTATING OPTICS FOR LIGHTHOUSES	3.10
1873	OLDBURY RAILWAY CARRIAGE & WAGON WORKS	TRAMCAR BUILT WITH MERRYWEATHER & SONS	2.11
1874	SANDWELL PARK COLLIERY CO	THICK COAL FOUND & 2ND SHAFT STARTED	2.7

Year	Site	Event	Ref
1875	BLAKELEY HALL, BROMFORD & SPON LANE COLLIERIES, JENSEN MOTOR LTD	BLAKELEY HALL & BRONFORD COLLIERIES PUT UP FOR SALE. SPON LANE COLLIERY STARTED	2.10
1876	SANDWELL IRON & AXLE WORKS	CHANGED FROM LONES, RAYBOULD & VERNON TO SANDWELL IRON & AXLE WORKS	2.3
1877	CORNWALL WORKS	TANGYE JACKS ARE USED TO ERECT CLEOPATRA'S NEEDLE IN LONDON	1.7
1877	RUSKIN POTTERY	EDWARD RICHARD TAYLOR AND SON WILLIAM HOWSON TAYLOR START RUSKIN GLASS	3.2
1877	RUSKIN POTTERY	EDWARD R TAYLOR BECOMES PRINCIPAL OF BIRMINGHAM SCHOOL OF ART	3.2
1879	CAPE HILL BREWERY	FIRST BEER PRODUCED	1.2
1880	CORNWALL WORKS	BIRMINGHAM CITY IS DONATED £100,000 BY TANGYE BROTHERS TOSTART AN ART GALLRY	1.7
1880	SPON LANE FOUNDRY & HORSELEY IRON WORKS	SPON LANE FOUNDRY SOLD	2.9
1880	CREDENDA WORKS	WILLIAM MICKLEWIGHT MADE MANAGER	3.6
1881	W & T AVERY	THOMAS AVERY IS MAYOR FOR SECOND TIME	1.5
1881	CORNWALL WORKS	TANGYE BROTHERS MAKE A DONATION TO FOUNDATION OF A SCHOOL OF ART	1.7
1884	SURREY WORKS	RICHARD EVERED BECOMES EVERED & CO	2.1
1885	CORNWALL WORKS	BIRMINGHAM MUSEUM & ART GALLERY OPENED	1.7
1885	RUSKIN POTTERY	BIRM.SCH. OF ART BECOMES THE FIRST MUNICIPAL SCHOOL OF ART	3.2
1886	DISTRICT IRON WORKS	JOHN BROCKHURST COMPANY STARTED	2.4
1887	LONDON WORKS	THOMAS ASTBURY WAS SELLING SHELLS TO THE BRITISH GOVERNMENT	3.9
1888	THOMAS ADKINS, HENRY WIGGIN	THOMAS ADKINS SOLD TO SIR HENRY WIGGIN	1.4
1888	CREDENDA WORKS	SEAMLESS STEELTUBE CO.CREATED	3.6
1889	JAMES WATT	THE UNIT OF POWER = A WATT	1.5
1889	CORNWALL WORKS	SIR RICHARD TANGYE WROTE HIS MEMOIRS	1.7
1889	CREDENDA WORKS	CREDENDA SEAMLESS TUBE LTD BOUGHT BIRMINGHAM PLATE GLASS CO	3.6
1890	SMETHWICK GAS WORKS	OPENED	1.6
1890	ALLEN EVERITT & SONS	ACQUIRED KINGSTON WORKS	3.7
1892	BIRMINGHAM CARRIAGE & WAGON CO.	DURING 2ND BOER WAR; DESIGNED HOSPITAL TRAINS	2.2
1892	THOMAS ADKINS, HENRY WIGGIN	DR LUDWIG MOND JOINED HENRY WIGGIN HENRY WIGGIN IS ELECTED MP	1.4
1892	BRITISH TUBE MILLS	FRANCIS HENRY GRIFFITHS MADE MANAGER	1.8
1892	SMETHWICK NEW PUMPING STATION	OPENED	2.5
1894	DISTRICT IRON WORKS	MANUFACTURED CLOSE-JOINT TUBES	2.4
1896	CREDENDA WORKS	CREDENDA WAS SOLD TO NEW CREDENDA TUBE CO & THEN TO BIRMINGHAM STAR TUBE CO	3.6
1897	CREDENDA WORKS	WELDLESS TUBES LTD TOOK OVER STAR TUBES	3.6
1898	RUSKIN POTTERY	THE TAYLORS START A SMALL POTTERY WORKS IN SMETHWICK & CALLED IT BIRMINGHAM TILE & POTTERY WORKS	3.2
1900	GKN	ARTHUR KEEN BOUGHT DOWLAIS IRONWORKS	1.3
1902	GKN	COMPANY CREATED BY MERGER	1.3
1904	INCANDESCENT HEAT COMPANY WORKS	COMPANY FORMED AT BRITISH MILLS	1.8
1904	RUSKIN POTTERY	NAME CHANGED TO RUSKIN POTTERY AFTER JOHN RUSKIN	3.2
1905	W & T AVERY	WILLIAM IS CREATED BARONET	1.5
1906	CREDENDA WORKS	ALLEN EVERITT & SONS MOVED TO ADJACENT KINGSTON WORKS AS TUBES LTD & THEN ABSORBED BY ICI	3.6
1907	CREDENDA WORKS	CREDENDA BOUGHT BY J.A.PHILLIPS & CO	3.6
1907	OLDBURY RAILWAY CARRIAGE & WAGON WORKS	COMPANY ACQUIRED DOCKER BROTHERS	2.11
1909	DISTRICT IRON WORKS	JOHN BROCKHOUSE MAYOR OF WEST BROMWICH	2.4
1910	RETAINING WALL TO CORPORATION YARD, SMETHWICK	THE 10M REINFORCED CONCRETE WALL IS FORMERLY OPENED	3.4

Year	Works	Event	Ref
1912	OLDBURY RAILWAY CARRIAGE & WAGON WORKS	SIR DUDLEY DOCKER CHAIRMAN	2.11
1912	RUSKIN POTTERY	EDWARD TAYLOR DIED	3.2
1914	DISTRICT IRON WORKS	STEEL ROLLING MILL & CLOSE-JOINT & ELECTRIC WELDED TUBES	2.4
1914	SANDWELL PARK COLLIERY CO	PRODUCTION CEASED	2.7
1914	CHANCE BROTHERS	ONLY COMPANY MAKING OPTICAL GLASS IN UK	3.1
1916	CREDENDA WORKS	J.A.PHILLIPS AMALGAMATED WITH ROLFE MANUFACTURING CO	3.6
1919	SANDWELL IRON & AXLE WORKS	JOHN BROCKHOUSE & CO TOOK CONTROL	2.3
1920	CREDENDA WORKS	SMETHWICK TUBE CO BECAME PART OF GEORGE BURN LTD & TUBE INVESTMENTS ACQUIRED J.A PHILLIPS	3.6
1925	FRENCH WALLS	MUNTZ METALS AMALGAMATED WITH ELLIOTS METALS CO OF SELLY OAK	3.8
1926	BLAKELEY HALL, BROMFORD & SPON LANE COLLIERIES, JENSEN MOTOR LTD	JENSEN BROTHERS START TO DESIGN CARS	2.10
1929	THOMAS ADKINS, HENRY WIGGIN	INTERNATIONAL NICKEL CO OF CANADA LTD TOOK OVER MOND NICKEL	1.4
1929	ALLEN EVERITT & SONS	ICI ACQUIRED ALLEN EVERITT & SONS	3.7
1932	FRENCH WALLS	ICI METALS ABSORBS MUNTZ METALS	3.8
1935	RUSKIN POTTERY	WORKS CLOSED WHEN WILLIAM HOWSON TAYLOR DIED	3.2
1936	DISTRICT IRON WORKS	JOHN BROCKHOUSE & CO ACQUIRED THE WORKS	2.4
1937	INCANDESCENT HEAT COMPANY WORKS	FURNACE PRODUCERS & SPECIALISTS OF NOTE	1.8
1937	CREDENDA WORKS	THE COMPANY BECAME GEORGE BURN City TUBE & CONDUIT MILLS	3.6
1939	BIRMINGHAM CARRIAGE & WAGON CO.	BUILT A10 NUMEROUS DESIGNED TANKS FOR WW2	2.2
1945	CHANCE BROTHERS	PILKINGTON GLASS ACQUIRED 50% COMPANY	3.1
1948	GKN	GUEST KEEN & NETTLEFOLD (MIDLANDS) LTD ESTABLISHED	1.3
1951	DISTRICT IRON WORKS	NATIONALISED	2.4
1953	DISTRICT IRON WORKS	JOHN BROCKHOUSE & CO ACQUIRES WORKS AFTER ENFORCED NATIONAISATION	2.4
1959	BLAKELEY HALL, BROMFORD & SPON LANE COLLIERIES, JENSEN MOTOR LTD	JENSEN MOTORS SOLD TO NORCROSS LTD	2.10
1971	CREDENDA WORKS	SMETHWICK PREMISES CLOSED & MOVED TO SHIRLEY	3.6
1981	CHANCE BROTHERS	THE WORKS CLOSED IN SMETHWICK & MOVED TO MALVERN	3.1
1982	SMETHWICK NEW PUMPING STATION	RENOVATION COMMENCED	2.5
1984	SURREY WORKS / DISTRICT IRON WORKS	ACQUIRED BROCKHOUSE GROUP	2.1 / 2.4
2000	SMETHWICK NEW PUMPING STATION	OPENED TO THE PUBLIC	2.5

A   W. & T. Avery bill dating from 1912

PART F.   REFERENCES

1. Historic England; Britain from Above. www.Britainfromabove.org
2. Grace's Guide to Industry. www.Gracesguide.co.uk
3. West Bromwich History www.westbromwichhistory.com/people-places/archibald-kenrick/
4. TANGYE Richard; "One and All" Autobiography of Richard Tangye of the Cornwall Works, Birmingham 1889.
5. British History BHO Smethwick: Other estates. www.british-history.ac.uk/vch/staffs/vol17/pp99-107
6. Historic England Britain from Above
7. O/S Maps: 1888, 1904 25":mile
8. GILLOTT Joseph; https://en.m.wikipedia.org/wiki/Joseph_Gillott
9. BLACK COUNTRY HISTORY. http://blackcountryhistory.org/collections/getrecord/GB146_PHS_3101/
10. Birmingham Museum & Art Gallery. Wikipedia https://en.wikipedia.org/wiki/Birmingham_Museum_and_Art_Gallery
11. George Tangye: Grace's Guide https://www.gracesguide.co.uk/George_Tangye
12. Gilbertstone; home of Sir Richard Tangye https://en.wikipedia.org/wiki/Gilbertstone
13. Black Country Living Museum. https://www.bclm.co.uk/
14. BODFISH Mary, Smethwick Local History Society: Smethwick Grove, Jean-Louis Moilliet, James Keir ; http://www.moilliet.ws/Smethwick_Grove.html
15. Richard Lovell Edgeworth : https://gracesguide.co.uk/Richard_Lovell_Edgeworth
16. GKN plc; Grace's Guide https://gracesguide.co.uk/GKN
17. Dowlais Ironworks, Merthyr Tydfil [Grace's Guide] https://gracesguide.co.uk/Dowlais_Ironworks
18. Guest, Keen & Co [Grace's Guide] https://gracesguide.co.uk/Guest,_Keen_and_Co
19. Nettlefold & Chamberlain [Grace's Guide] https://gracesguide.co.uk/Nettlefold_and_Chamberlain
20. John Sutton Nettlefold [Grace's Guide] https://gracesguide.co.uk/John_Sutton_Nettlefold
21. Nettlefolds [Grace's Guide] https://gracesguide.co.uk/Nettlefolds
22. Guest & Co [Grace's Guide] https://gracesguide.co.uk/Guest_and_Co_(2)
23. Ivor Bertie Guest [Grace's Guide] https://gracesguide.co.uk/Ivor_Bertie_Guest
24. Malta; Welsh Brummie Guest family : https://birminghamhistory.co.uk/forum/index.php?threads/nettlefolds-limited.9730/
25. Black Country History: Guest, Keen & Nettlefolds Midlands) Ltd, Nut, Bolt, Screw & Fastener Manufacturers, Smethwick http://blackcountryhistory.org/collections/getrecord/GB146_BS-GKN/
26. Wikipedia: Melrose Industries. https://en.wikipedia.org/wiki/Melrose_Industries
27. Muntz's Metals – Wikipedia: https://en.wikipedia.org/wiki/Muntz_metal#/media/File:Cutty_Sark_stern.jpg
28. HISTORIC ENGLAND SCHEDULED MONUMENTS: www.historicengland.org.uk/listing/what-is-designation/scheduled-monuments/
29. HISTORIC ENGLAND – INDUSTRIAL SITES: https://historicengland.org.uk/images-books/publications/dssg-industrial-sites/heag246-industrial-sites-ssg/
30. Department for Digital, Culture, Media & Sport (DCMS) https://www.gov.uk/government/organisations/department-for-digital-culture-media-sport

31. National Planning Policy Framework [2012 revised 2019]: https://www.gov.uk/government/publications/national-planning-policy-framework--2
32. Scheduled Monuments Policy Statement [2013] https://www.gov.uk/government/publications/scheduled-monuments-policy-statement
33. HISTORIC ENGLAND – PROTECTING INDUSTRIAL SITES https://historicengland.org.uk/advice/heritage-at-risk/industrial-heritage/protecting-industrial-sites/
34. HISTORIC ENGLAND – SOHO FOUNDRY Listed Building Grade II* [1268451] https://historicengland.org.uk/advice/heritage-at-risk/search-register/list-entry/47046
35. HISTORIC ENGLAND – BUILDINGS AT RISK https://historicengland.org.uk/advice/heritage-at-risk/buildings/buildings-at-risk/buildings-at-risk-sale/
36. HISTORIC ENGLAND – HERITAGE AT RISK REGISTER: ;SOHO FOUNDRY' https://historicengland.org.uk/advice/heritage-at-risk/search-register/results/?searchType=HAR&search=SOHO+FOUNDRY
37. Department for Culture Media & Sport: - Scheduled Monuments 2013 https://assets.publishing.service.gov.uk/government/uploads/system/uploads/attachment_data/file/249695/SM_policy_statement_10-2013__2_.pdf
38. Ancient Monuments & Archaeological Areas Act 1979 http://www.legislation.gov.uk/ukpga/1979/46
39. HISTORIC ENGLAND – REMAINS OF THE BOULTON & WATT SOHO FOUNDRY & MINT, BIRMINGHAM CANAL, SMETHWICK: https://historicengland.org.uk/listing/the-list/list-entry/1021388
40. Science Museum: James Watt Garret Collection https://www.sciencemuseum.org.uk/
41. Historic England: Britain from Above www.britainfromabove.org/image/EPW053086
42. Whitehouse S. : J.A. Phillips, Credenda https://gracesguide.co.uk/Renowned_The_World_Over_-_The_Phillips_Cycle_Company_by_Sam_Whitehouse
43. BRITISH HISTORY ON LINE: SMETHWICK ECONOMY https://www.british-history.ac.uk/vch/staffs/vol17/pp107-118
44. Soho Manufactory; Wikipedia https://en.wikipedia.org/wiki/Soho_Manufactory
45. FISHER H.A.L. "A History of Europe" Vol. II [1935] Fontana Classics
46. James Watt 1736-1819 http://en.wikipedia.org/wiki/James_watt
47. Horsepower https://en.wikipedia.org/wiki/Horsepower
48. James WATT Garret Workshop: https://collection.sciencemuseumgroup.org.uk/objects/co52335/james-watt
49. Google Earth aerial photos:
50. Grace's Guide: James Watt & Co. https://www.gracesguide.co.uk/James_Watt_and_Co
51. Birmingham Journal; 2 April 1859
52. SS Great Eastern; https://en.wikipedia.org/wiki/SS_Great_Eastern
53. TANGYE Sir Richard; autobiography "One and All" 1889
54. SCHRAEDER R. The Cartwheel Issue & Matthew Boulton http://numis.org/wp-content/uploads/2014/04/Watt-Cartwheel.pdf
55. SOHO MINT Wikipedia: https://en.wikipedia.org/wiki/Soho_Mint
56. WHITBREAD ENGINE; Wikipedia https://en.wikipedia.org/wiki/Whitbread_Engine
57. SOHO FOUNDRY; Wikipedia https://en.wikipedia.org/wiki/Soho_Foundry#cite_note-Martin-5
58. W & T Avery – Wikipedia; https://en.wikipedia.org/wiki/W_%26_T_Avery
59. SOHO FOUNDRY HISTORY: http://www.andrewlound.com/index_sohofoundry.htm

60. MURDOCH William; Wikipedia https://en.wikipedia.org/wiki/William_Murdoch
61. Allen Everitt & Sons; Grace's Guide https://gracesguide.co.uk/Allen_Everitt_and_Sons
62. George Allen Everitt Grace's Guide https://gracesguide.co.uk/George_Allen_Everitt
63. Nevill Everitt; Grace's Guide https://gracesguide.co.uk/Nevill_Henry_Everitt
64. HISCOCK Ted: Brindley Out Telford Home https://www.amazon.co.uk/Brindley-Out-Telford-Home-Birmingham-ebook/dp/B082P6WM75
65. Boydell & Glasier; Anchor Works. [Grace's Guide]. https://gracesguide.co.uk/Special:Search?search=Boydell%20and%20Glasier
66. W & T AVERY of Soho Foundry. https://gracesguide.co.uk/W._and_T._Avery
67. Soho Manufactory; Boulton & Fothergill. https://en.wikipedia.org/wiki/Soho_Manufactory
68. BIRMINGHAM CARRIAGE & WAGON COMPANY. Wikipedia https://en.wikipedia.org/wiki/Birmingham_Railway_Carriage_and_Wagon_Company#:~:text=The%20Birmingham%20Railway%20Carriage%20and,company%20was%20established%20in%201854.
69. GOLDEN ARROW. Wikipedia https://en.m.wikipedia.org/wiki/Golden_Arrow_(train)
70. BIRMINGHAM RAILWAY CARRIAGE & WAGON Co. Ltd [1855-1964]. Science Museum Group https://collection.sciencemuseumgroup.org.uk/people/cp6676/birmingham-railway-carriage-wagon-company-limited
71. CHANCE BROTHERS & CO; https://gracesguide.co.uk/Chance_Brothers_and_Co
72. CRYSTAL PALACE. Wikipedia ; https://en.wikipedia.org/wiki/The_Crystal_Palace
73. CHANCE GLASS WORKS HERITAGE TRUST https://www.chanceht.org/
74. REVOLUTIONARY PLAYERS. https://www.revolutionaryplayers.org.uk/#:~:text=The%20Revolutionary%20Players%20were%20the,beyond%20from%201700%20to%201830.
75. Sandwell Park Colliery www.sandwell.gov.uk
76. RICHARD EVERED & CO https://gracesguide.co.uk/Evered_and_Co
77. GALTON BRIDGE; Nigel CROWE CRT https://canalrivertrust.org.uk/news-and-views/blogs/nigel-crowe/galton-bridge
78. ENGLISH HERITAGE GALTON BRIDGE GRADE ONE LISTING. https://historicengland.org.uk/listing/the-list/list-entry/1214833
79. James KEIR; https://en.wikipedia.org/wiki/James_Keir
80. LUNAR MOONSTONES; https://en.wikipedia.org/wiki/Lunar_Society_Moonstones
81. LUNAR SOCIETY OF BIRMINGHAM: https://en.wikipedia.org/wiki/Lunar_Society_of_Birmingham
82. William SMALL: https://en.wikipedia.org/wiki/William_Small
83. SMETHWICK ENGINES: https://gracesguide.co.uk/Smethwick_Engine
84. GEORGE BURN & CO: https://gracesguide.co.uk/George_Burn
85. Thomas ADKINS family histories: https://adkins-family.org.uk/hist-thomas_b1792.htm
86. Henry WIGGIN: Wikipedia https://en.wikipedia.org/wiki/Henry_Wiggin
87. John SMEATON: Wikipedia https://en.wikipedia.org/wiki/John_Smeaton
88. Eddystone Lighthouse: John SMEATON: Wikipedia https://en.wikipedia.org/wiki/Eddystone_Lighthouse
89. Birmingham & Fazeley Canal: Wikipedia https://en.wikipedia.org/wiki/Birmingham_and_Fazeley_Canal
90. Summit Bridge, Smethwick: Wikipedia https://en.wikipedia.org/wiki/Summit_Bridge%2C_Smethwick
91. Walter George KENT: Grace's Guide: https://gracesguide.co.uk/Walter_George_Kent_(d.1921)

92. RUSKIN POTTERY; Wikipedia https://en.wikipedia.org/wiki/Ruskin_Pottery#:~:text=The%20Ruskin%20Pottery%20was%20an,Taylor%2C%20formerly%20a%20student%20there.
93. BIRMINGHAM SCHOOL OF ART; Wikipedia https://en.wikipedia.org/wiki/Birmingham_School_of_Art
94. Peter Duckworth BENNETT: Grace's Guide https://gracesguide.co.uk/Peter_Duckworth_Bennett
95. Annals of Tipton Industries : http://www.historywebsite.co.uk/articles/Tipton/Horseley.htm
96. HORSELEY IRONWORKS: Grace's Guide: https://gracesguide.co.uk/Horseley_Ironworks
97. SANDWELL IRON & AXLE WORKS Grace's Guide: https://gracesguide.co.uk/Lones,_Vernon_and_Holden
98. STEWART AQUEDUCT; Grace's Guide: https://gracesguide.co.uk/Stewart_Aqueduct
99. SPON LANE COLLIERY MINERAL RIGHTS https://www.mindat.org/loc-381636.html
100. SPON LANE ACCIDENT ; Grace's Guide https://www.gracesguide.co.uk/Spon_Lane_Colliery
101. BRITISH MINING No 57 MEMOIRS: https://www.nmrs.org.uk/assets/pdf/BM57/BM57-125-133-blakeley.pdf
102. JENSEN MOTORS LTD Wikipedia: https://en.wikipedia.org/wiki/Jensen_Motors
103. MERRYWEATHER & SONS: Grace's Guide. https://gracesguide.co.uk/Merryweather_and_Sons
104. JOHN GRANTHAM: Grace's Guide. https://gracesguide.co.uk/John_Grantham
105. PERCY WHEELER; Grace's Guide. https://gracesguide.co.uk/Percy_Wheeler
106. METROPOLITAN AMALGAMATED RAILWAY CARRIAGE & WAGON Co. Grace's Guide. https://gracesguide.co.uk/Metropolitan_Amalgamated_Railway_Carriage_and_Wagon_Co
107. METROPOLITAN CARRIAGE, WAGON & FINANCE CO LTD: Grace's Guide. https://gracesguide.co.uk/Metropolitan_Carriage,_Wagon_and_Finance_Co
108. "Short Hop to brewing empire" UPTON Chris, Birmingham Post, Sat. April 15. 2006
109. Sandwell Hall: Wikipedia https://en.wikipedia.org/wiki/Sandwell_Hall
110. BROOKSBANK B.W.L. "Railway Damage & Disruption in World War II. Part 2: p. 157
111. SMETHWICK NEW PUMPUNG STATION: CRT: Information board at the Smethwick Pumping Station
112. Erasmus DARWIN; Wikipedia: https://en.wikipedia.org/wiki/Erasmus_Darwin
113. James WATT; Wikipedia: https://en.wikipedia.org/wiki/James_Watt
114. William MURDOCH; Wikipedia: https://en.wikipedia.org/wiki/William_Murdoch
115. Matthew BOULTON; Wikipedia: https://en.wikipedia.org/wiki/Matthew_Boulton
116. John FOTHERGILL; Wikipedia: https://en.wikipedia.org/wiki/John_Fothergill_(merchant)
117. Soho House, Birmingham; Wikipedia: https://en.wikipedia.org/wiki/Soho_House
118. Boulton & the Birmingham Triennial Festival; Wikipedia: https://en.wikipedia.org/wiki/Birmingham_Triennial_Music_Festival
119. DEAN Richard: "Historical Maps of the Birmingham Canals – 1989"
120. "SPON LANE BRIDGE" Smethwick Telephone: 9th January 1926. County Borough of Smethwick to Public Works Contractors. "Spon Lane Bridge Widening".
121. François Hennebique & system: https://en.wikipedia.org/wikiFrancois_Hennebique

INDEX

A

AARON MANBY SHIP	97, 100
ADKINS Thomas, & family, Soap Works	29-30, 140
AGUSTAWESTLAND	26
ALLEN EVERITT & SONS	130, 133-134
ANCHOR IRON WORKS	127-128
ARCHIBALD KENRICK WORKS	93-94
ASTBURY Hannah	23, 143
Thomas	23, 143
ASTBURY & SONS	24
AVERY family	43
AVERY Thomas	43-44
AVERY MUSEUM	47
AVERY William	43-44
AVERY; Sir William Beilby Bart.	44-45
AVERY-HARDOLL	46
AVERY-WEIGH-TRONIX	46
W & T AVERY	43-49

B

BACCHUS George	140
BENNETT Peter Duckworth	98-101
BIRFIELD GROUP	26
BIRMINGHAM & MIDLAND BANK	24
BIRMINGHAM CARRIAGE & WAGON CO.	78-80
BIRMINGHAM LUNAR SOCIETY	156
BIRMINGHAM MUSEUM & ART GALLERY (Tangye)	61
BIRMINGHAM PATENT IRON & BRASS TUBE CO	22, 25, 140
BIRMINGHAM PLATE GLASS CO	129, 138
BIRMINGHAM SCHOOL OF ART	117
BIRMINGHAM SCREW CO	21
BIRMINGHAM STAR TUBE CO	129
BIRMINGHAM TILE & POTTERY WORKS	117
BLAIR; Captain Alexander (James Keir)	163
BLAKELEY HALL, BROMFORD & SPON LANE COLLIERIES	102-103
BLOYE William (Sculptor of Boulton, Watt & Murdoch, Birmingham)	164
BOHLE Ernest William	130
BOULTON Matthew Robinson	155-157
BOULTON & WATT	32-49, 125, 157
BOULTON & FOTHERGILL	155-156
BRAMAH John Joseph & family (London Works)	98, 141
BRAMAH, FOX & CO	141
BROCKHOUSE & CO, (JOHN BROCKHOUSE)	83
BRIGHT John	57
BRINDLEY James	**145-147, 156**
BRINDLEY CANAL	8, 10-108
BRITISH CROWN GLASS CO	110
BRITISH TUBE MILLS	8
BROMFORD & SPON LANE COLLIERIES	102-103
BRUNEL Isambard Kingdom	55
BUTLER William	14

C

CAMERON A.S. (New York)	58
CANAL FEEDER CONDUIT	12-13
CAPE ARM LOOP	10
CAPE HILL BREWERY	14
CARTWHEEL PENNIES	39-40
CHAMBERLAIN Joseph Jnr. MP	20-21
CHAMBERLAIN Joseph Snr.	20

CHAMBERLAIN Martha (m. NETTLEFOLD J. S.)	20
CHANCE BROTHERS	31, 110-116
CHANCE; Alexander M.	114
George	111
James Timmins	111-113, 116
Robert Lucas	111, 116
William Jnr.	113
William Ser.	111-113
CHANCE & HARTLEY	111
CHARRINGTON UNITED BREWERIES	16
CHATSWORTH HOUSE (Chance Brothers)	112
CITY TUBE & CONDUIT MILLS	138
CLEOPATRA'S NEEDLE (Tangye)	58-60
CORNWALL	38
CORNWALL WORKS	58, 67
CRAIG John (James Watt)	158-159
CREDENDA WORKS	129-132, 138
CROWN INN, Oldbury Road	14
CRYSTAL PALACE (Chance Brothers)	113
(Fox Henderson & Co)	142
CYLINDER GLASS SHEET	111

D

DARWIN Erasmus (Lunar Society, Galton)	121, 154
DAVY; Sir Humphry (James Watt)	159
DAWES Samuel J.	103
DAWES William Henry	103
DICTIONARY OF CHEMISTRY – James Keir	163
DIFFERENTIAL PULLEY BLOCK (T.A.Weston)	57
DIOPTIC LENSES (Chance Brothers)	112
DISTURNAL R.& CO	82
DISTRICT IRON WORKS	82, 83
DOCKER; Sir Dudley	106
DOCKER BROTHERS	106
DOWLAIS IRONWORKS	17-19, 25
DOWNING Henry	135-136

E

EAGLE IRON WORKS	127-128
EDGEWORTH Maria	140
Richard Lovell	140
ENGINE ARM & AQUEDUCT	123-126
ETNA IRON WORKS	127-128
EVERED & CO HOLDINGS / EVERED INDUSTRIAL PRODUCTS EIP	76
EVERITT George Allen	133
Neville Henry	133

F

FAIR HOUSE (William Murdoch)	161
FAIRFIELD, Handsworth	53
FARADAY Michael (Chance Brothers)	113
FINMECCANICA	26
FOTHERGILL John	155-156
FOX; Sir Charles	141
FOX HENDERSON & CO	99, 139-144
FRANKLIN Benjamin	154
FRENCH WALLS	135-138
FRENCH WALLS WORKS (James Watt Jnr)	136
FRESNEL LENSES (Chance Brothers)	113-114

G

GALTON BRIDGE	119-122
GALTON family	121, 140

GALTON HOUSE	121
GEC & AVERY-HARDOLL, GEC- AVERY	46
GEORGE BURN LTD	131-132, 138
GEORGE MUNTZ	135-137
GILBERTSTONE (Sir Richard Tangye)	53
GILLOTT Joseph	57
GKN; [GUEST, KEEN & NETTLEFOLDS]	17-19, 22, 25 – 27, 144
GREAT BARR HALL (Galton)	121
GREAT EASTERN SS; (Brunel)	40-41, 55-56
GREAT EXHIBITION 1851 (Crystal Palace)	20
GROVE, The – (Smethwick Grove)	30
GUEST Lady Charlotte	19
GUEST Ivor Bertie	18-19
GUEST & CO	17
GUEST John	17-18
GUEST John Josiah	17-19
GUEST Thomas	17

H

HAMMEL HILL, Ladywood (James Tangye)	53
HAMPSTEAD HALL (Moilliet)	140
HEATHFIELD HALL, Handsworth	40, 49, 63, 159
HENNEBIQUE Francois	119
HENDERSON John	141
HOPKINSON John (Chance Brothers)	113
Horsepower definition (James Watt)	38
HORSELEY IRON WORKS CO	96-99, 120
HYDRAULIC JACK (Tangye)	55

I

I.C.I	130, 134, 137
IMPERIAL MILLS	**21**
INCANDESCENT HEAT COMPANY WORKS	70-71
INTERNATIONAL NICKEL CO. OF CANADA LTD	31

J

J.A. PHILLIPS & CO	130-132, 138
JAMES WATT & CO	38
JAMES WATT ENGINE	17
JENSEN MOTOR LTD	103-104
JOHN BROCKHOUSE & CO LTD	81
JOHN RIGBY & SONS	82

K

KEEN Arthur	23-25, 143
KEIR James	38, 139-140, 163-164
KENT; Engineer-Captain Walter George, CBE., RN (Allen Everitt)	134
KINGSTON METAL WORKS	130, 133-134
KJELL OVALE	104

L

LATENT HEAT & JAMES WATT	37
LEAD: RED & WHITE MANUFACTURERS	30
LIGHTWOODS PARK & HOUSE, Bearwood, Birmingham	30
LONDON & NORTH WESTERN RAILWAY	54
LONDON WORKS	24, 98, 137, 139-144
Old Site Works A (Muntz)	137
New Site Works B (Muntz)	137
LONDON WORKS TAVERN, Smethwick	15
LOUND Andrew (Avery Archivist)	32
LUNAR SOCIETY	37, 121, 139, 140, 152-164

M

MACFARLANE Alexander (James Watt)	158
MANBY Aaron (Horseley Works)	97-99
MELROSE INDUSTRIES	27
MERRYWEATHER & SONS	105
METROPOLITAN AMALGAMATED RAILWAY CARRIAGE & WAGON CO	105
MICKLEWIGHT William	129-130
MINEROLOGY OF STAFFORDSHIRE – James Keir	163
MINT (Matthew Boulton)	39-40
MITCHELL Henry Jnr.	14
MITCHELL Henry Snr.	14
MITCHELLS & BUTLERS BREWERY	14
MOILLIET James & Jean-Louis	30, 49, 139-140
MOND Dr Ludwig	30-31
MOSER'S SCREW CO	26
MOUCHEL & partners Ltd	119
MUNICIPAL SCHOLL OF ART	61-2, 117
MUNTZ George	135-137
MUNTZ Phillip Frederick	135
MUNTZ'S METAL	135-138
MURDOCH William	38-39, 51, 54, 156, 160-162

N

NASH; Dr John (Matthew Boulton)	156
NETTLEFOLD & CHAMBERLAIN	21
NETTLEFOLD & SONS	20
NETTLEFOLDS	20-21
NETTLEFOLD Edward	20-21,25
NETTLEFOLD FREDERICK	21-22
NETTLEFOLD John Sutton	20-21
NETTLEFOLD Joseph Henry	21-22
NEWCOMEN Thomas & atmospheric engine	37
NORCROSS & JENSEN MOTIRS	104

O

OLD SITE WORKS (Muntz)	137
OLDBURY RAILWAY CARRIAGE & WAGON WORKS	105-106
"ONE & ALL" – autobiography by TANGYE Richard Sir	54, 59-66
OPTICAL GLASS (Chance Brothers)	112
ORMOLU (Soho Manufactory)	157
OWEN George – Crown Pub, Broad St, Birmingham	15

P

PARALLEL MOTION ENGINE	38
PATENT IRON & BRASS TUBE CO	22-23
PATENT METAL CO	137
PATENT NUT & BOLT CO	24, 139-144
PATENT SHAFT & AXLE CO	133
PATENT PLATE GLASS	112
PATRICK MOTORS, (Bournebrook, Birmingham)	103
PAXTON Joseph	112, 142
PENGE COMMON (Chance Brothers)	113
PHILLIPS J.A. & CO	130
PILKINGTON GLASS (Chance Brothers)	114
PRIESTLEY Joseph (James Keir)	163
Pump, BOULTON & WATT	85

Q

QUEEN CHARLOTTE (Queen to George III)	156

R

RABONE HALL	57
RECIPROCATING MOTION PUMP	38
REGENERATIVE FURNACE by William SIEMENS (Chance Brothers)	113
RETAINING WALL TO CORPORATION YARD, SMETHWICK (Grade 2 Listed)	122
RICHARD EVERED & CO LTD (SURREY WORKS)	74-77
ROEBUCK Dr. John	38
ROBINSON Anne (Matthew Boulton)	155
Luke (Matthew Boulton)	155-156
Mary (Matthew Boulton)	155
ROTATING OPTICS; lighthouses (Chance Brothers)	113
ROTTON PARK RESERVOIR	125
ROVING BRIDGE: DEFINITION	11
RUSKIN John	117
RUSKIN POTTERY	117-119

S

ST. GEORGE'S WORKS	21
STEAM BEAM ENGINES; Boulton & Watt	38
SANDWELL HOSPITAL	17
SANDWELL IRON & AXLE WORKS	81, 127-128
SANDWELL PARK COLLIERY	90-93
SEAMLESS STEEL TUBE CO. LTD	129
SELBY George	22, 140
SIEMENS William & Regenerative Furnace (Chance Brothers)	113
& Regenerative Steam-engine & condenser (Fox, Henderson & Co)	141
SMALL William	154, 162
SMEATON John	87, 124, 148-149
SMETHWICK ENGINES (Boulton & Watt)	125-126
SMETHWICK GAS WORKS	51-2
SMETHWICK IRON ROUNDRY	127-128
SMETHWICK TUBE CO	131, 138
SMETHWICK HALL	57
SMETHWICK GROVE	22, 49, 139-140
SMETHWICK LOCKS	72-3
SMETHWICK NEW PUMPING STATION	84-86
SOHO LOOP	10
SOHO FOUNDRY	32-49, 125, 129, 136, 139
- AN AT RISK SCHEDULED MONUMENT	33
- REMAINS OF SOHO FOUNDRY	34
- SOHO FOUNDRY TODAY	48-9
- UNIQUE HISTORY OF BOULTON & WATT	37
SOHO HOUSE (Boulton)	49, 155-156
SOHO MANUFACTORY – BOULTON & FOTHERGILL	36, 155
SOHO MANUFACTORY	49, 155
SPON LANE BRIDGE	119
SPON LANE LOCKS	95-96, 103
SPON LANE FOUNDRY & HORSELEY IRON WORKS	96-101
SPON LANE COLLIERIES, BLAKELEY HALL, BROMFORD COLLIERY	102-103
STAR TUBE CO	138
STEER Edward	21
STEPHENSON Robert	141
STEWART AQUEDUCT	107-108
SUMMIT TUNNEL	87-89, 124
SUN & PLANET GEAR (Murdoch)	38, 161
SURREY WORKS	74-77
SYCAMORE HILL (Murdoch)	49

T

TANGYE	Edward	53
	George	53
	James	53
	Joseph Jnr.	53, 55,
	Joseph Snr.	54

TANGYE	Sir Richard	32, 42, 53-66
TAYLOR	Edward Richard (Ruskin Pottery)	117
	William Howson (Ruskin Pottery)	117
TELFORD Thomas		107-109, 120-122, 125, 140, 150-151
TELFORD'S MAIN LINE		129, 107-144
THINKTANK MUSEUM		12, 38, 126
THOMAS ADKINS, HENRY WIGGIN		29-31
THOMAS ASTBURY & SONS		139-144
THOMAS PIGGOTT & CO		133
THOMPSON, ASBURY & CO		143
TUBES LTD		138

W

WATKINS & KEEN	23-24, 139-144
WARLEY WOODS HOUSE (Galton family)	121
WATT James Jnr	135
WATT James Snr.	37-42, 129, 158-159
- Garrett workshop	49
- WAY; Sir Samuel James	57
WESTLAND HELICOPTERS	26
WESTON T.A. (differential pulley block)	57
WHATELY family	135
WHEELER Percy	105-106
WHITBREAD ENGINE (James Watt)	39
WHITWORTH; Sir Joseph	129
WHITE William (Mayor of Birmingham)	55
HENRY WIGGIN, THOMAS ADKINS	30-31
WINSON GREEN STOP	11
WOODFORD IRON WORKS	68-69
WORSDELL Thomas	54
WYATT Samuel Architect of Soho Manufactory	36-37, 157

Y

YORKSHIRE IMPERIAL METALS LTD	134